WISCONSIN WOMEN:
a gifted heritage

To my dear friend Mary –

Christmas 1982,
A book of inspiration and awe–

love– Jan

project directors:
JEANNINE WADOZ GOGGIN
PATRICIA ALLAND MANSKE

editors:
ANDREA BLETZINGER
ANNE SHORT

WISCONSIN WOMEN:

a gifted heritage

A Project of
THE AMERICAN ASSOCIATION OF UNIVERSITY WOMEN
WISCONSIN STATE DIVISION

WISCONSIN WOMEN
PO BOX 646
NEENAH, WI 54956

Printed in the United States of America.

First edition.

First printing, January 1982.
Second printing, November 1982.

ISBN: 0-910122-63-6
Amherst Press

from the governor

When one examines the quality of life in Wisconsin, it becomes apparent that women have played an enormous role in shaping its destiny.

An emerging interest in the role women have played in society has resulted in serious research and discovery. The book, *Wisconsin Women: A Gifted Heritage,* is an important consequence of that research. Its pages are filled with the contributions of accomplished women, as transmitters of our history, culture, values and beliefs.

More importantly, the book goes beyond their contributions and delves into the backgrounds and motivations of these women, tracing the steps toward achieving their goals. These women are examples of lives well lived. Their stories serve as an inspiration to women of all ages who are in need and are seeking direction.

If I may add a personal note, I can say from experience that these women can be role models for men as well as women. My own mother, Clare Dreyfus, has greatly influenced my career goals and commitment to public service.

I congratulate you on a publication that will be well read and long remembered.

Lee Sherman Dreyfus
Governor of Wisconsin

contents

acknowledgements	10	State Project Committee
foreword	12	Jeannine Wadoz Goggin & Patricia Alland Manske
brief history of aauw	14	Sally A. Davis
section I		
glory of the morning	22	Joann L. Oh
rosaline peck	26	Betty Schlimgen Geisler
clarissa tracy	29	Beverly Thomann
frances willard	32	Ann Allen
kate pier	35	Joan Stebbins Des Isles
lucy smith morris	40	Vicki Gooding & Joan Wucherer
mother m. agnes hazotte	43	Sr. Margaret Lorimer, CSA
ella wheeler wilcox	46	Kathy Van Sistine & James Koltes
elizabeth peckham	50	Annabel Douglas McArthur
belle case la follette	53	Maria Bode
helen thompson	58	Grace Draxler
mary spellman	60	Margaret Lamoreaux Macfarlane
jessie jack hooper	63	Dorothy & Lee Newcomer
evangeline bergstrom	66	Andrea Bletzinger
zona gale	70	Judith Eulberg
lillie rosa minoka-hill	75	Rima D. Apple
ada james	79	Jane Nee Marr
fay crow	82	Geri Nikolai
emma duerrwaechter	84	Janice Straus & Lois Turba
elma spaulding schuele	86	Shirley Whipple Hinds
edna ferber	89	Beverly Prieto
marguerite davis	92	Elizabeth Walker
rosalie ganz	94	Blanche Schneider
georgia o'keeffe	96	Catherine Krueger
emily cowles	101	Diana Margotto
peg bradley	104	Margaret Jane Park
edith heidner	106	Marion Haebig
clare bluett dreyfus	109	E. Frankie Dreyfus
greta celia lagro potter	112	Dr. Paul H. Gaboriault

section II

edna frida pietsch	116	Gloria Prince
gladys mollart	120	Evelyn Rose
helen c. white	122	Hazel McGrath
breta luther griem	126	Maxine Ellis
harriet harmon dexter	128	Eileen Carlson & Ida Bobb
maurie applegate clack	130	Patt Boge
ruth west	133	Dolly Stokes
golda meir	136	Mary Podell
maren christine pedersen	140	Jane Huelskamp
frances cline	142	Marion E. Miller & Liz Kretlow
bernice scott	145	Betsy Hodson
lois almon	148	Allan Bell
della wendt	151	Esther Kaufmann
anita hankwitz kastner	154	Frank J. Prince
ruth de young kohler	156	Dolores C. Flader
hildegarde	160	Alice Zillmer
lillian mackesy	162	Anne Biebel
mabel mannix mc elligott	164	Violet E. Dewey
marie sperka	166	Cheryl Maxwell
monica bainter	168	Marilyn Thompson
marguerite henry	170	Anna Megna Dunst
lillian leenhouts	173	Ruth Swaziek
dorothy von briesen	176	Ann Andersen
sister thomasita fessler, osf	178	Sr. Margaret Peter
hannah swart	182	Jean Tyler
catherine cleary	186	Patricia Smith Wilmeth
madame liane kuony	189	Marilyn Stuckey
clare kiepke	192	Marilynn Richter
ellen benson humleker	194	Mary D. Fischer
mabel ruby mc clanahan	196	Jean Gaechke

section III

| margaret mary abaravich | 202 | Vincent Abaravich |
| florence parry heide | 205 | Linda S. Noer |

kathryn clarenbach	208	Constance Threinen
sister remy revor	212	Phyllis Tikalsky Casey
signe skott cooper	216	Anne G. Niles
isabel brown	220	Bette Brown & Mary Ellen Stone
ruth clusen	223	Lucille H. Katas
angeline thompson	226	Jane Manske
barbara thompson	229	Myrna M. Toney
mary lou munts	232	Marion Bates
sister joel read	236	May Murphy Thibaudeau
audrey jane dernbach	240	Barbara Zellmer
gene boyer	244	Iris Grundahl
mary linsmeier	247	Kathleen Winkler
lorna balian	250	Sue Roemer
roberta boorse	254	Patricia Smith Wilmeth & Alice Sedgwick
carol hough merrick	258	Elaine Edwards
audrey sickinger	260	Anne Ernst
shirley abrahamson	263	Marion Bates
ada deer	265	Lois Tate Kliefoth
helen barnhill	268	Mary Lueck Crouse
margaret hawkins	272	Marie Frank
sarah harder	274	Kathy Mitchell
barbara nichols	278	Louise C. Smith
marlene cummings	280	Jeanne Lamsam
jill geisler	284	Barbara Clapp
ferne caulker-bronson	286	Olive Caulker
sheila young ochowicz	289	Anne Silvis O'Brien
susan shannon engeleiter	292	Catherine DePledge
jill ann lieber	295	Jann McBride
beth heiden	298	Mary Helen Becker
appendix a	303	Bibliography
appendix b	306	Selected Honors, Accomplishments, Publications
appendix c	316	Source Listing
index	324	Alphabetical Listing
the committee	326	Wisconsin State Division State Project Committee

acknowledgements

Preparation of this book began in the summer of 1980 with the search for nominations. We wish to thank all who responded.

Special recognition is due AAUW's State Division Board of Directors and Division Presidents, Janice McCarthy (1979-81) and Dorothy Dedo (1981-83). State Division sponsorship provided generous financial and moral support, program opportunities at Division meetings and publicity in the quarterly publication, *Badger Briefs.*

We are grateful to the nominees who graciously told their life stories, answered innumerable questions and loaned cherished photographs. Their friends, spouses and relatives enriched the narratives with details of special moments. Biographers spent many hours interviewing, writing and revising.

Committee meetings were held at Hartford's United Methodist Church, a serene and comfortable setting for the all-day sessions. Our thanks to Hartford's AAUW member hostesses.

The State Project Chairmen in each branch were the vital communication links between the committee and branch members all over the state. They contributed ideas, helped with publicity and took responsibility for the sale and distribution of books.

The committee gratefully acknowledges the special contributions of:

Linda Parker, Women's Studies Librarian-at-large, University of Wisconsin System, for *Wisconsin Women: A Bibliographic Checklist.*

Editors Andrea Bletzinger and Anne Short reviewed each manuscript. Their efforts provide cohesive style to the book

We also appreciate the contributions of editorial advisor, Lois Kliefoth and of Janet Robertson, project business manager.

Jeannine Goggin and Patricia Manske served as dauntless project co-directors. Jeannine's enthusiastic leadership and resourcefulness in fielding problems were an inspiration to all. Patricia's rich artistic talent is responsible for the book's striking design.

The book represents the collective efforts of AAUW members and community volunteers. For everyone involved in the project, it has been a labor of love. It is AAUW's gift to Wisconsin.

The State Project Committee

foreword

"It might be interesting to compile a book of biographies of outstanding AAUW members from Wisconsin as a means of recognizing their contributions and preserving local history. The criterion could be the demonstration of AAUW's goals in their lives."

The proposal of a member from Madison was the nucleus from which this book evolved as a Wisconsin State Division project to celebrate the American Association of University Women's centennial year, 1981.

Approved at the Division convention in June, 1980, the scope was expanded to include not just AAUW members, but Wisconsin women of historical significance and women who are emerging as leaders of the 1980's.

The response to the call for nominations was immediate and gratifying. From some 300 nominations, 90 women were selected on the basis of their achievements in promoting educational opportunities, providing leadership in the advancement of women, sharing their unique talents and dedicating their lives to the solution of social and civic problems. Included were women from all parts of the state in many different fields of endeavor.

This is a panorama of Wisconsin women spanning three centuries. Beginning with Winnebago chieftess Glory of the Morning and closing with Olympic medalist Beth Heiden, we meet pioneers, suffragettes, homemaker volunteers, community leaders, lawyers, educators, doctors, artists, musicians, businesswomen. Their cumulative impact upon Wisconsin is beyond measure.

These women are significant for what they

accomplished in the context of their times. They are more than a parade of notable women—they are pages in the life of America. Their struggles and aspirations reflect the development of the state and the nation.

Some of them began moving mountains when they were young, others later in life. Some did a little in a big way; others did much in small ways. All had dreams and the determination to make those dreams come true. Their enthusiasm and eternal optimism make a strong statement about the value of individual effort.

The book is divided into three sections representing major periods in history. Because social change is subtle and gradual, the periods overlap to some degree.

In the Beginning. . .

For both Native American and pioneer white women, maintenance of day-to-day existence was totally time and energy consuming. Cultural values defined the positions of men and women within the family or tribal structure. In the struggle for survival, few were concerned about role definition.

Changes. . .

The Industrial Revolution in the wake of the Civil War brought profound changes throughout the nation. Women began to resist the constraints of male-dominated society and suffragettes led the fight for intellectual equality. Women were prime movers in reform movements striving to combat social and economic evils.

The country weathered the first World War and Great Depression. Mechanical servants and modern conveniences relieved the drudgery of household tasks. Many women invested their leisure time in community service as career volunteers.

Hospitals, libraries, churches, community organizations owe their vitality to the dedication of these women. AAUW and the League of Women Voters became powerful voices for the advancement of women.

Today. . .

The decades of the 1960's and 1970's represent a social revolution. Economic pressures as well as the quest for personal fulfillment took women out of the home and into the work force. Well-qualified women competed with men for positions of authority and responsibility. Inequities within the system became obvious and intolerable. The civil rights and women's liberation movements gave voice to demands for justice and equality.

Today's women are struggling, as their counterparts of earlier eras struggled to develop and use their talents to build a better world.

Project co-directors:
Jeannine Wadoz Goggin
Patricia Alland Manske

brief history of AAUW *written by SALLY A. DAVIS*

On the 28th day of November, 1881, at the Massachusetts Institute of Technology, 17 university-educated women met to form a new organization, the Association of Collegiate Alumnae (ACA). The women represented eight colleges—Oberlin, Vassar, Cornell, University of Michigan, Boston University, Smith, Wellesley and the University of Wisconsin. ACA's purpose was to "draw together in a great body for the advancement of human folk," young women who

Far Left: (Above) Chauncey Hall School, Boston, was the site of the January 1882 meeting at which the bylaws of the ACA were adopted by the 65 young women college graduates present;
(Below) AAUW's second home located in Washington, DC, one block from the White House
Left: AAUW Headquarters today, Washington DC
Near left: Marion Talbot (child on left) with her family. She was active in the fight for women's rights. Marion grew up to found the AAUW.

(courtesy, AAUW Educational Foundations Program)

had college educations, similar training and similar tastes. These women would set the path for education, encourage women to set goals for their lives, and give support to the economically impoverished.

From its inception, Wisconsin contributed to the growth of the organization through its University of Wisconsin graduates. Two of the original founders were Marie Dean, 1880 UW graduate, and Alma F. Frisby, Class of 1878.

On January 14, 1882, 65 women gathered at Chauncey Hall School in Boston. After a number of speeches, the group adopted a constitution that stated, "The object of this association shall be to unite alumnae of different institutions for practical educational work." The assemblage elected officers and Jennie Field Bashford, an 1874 University of Wisconsin graduate, became the first president and served two terms. Mrs. Bashford, described as a gentle, charming woman was a graduate in one of the early classes that admitted women.

It soon became apparent that membership could not be restricted to the original eight colleges/universities. Graduates of Wesleyan University and Massachusetts Institute of Technology requested inclusion, which was granted. By 1884, the first Association branch was established in Washington, D.C. and the ACA's constitution was broadened to include branches.

By the time the Association celebrated its 25th birthday (1906), there were 35. Milwaukee, the first in Wisconsin, was the 20th community to establish a branch (1896).

By 1886, ACA had established its policies, some of which are still carried on today.

Meanwhile, a group of college women in the Chicago area had shown interest in joining. When the two groups could not work out their philosophical differences, the Chicago group, in late 1883, organized the Western Association of Collegiate Alumnae. Until 1889, they worked as separate entities and, after much discussion, finally merged with the ACA. Their particular contribution to the larger association was the establishment in 1888 of "a fund offered by a group of organized college and university alumnae for a woman in competition with other women, for the purpose of pushing out farther the bonds of knowledge and truth." This was one of the first of such fellowships in any country.

In July of 1903 in Nashville, Tennessee, a group of 17 women banded together to form yet another association, the Southern Association of College Women.

Because of the geographical and specific educational interests of the southern group, a number of years passed before differences between it and the ACA could be resolved. However, cooperation was strong between them. Many women had memberships in both.

Concern over high school girls and their opportunities for education in the South resulted in scholarships for seniors, "college day" in the high schools, and other activities to promote quality university education. When the Southern Association merged with the ACA, it brought along its interest in senior high school girls and many AAUW branches today carry out similar activities.

Merger of the two associations became a reality in 1921 after months of discussion and planning. The new association adopted a new name, the American Association of University Women (AAUW). This merger was captained by a remarkable Wisconsin woman, Lois Kimball Mathews Rosenberry, president of the ACA from 1917 to 1921.

Merger and Lois Rosenberry

Lois Kimball was born in Cresco, Iowa, in 1873. As a young woman of 17, she graduated from Normal School at Winona, Minnesota. For the next seven years she taught, first in Minnesota and then in Salt Lake City, Utah. At 24, she married George Reynolds Mathews, a professor of modern languages at the University of Utah. Two years later, Lois Mathews found herself a widow, and in the early 1900's, she returned to college. She attended Stanford University in Palo Alto, California, where she received a bachelor's degree in 1903 and a master's in 1904. From California, she went to Radcliffe, where she earned a PhD in 1906. It is said she was the first woman to pass Harvard University's doctoral examination in the combined fields of history, economics and political science.

Lois Mathews taught history at Vassar from 1906 to 1910 and then received an appointment as associate professor of history at Wellesley College. From this post, she accepted the position of Dean of Women and Associate Professor of History at the University of Wisconsin in Madison, (1911-1918). She served until 1918, the first Dean of Women in the country, and the first woman to become associate professor in the history department. In 1918, she married Marvin Rosenberry, who became Chief Justice of the Wisconsin Supreme Court in 1929.

During this time, she was an active member of

Two early leaders: (Above) Eva Perry Moore, president of ACA, 1903-07; and (right) Laura Drake Gill, president of ACA, 1907-11.
(courtesy, AAUW Educational Foundations Program)

the Association of Collegiate Alumnae on the national level and in the Madison Branch, the second Wisconsin branch to be founded (1908). She was national president of the ACA from 1917 to 1921. She presided over the dissolution of the ACA and the birth of the AAUW. She also was instrumental in the purchase of the property that is today AAUW's national headquarters in Washington, DC. It should be noted that both the first president of ACA and the last were Wisconsin women.

Wisconsin Beginnings

The Milwaukee Branch, first in Wisconsin, had an interesting history. In 1894, eight young women banded together to form a support group for the miniscule number of women college graduates in the area. The aim was to interest parents in the value of higher education for girls while demonstrating that the girls would not lose their femininity.

In 1896, the national ACA recognized the Milwaukee Branch. It became involved in a number of causes and studied such issues as child labor, sweat shops, settlement and social work and education. It developed and maintained a placement bureau and supported women's suffrage.

Ellen C. Sabin served as president of the still infant Milwaukee Branch in 1900-1902. No branch could have had a more impressive mentor and guide. Ellen Clara Sabin was born in Sun Prairie, Wisconsin, in 1850. At 15, she enrolled at the University of Wisconsin and, at the same time, taught school in Sun Prairie. Her teaching gifts came to the attention of other educators and she was offered a position in the Madison Schools. In 1870, she became principal of the Fourth Ward (Doty) School.

In 1872, the Sabin family migrated westward to Eugene, Oregon. Ellen Sabin taught in Portland, Oregon, became principal of an elementary school, and finally, in 1887, was appointed Superintendent of the Portland Schools—the first woman in the country to hold such a position in a large city.

Ellen Sabin returned to Wisconsin in 1890 to assume the presidency of Downer College in Fox Lake. In the next 10 years, she saw the institution grow, merge with Milwaukee College, move to Milwaukee and occupy a new campus. For 30 years, Ellen Sabin who "never graduated from anything" served as president of Milwaukee-Downer College (now part of Lawrence University).

Because of the dedication of these and many similar women, AAUW has developed into an impressive 190,000 member Association. The Association's current program seeks equity for women, expansion of education and employment opportunities.

The fellowship program continues to provide opportunities for women scholars throughout the world to continue their academic study and research. Since its beginning in 1888, more than 3900 fellowships have been awarded to 2138 American women and 1502 women from 93 other counties. AAUW fellowships are unique because there are no restrictions on age, field of study or place of study.

In 1971 research and project grants were introduced to increase members' opportunities to work on projects in the public interest that reflect

Right: Hospitality Committee, AAUW National Convention, Washington, 1924. (Note those outfits down to the shoes—and what marvelous hats!)
(courtesy, AAUW Educational Foundations Program)

Association interests and goals. Recently, Project RENEW was begun to enable members to take courses to upgrade marketable skills or change professional objectives.

The road has been long and varied since that small group met in Boston in 1881. This book, *Wisconsin Women: A Gifted Heritage,* is our effort to salute yesterday's and today's Wisconsin women. The vision of the women in Boston one hundred years ago has been fulfilled.

section I: in the beginning . . .

*Ho-po-ko-e-kaw was the founder of the largest
and most powerful family of the Winnebago Indians.*

glory of the morning

In 1766 an English explorer named Jonathan Carver visited the Winnebago Indian tribe on Doty Island where he found 50 strongly palisaded "houses," 200 warriors and 1000 people. Among their leaders was a woman, a chieftess named Ho-po-ko-e-kaw or Glory of the Morning. He wrote:

> She received me with great civility, and entertained me in a very distinguished manner, during the four days I continued with her . . . She was a very ancient woman, small in stature, and not much distinguished in dress from several young women who attended her. These her attendants seemed greatly pleased whenever I showed any tokens of respect to their queen, particularly when I saluted her, which I frequently did to acquire her favour. On these occasions the good old lady endeavored to assume a juvenile gaiety, and by her smiles showed she was equally pleased with the attention I paid her.

His is the only eyewitness account of this remarkable woman. So impressed was he that he devoted more space to her than to any other individual in the village.

Who was this "ancient" woman? She was born in the early 18th century when the Winnebago were living a comfortable life on their island in the middle of the Fox River on the western side of Lake Winnebago. They ate well from their own gardens of corn, beans, pumpkins, watermelons and squash and from the natural harvest of grapes, plums, nuts, berries, wild rice, fish, ducks and geese. During Glory of the Morning's childhood, the Winnebago began to regain some of the strength they had lost in the preceding two generations.

As she grew, she learned from tribal tradition that when the first white man visited Wisconsin in

24

1634, the Winnebago were very powerful. Her great-grandfather was chief of the Winnebago at Red Banks near Green Bay when Jean Nicolet stepped ashore; 4000 Winnebago warriors ate roasted beaver at the feast in Nicolet's honor. She learned that in her grandmother's time the once powerful Winnebago tribe had come close to extinction and had dwindled to about 150 warriors, primarily by a long, fierce war with the Illini tribe. This knowledge may well have intensified her commitment to peace.

In 1728 Sabrevoir Des Carrie (also spelled De Carry, Descaris, De Khaury, De Kau-ray, and finally Decorah) marched with an army from the French fort at Green Bay south along the Fox River and stopped at the Winnebago village on Doty Island. There he met Glory of the Morning, the head chief's daughter; he left the army, married her and became the first white fur trader in the area.

Why did the daughter of a Winnebago chief marry a white man? A possible answer is implied in the Decorah family account of the marriage, which emphasizes the benefits which the Indians felt their culture derived from the infusion of white blood:

> Des Carrie lived there and worked for the Indians and stayed with them for many years and he taught them the use of many tools. He went home every once in awhile and his wife went with him, but he always came back again . . . A person with French blood had always been chief. Only they could accomplish anything among the whites.

The Winnebago were impressed by the knowledge and abilities of the French in general, and by Des Carrie in particular.

In about 1748 after 20 years of marriage and

birth of two sons and a daughter, Des Carrie suddenly left Doty Island and did not return. He took his daughter with him to Canada to be educated, but Glory of the Morning remained behind. He was wounded at the Battle of Quebec during the French and Indian War and was taken to Montreal where he died on April 28, 1760.

Whether Glory of the Morning was deserted by her French husband or whether she chose to

remain behind is irrelevant. What is significant is the use to which she put the remaining years of her long life.

To understand Glory of the Morning's contribution to her own culture and to the future white settlers of Wisconsin, several facts must be understood. First of all, the peace chief of the Winnebago was chosen from the Thunder clan to which Glory of the Morning belonged. Second, the peace chief was chosen for his exceptional concern for the total welfare of his people and his ability to resolve problems by peaceful means. Glory of the Morning apparently combined this hereditary eligibility with her personal exceptional abilities, for when her father died, she, like several generations of her family before her, was chosen peace chieftess, a very unusual rank for a woman in the Winnebago tribe. As chieftess she worked for the peace and well-being of her people until she was an old woman.

She then passed on her dedication to peace and the welfare of her people to her descendants, who became the most powerful family in the Winnebago tribe. The Decorah family history says that Glory of the Morning's son Chou-ke-ka, when forced to fast for a long time, ran away into the woods for a month and returned with a drum, which he said was not to be used in war, but "to obtain life." He also said that the Earth-maker had blessed him and told him to give his life in the service of the Winnebago. He thus expressed the very same strong commitment to peace and to the welfare of the tribe that Glory of the Morning stood for. Both of Glory of the Morning's sons, as well as three grandsons and one great-grandson became outstanding peace chiefs of the Winnebago. They ultimately gave up their lands in peace treaties rather than resist the advance of white settlement.

One mystery about Glory of the Morning remains. Why is there any record at all of her life? She was a woman, not a warrior, who lived in a time when the "greatest honor was to be a brave man." Her tribe was relatively small; she had no access to the permanent record-making equipment that we take for granted: a written language, a pen, a piece of paper. Her access to the people who did keep records, like Jonathan Carver, was limited by a language barrier. No picture of her is known. Yet her name survives. Why wasn't it lost in the grand sweep of history along with the names of thousands of other Indian women?

Glory of the Morning's memory survives because she herself was a survivor. She accepted the burden of leadership that her ancestry and her own abilities equipped her to carry. She reached out warmly to others and passed on to her descendants the clan's dedication to cooperation and peace. She and her descendants maintained their cultural identity. She gave of herself to her own time and to her people's future.

(See Selected Honors, Accomplishments, Publications, page 309)

written by BETTY SCHLIMGEN GEISLER

rosaline peck

Rosaline Willard Peck may have become just another name on the genealogy page of a family Bible, if she and her husband, Eben, had not decided to set up housekeeping in 1837 in the capital of the new Wisconsin Territory. Rosaline has a claim to fame as the first white woman settler in Madison, and the mother of the first white child born there. In 1840, she was also the first white woman in Baraboo, Wisconsin.

She was a dynamo pioneer "woman's libber," not reluctant to speak her mind. Many of her statements were recorded, giving her views about the hardships and frustrations of pioneer life in Wisconsin.

Rosaline Willard Peck was born February 24, 1808, in Middletown, Vermont of Yankee stock. Her ancestors fought in the American Revolution. On her 21st birthday, in 1829, Rosaline married Eben Peck. He was a Green Mountain boy who had established a business in Middletown, where they stayed for three years. They moved to Middlebury, New York, where their first child, Victor, was born in 1833. Eben caught the wanderlust and left temporarily to look for land. He took his time. According to Rosaline, it was "some 18 or 20 months before returning to New York State and conveying us hither!"

When he returned, they packed their gear and were on their way to Wisconsin. They arrived in July, 1836, and took over management of Colonel Ebenezer Brigham's inn at Blue Mounds. Judge James Doty soon came into their lives to convince them to build boarding house facilities for the construction crew of his Capitol building.

Rosaline never forgot that trip to Madison. She

was five months pregnant. She rode on her pony, carrying Victor, while the team pulled the wagon loaded with supplies. "We camped the first night in a half-made cabin, and put the tent over us. We pushed on on the 14th (April), a more pleasant day I never wish to see. . .but I had a severe headache before night, so we pitched our tent. . .about three miles from Madison. . .spread out our beds and near three o'clock, we were awakened by a tremendous windstorm, the howling of wolves. . .and found snow six inches deep. . .which continued to fall until after we arrived in Madison. . .

"Well, now, here we are in Madison, sitting in a wagon under a tree, with a bed-quilt thrown over my head and my little boy's head . . . in a tremendous storm of snow and sleet, 25 miles from any inhabitants on one side and near a hundred on the other."

Rosaline cajoled Eben, "just build me a pen under this tree, move in my stove, and we will crawl in there."

Two weeks later, Augustus Bird, in charge of building the Capitol, came along with 15 workmen. Rosaline spread tables "under the broad canopy of heaven." Ten days later, Judge Doty arrived, with Bird and Brigham, and about 30 men.

The Pecks still had not moved from their lean-to under the tree. When Doty asked why, Rosaline said, "My dear Sir, I must have it plastered with lime first!" With no lime quarry within 100 miles, Doty reported, "Everyone pitched in and helped daub up the kitchen on the outside with mud, so,

by night, we were all comfortably situated in the kitchen!" Later, two additions were built on the northeast and southeast corners. A frame hall, where weary travelers were fed and entertained, was built in the passage between.

A confrontation with one of her early boarders illustrates what Rosaline was really like. Scottish geologist G.W. Featherstonaugh came up from St. Louis expecting to find Madison a flourishing metropolis. After returning to England, he published disparaging remarks about Peck's Place.

In an account by W.H. Canfield in the *Baraboo Republic,* Rosaline defended herself. She considered his criticisms "squibs", unmerited attacks upon her fair name and character. He came in May, when they had been open a little over a month, and he had the nerve to complain about her coffee, suggesting she used acorns and tincture of myrrh. "If there is anything I took pride in, it was in making good coffee. I guarantee I could manufacture better coffee from parsnips and catnip than crack hotels of the present day do from the imported article."

He complained he had to sleep between two barrels. Rosaline replied, "If a bed with over 30 pounds of fresh geese feathers laid on a good clean backwoods bedstead, with plenty of clean bedding, was not good enough for His Majesty, he should carry his own accommodations!" She described him as an "old gray-haired idiot. . .troubled with worms or the gout." The prize is that "this ungrateful gentleman stayed the three nights gratis—and if he got nothing but a crust given in kindness, he ought to have been thankful!"

At Peck's Place, hog and hominy were "common doings". Sleeping rooms sold at two pence a square foot, or one could occupy a "field bed" where sleepers arranged themselves "spoon fashion". Fish

Mrs. Rosaline Peck
(courtesy, State Historical Society of Wisconsin)

Rosaline Peck (courtesy, State Historical Society of Wisconsin)

were plentiful, summer and winter, there were prairie chickens and quail roaming Capitol Park. Wild turkey was a specialty, while squirrel, rabbit, and venison graced many a platter.

There were also memorable euchre parties, Christmas and New Year's suppers, dances when her brother-in-law, Luther Peck, provided some mean fiddling. Rosaline had talent with the violin, too, but she was in constant demand as a dancing partner and could rarely be spared for the orchestra. One party she never forgot was the turtle soup supper. Pioneer Abel Rasdall brought a wagon load of turtles he had chopped out of the ice of Lake Wingra, dumping them, like frozen stones, into the basement. When she went down a few days later, they were crawling all over the place. In 1837, the New Year's Eve party lasted two nights and two days. Most parties ended only when the spirits ran out.

Rosaline's daughter was born September 14, 1837. When the baby was less than a week old, Judge Doty arrived and ordered a table spread with wine. The entire party standing around it, solemn as a funeral, sipped the wine. The baby was named "Wisconsiana". Victoria was added in honor of the young Queen of England who had ascended the throne a few weeks before. Wisconsiana Victoria Peck was the first white child born in Madison.

The Pecks ran their hotel for two years. Rosaline relates, "I soon got weary of being a slave to everybody, and we finally rented our tavern stand to Mr. Ream and turned our attention to farming." In the autumn of 1840, they arrived in Baraboo. "Our nearest neighbors were on the other side of the Baraboo River. We made a claim of a mill privilege, and claimed a piece of farming land on the other side . . . got it fenced in, and a larger part improved when my husband left, under the

pretense of going to Oregon."

"From that time, I have struggled alone to bring up my little family . . . for seven long years . . . and then the land was thrown into market . . . and no money to be got . . . I was informed I must show proof of my husband's death or no pre-emption!" She was swindled out of her land, and never got the money she paid for it. "After I lost my improvements, I sold my last cows . . . and thereby raised enough money and bought the piece of land I now live on (1860)."

From her earliest days in Baraboo, before there was a resident physician, Rosaline treated the sick. On one occasion she set the broken leg of a child that lived five miles away. She had to work with the light of a "grease dip", but successfully performed the operation. She was quoted as saying there were "no deaths in the valley until after the doctors came!"

As for Eben, most reports assume he was drowned or massacred by Indians. Rosaline never heard from him again.

In an era when women usually succumbed at an early age, Rosaline survived into her nineties. She died October 28, 1899.

(See Selected Honors, Accomplishments, Publications, page 313)

written by BEVERLY THOMANN

Clarissa Tracy

Known as the mother of Ripon College, she was for 46 years its intellectual and spiritual force. She was truly an indomitable woman.

clarissa tracy

Clarissa Tucker Tracy, the "Mother of Ripon College," supported herself from the time she started teaching as a 14-year-old girl until her death the day after her 87th birthday. Scholarly and intellectual, she demonstrated strength of character, self-confidence and faith in God throughout her life.

Clarissa Tucker was born in a log house in Susquehanna County, Pennsylvania, in 1818 to parents emigrated from Vermont. She started school at three and a half, and in three months learned to read and spell well. At home she was taught to knit, sew, spin and to tend the younger children.

Because times were hard, Clarissa started teaching near her home when she was 14. She had 13 pupils. Later, she attended an academy and went on to continue her studies and assist at Honesdale Seminary in Pennsylvania. She married Horace Hyde Tracy in May, 1844.

Their marriage was a happy one, in spite of Tracy's poor health. Two children were born, Horace James and Clarissa Aurelia. Mrs. Tracy continued teaching for a year and a half but quit to nurse her ailing young husband, who died in 1848. More sorrow followed as little Clarissa died of measles in 1851. Mrs. Tracy, who had resumed teaching following her husband's death, decided to move West—to a "less favored place" as she put it. She spent three years teaching in Neenah, Wisconsin, but was not happy there, so returned to Pennsylvania in 1859.

Soon afterward, she received a letter from a trustee of Brockway (Ripon) College offering her a position as teacher and superintendent of the

Ladies' Department. After serious consideration and prayer, she accepted and began her work on October 4, 1859. Her association with the College continued until her death 46 years later in 1905.

When she arrived, the campus consisted of two partially completed buildings. Her salary was $300 a year. But to Clarissa Tracy, the position was a challenge which she met so well that the president of the College declared her service of more importance than his own.

Although she was a career teacher, in her early years at Ripon College, Mrs. Tracy was most appreciated as head of the kitchen. She had to provide food for about 100 boarders a day with very little equipment and no trained helpers. In the early years, her meager salary came from the income of the boarding department. Clarissa Tracy was proud of her culinary skills and frequently came to class with pie crust dough on her fingers. Holidays and commencements were special occasions, and she delighted in serving excellent food. She often arose at 4 a.m. to make preparations.

Mrs. Tracy taught algebra, arithmetic, English literature and botany, which was her favorite subject. Her specialty was analyzing flowers, and she confessed that she often found herself analyzing posies on ladies' bonnets in church. She

*She was a Victorian in many ways. She had a firm faith
in God which gave her the strength to face the tragedies in her life.*

31

was responsible for the publication in 1889 of a catalog of *Plants Growing without Cultivation in Ripon and Near Vicinity.*

Students recalled Clarissa Tracy as an exacting teacher, never satisfied with less than their best. One pupil put it, "Those eyes tested your mettle; her voice demanded the best that was in you." Students remembered her abrupt ways and sharp voice but also recognized that she was kind and helpful when they needed her. One commented that he could still repeat the 26 prepositions that govern the accusative—50 years later.

Although she was slight of build, Clarissa Tracy enjoyed good health all her life. During Wisconsin winters, she ate mince pie for breakfast and dinner because she felt it was nutritious.

Mrs. C.T. Tracy, as she always signed her name, was an active member of the Congregational Church for 46 years with a deep commitment to missions. When the town women met to promote their first female candidate for the School Board, Mrs. Tracy presided. She was active in the Temperance Movement. During the 1870's Ripon ladies, led by Clarissa Tracy, descended upon local saloons where they read Scripture, sang hymns and prayed.

A cause that did not receive Mrs. Tracy's support was suffrage. A student reported hearing a proponent of women's rights ask her if she had felt "put upon" because she was a woman. "No, I never noticed it," was Mrs. Tracy's reply.

When this able and versatile teacher died November 13, 1905, students and faculty walked together to the funeral service, and public school classes were dismissed.

A simple stone marks her grave in the cemetery adjoining the College she served so long and faithfully. On it are these words of her choice: "A Teacher in Ripon College."

(See Selected Honors, Accomplishments, Publications, page 314)

Tracy Hall, Ripon College

Frances Willard, 1898.
(courtesy, State Historical Society of Wisconsin)

frances willard

"Ma, is the baby dead?" little Oliver Willard would call out every morning. He would run downstairs in fear because another infant sister had died the year before. When Oliver found that this new baby endured, he would still come and say, "Ma, is the baby well?"

Frances Willard was well in that autumn of 1839. "She was a very affectionate creature," her mother said years later. "She could talk some time before she could walk, speaking quite wisely at 14 months but not walking until 24 months old." The Willards were to see their "Frank" become a renowned speaker and a world leader for social reform. Though admired today as a crusader to improve the status of women, as an international politician and as a college president, Frances Willard is more often remembered for her role as Women's Christian Temperance Union campaigner. Mrs. Willard, in a flash of humor, once said of her famous daughter, "But I ought to add for her present reputation's sake, she has no affinity for the bottle—putting it away when 10 months old with no regret."

Frances Elizabeth Caroline Willard was born in Churchville, New York, on September 28, 1839. Her mother had been a teacher, her father, a store manager with aspirations to the ministry. Seven years after Frances was born, when ill health made ministerial pursuits impossible, Josiah Willard moved his young family—his wife, Frances, her elder brother Oliver and sister Mary—to Wisconsin, where they settled on a bluff overlooking the Rock River, about six miles south of Janesville. The Willard farm, Forest Home, came to be recognized as one of the finest stock farms in Wisconsin.

Frances Willard, 1872.

There was no formal schooling at Forest Home, but within three years, Mr. Willard improvised a room that served as a place of learning for Frances, her sister and two neighbor girls. Eventually a small schoolhouse was built by Mr. Willard on the river bank about a mile away from Forest Home, which served as a "temple of learning" in the years to come.

In 1857, at the age of 18, Frances left home to continue her education at Milwaukee Female College. By age 32, she had accepted the presidency of the newly organized Evanston College for Ladies. Upon the merger of the college with Northwestern University in 1873, she became Dean of Women.

Meanwhile Frances had become increasingly aware of and sympathetic toward the temperance movement. Following her resignation as Dean in 1874, she forsook a $2,400 annual salary to become corresponding secretary for the fledgling National Women's Christian Temperance Union.

It was a risky undertaking, one which surprised her family and close friends and initially lost her much of the popular support she had enjoyed as an academician. But she was committed to the ideals and principles of the WCTU—"an organization of women banded together for the protection of the home, the abolition of the liquor traffic and the triumph of Christ's golden rule in custom and in law." The WCTU was later to be characterized by Frances as a "compact, organized army, a great educational agency for women, such as they could create to combat any of society's evils."

Frances' concern with the status of women was a natural outgrowth of her involvement in the temperance movement. Arguing that only through women's vote could the cause of temperance succeed, she became a suffragist to help insure "protection to the home" from the evils of liquor. In this position she was ahead of her time. Not until 1880 did the WCTU endorse woman suffrage, and it would be another 40 years before women gained the vote in national affairs. For Frances, the temperance cause was only the open door through which she entered into her service for the world. In the defense of women, her main task, Frances Willard belonged to no special cause.

Beginning in 1883, for the next seven years, Miss Willard traveled throughout the world, spreading her message in 50 countries. An excellent speaker, a successful lobbyist and an expert in public opinion and pressure politics, Miss Willard participated effectively in several political campaigns, ironically without herself being able to vote.

In 1891, with the founding and first biennial convention of the World's WCTU, Frances became an international figure. Following her mother's death that same year, Frances moved to England, where she was received with overwhelming enthusiasm. Three years later, she returned to New York to a public reception so hearty as to assure her of an equally positive following at home.

She died at Forest Home in Janesville on February 17, 1898.

(See Selected Honors, Accomplishments, Publications, page 314)

kate hamilton pier

The following are excerpts from her imaginary journal:

JUNE 22, 1893. Burlington, Vermont.
I just turned eight years old today and I'm so excited. Tomorrow our family is leaving for a new state and a new life a thousand miles from St. Alban's where my two brothers and I were born. So many people are leaving our beautiful state to

In 1891 Kate Pier and her three daughters constituted half of the total number of women lawyers in Wisconsin.

Kate Hamilton Pier
(left) and Katherine
Pier. Both graduated
UW Law School in
1887.
(courtesy, UW-Madison
Law School)

start homesteads on new land. Father knows some who are living in Fond du Lac where we are going so it won't be quite so strange. I'm not afraid, but I'll miss my friends.

AUGUST 1, 1853. Fond du Lac, Wisconsin.

The Hamilton family is getting settled at last in this wilderness called Wisconsin.

There are several other Vermont families here, too. One is the Pier family with five children, including twins, a boy and girl. The boy, Colwert Kendall, is four years older than I am but, even so, he is very nice to me.

JULY 2, 1858. Fond du Lac.

Father has become interested in buying farms in the surrounding county. When he goes out in his

buggy to look at farms, he takes me along for company and I am learning what makes the land worth buying. I am almost 13, and I think I would like to work with my father when I am older. He says I notice things he doesn't expect me to see, things grown men don't always notice.

JUNE 22, 1862. Fond du Lac.

My 17th birthday! I have graduated from Fond du Lac High School. I am going to teach school in the Town of Empire next fall for six dollars a month plus room and board.

The boys are going off to fight in the Union army to make those Southern states give up keeping slaves and become part of our country again. The first man in Fond du Lac to enlist was Colwert Pier. We have become good friends and he has asked me to write to him so he won't be so lonesome.

MAY 20, 1863. Fond du Lac.

I have accepted a position of teacher in the Fond du Lac schools for the next school term. I will be paid the grand sum of $22.50 a month. What a fortune for an 18-year-old!

APRIL 16, 1865. Fond du Lac.

The War Between the States is over at last. I hope Colwert will soon be home. He has been studying law in Albany, NY after fulfilling his term of enlistment. He intends to practice law here in the Gillet and Conklin law office. I wonder if he will ask me to marry him?

JUNE 25, 1866. Fond du Lac.

Our wedding day!! Today I became the wife c

Lieutenant Colonel Colwert Kendall Pier at my parents' home. Three days ago, I turned 21. I wonder where life will lead us in the next 21 years. . .

Colwert is busy in this fast-growing city with his law practice and real estate holdings. I think I can be of some help to him in handling his property.

. . . . 1871. Fond du Lac.

My father is dead. How I shall miss him and all his wisdom and companionship! There seems to be no one in the family except me who can take over Father's real estate business and manage his land. Since I have been helping him the last few years, I won't find it too difficult to continue the work. I am not afraid of functioning in the male world of business.

. . . . 1879. Fond du Lac.

Colwert and I have four daughters, Kate Hamilton, Mary, Harriet, and Caroline. They are all sweet, loving and lively, though Mary is a bit weaker physically. Of course, they are all very smart! We are living in the Pier homestead south of town built more than 30 years ago by Colwert's father, Edward Pier. It is larger now since we added several rooms for our growing family.

. . . .   Fond du Lac.

Our dear Mary has rejoined her Creator. How empty our lives will be without her. Colwert and I must be strong for the girls' sakes.

JUNE 15, 1886. Fond du Lac.

Kate has graduated from high school and wants to go to the University in Madison to study law. She has always had an interest in her father's profession and he has encouraged her. She has a bright, quick mind, is an apt student and pretty, too, which may make it hard for the boys to keep their minds on their studies.

I am thinking of going with her. I don't think she should be down there alone. Besides, I could benefit from studying law, too. It would help me in taking care of our real estate. Harriet and Caroline could go to high school there and I could

The kind of scenery Kate Pier enjoyed in her travels between Milwaukee and Fond du Lac.

take care of them all. Colwert will have to get along by himself which I am sure he can do. He thinks I should do this.

JUNE 22, 1887. Madison

We have graduated, my daughter Kate and I. Imagine, I am 42 today with a college diploma for a birthday present! We are going back to Fond du Lac and will open a law office.

It has been a gratifying experience to go to college with my oldest daughter and live in our state capital. The members of the legal profession have shown us every kindness.

The only case of "direct partiality" was when the men in our class made a list of members and registered "Mrs. Pier at 26 and Miss Pier at 18." Very flattering, I must say—but not very accurate!

OCTOBER 15, 1888. Milwaukee.

We opened a law office here after practicing law in Fond du Lac for a year. We bought a house near Lake Michigan but are keeping our home in Fond du Lac so that we can go back to visit and continue to oversee our properties. We own a great deal of land in Oneida, Lincoln and Vilas counties much farther north that requires our attention several times a year, too.

Our law practice here consists of corporation, real estate and probate cases. I am in charge of the office and Kate usually takes the court cases. Colwert is involved with businessmen in the city regarding their problems.

JUNE 25, 1891. Madison.

Caroline and Harriet have completed the law course at the University of Wisconsin and will join us in our Milwaukee office. Already Kate has distinguished herself in court. She has pleaded ten

Well known in the law profession, she became the first woman in the United States to serve on Circuit Court commissions.

39

cases in the Supreme Court quite successfully, too. She was the first lady attorney to address that body two years ago.

We have promoted the passage of two laws in the state legislature that have a direct bearing on women attorneys. One states that a married woman is capable of acting as an assignee so property may be legally transferred to her and the other permits a woman attorney to be a court commissioner.

The first will help women who may inherit property from their husbands and the second will open wider the doors of courtrooms and judgeships for women.

JUNE 26, 1891. Milwaukee

Kate presented Caroline and Harriet to the court here and they have been admitted to the bar. What a great day for the Pier girls and their parents! Our practice is really thriving. Yesterday was a red letter day for us: we are now one-half of the women attorneys in the state.

SEPTEMBER 20, 1892. Milwaukee.

I have been appointed Circuit Court Commissioner in the county of Milwaukee, the first and only woman holding that position in the United States!

APRIL 14, 1895. Milwaukee

My husband has died . . . my beloved husband and partner for all these 29 years is dead at a young 54 years. He and his twin sister were the first children born in Fond du Lac, June 7, 1841. Many people will miss him sorely, his family most of all. However, we will continue to carry on our law practice here and maintain our real estate holdings in Fond du Lac. This is the second death in our family now.

POSTSCRIPT BY DAUGHTERS:

Our dear mother died June 23, 1925, at the family home in Fond du Lac after spending the morning visiting with Kate. She was eighty years old, a venerable age and a venerable woman. She had a reputation as "intelligent, gracious and womanly with Irish charm and instincts which made her a fine wife and mother." Not only was she our mother but she reared two orphan nephews, children of Father's brother.

She was laid to rest in the Hamilton plot in Reinzi Cemetery, 59 years to the day since she and Father were married.

(See Selected Honors, Accomplishments, Publications, page 312)

written by VICKI GOODING & JOAN WUCHERER

lucy smith morris

"Ability begets responsibility." That advice, offered by a contemporary, was the guide by which Lucy Smith Morris, one of Wisconsin's most active clubwomen and early suffragettes, patterned her life.

"Her words . . . have moved me to 'gird on my armor' when I have thought it would be very pleasant to 'let George do it'," Lucy said. This belief that those who had the ability "to do" must accept that responsibility led Mrs. Morris to promote the cause of women.

Lucy Smith was born August 28, 1850 on a farm north of Markesan on the shores of Little Green Lake. She was one of five children of Samuel and Almena Smith. Her father was a prominent flour and feed mill proprietor and politician in Markesan. Lucy received her early

Nationally known for her support of women's causes, Lucy Smith Morris founded the Wisconsin Federation of Women's Clubs in 1896.

41

education in a nearby rural school and then was sent to the Notre Dame Convent, now Mount Mary College, considered one of the best schools in the Midwest. She continued her education at the Musical Academy in Beaver Dam and taught school for several years.

After her marriage in 1876 to Charles S. Morris, she made her home in Berlin, Wisconsin. She and her husband were active in civic affairs, giving time and money for improvements in libraries, hospitals and schools in the area. She was known as a gracious and generous hostess.

"Our critics assert we as club women are given to the fad of 'organization' and that in our desire to be equal to men we are overdoing matters and that our restless activity will cause us to lose all repose of manner. But there . . . are multitudes of bright women, no doubt, whose household cares are such as to prevent them from participating in club life and to guard well the life

within the home is the first duty of women. But women, however immersed in home, can give moral support to the movement."

These words were spoken by Lucy Smith Morris 85 years ago when the Wisconsin Federation of Women's Clubs was formed, and they still reflect the views of women today. She and her contemporaries would have welcomed today's opportunities for women.

Lucy Morris founded the Athena Club, a literary study group, in 1890 and served as president for 25 years. Its primary study was Shakespeare, a subject on which Mrs. Morris was an authority. Her booklets "Shakespearean Study Outlines" have been used by Women's Clubs and college classes. In her honor, Women's Clubs established an annual scholarship, the Lucy Morris Memorial, for the best Shakespearean student at Ripon College.

Mrs. Morris was also active in Berlin Friends in

Left: Lucy Smith Morris and a Fourth of July Pageant. Billed as a patriotic celebration, it began on the steps of Lucy's home. An immense crowd of spectators was gathered in Nathan Strong Park across the street. The lady holding the torch could be Lucy Morris who would have been in her sixties at the time. This picture was reproduced from a postcard on which the flag was backward.
(courtesy, Thomas Wucherer)

Right: The home of Lucy Smith Morris and her husband Charles was Lucy's pride and joy. She had a skilled craftsman, Mr. Blieferknicht, brought to Berlin on a retainer and promised him a living wage if he would keep the ornate, carved woodwork in good repair. It is not known if the car is theirs. The postcard was dated 1919.
(courtesy, Thomas Wucherer)

Council, the oldest woman's club in Wisconsin, organized in 1873 to study historical literature. Through the efforts of this group, such speakers as Julia Ward Howe, Elizabeth Cady Stanton and Susan B. Anthony were brought to the small community of Berlin. Mrs. Morris noted "the slogan 'Votes for Women' was then quite unpopular and so the titles of their addresses were usually announced as related to some subject of general interest, but none of them hesitated to voice their inner convictions before leaving the platform. So I can truthfully say their speeches were of Women's Rights masked."

Mrs. Morris became known throughout the state and nation as a leading social worker. She fought for suffrage and started several branches of the League of Women Voters in Wisconsin, including the Fond du Lac branch. For this, her name was placed on the state roll of honor. Her influence and dedication helped women in Wisconsin gain political freedom.

Lucy was interested in the peace movement espoused by Julia Ward Howe and became a member of the Woman's International Peace Association in 1877. In a letter written in 1931, Lucy ruefully remarked that wars were still going on even though she had paid dues to the Peace Association for all those years.

The culmination of all these interests and commitments came in the founding of the Wisconsin Federation of Women's Clubs. Lucy wrote every postmaster in Wisconsin, asked for the names and addresses of the women's groups in the area, and contacted those groups to encourage federation. Her efforts succeeded, and on October 20, 1896, the Wisconsin Federation of Women's Clubs was founded in Milwaukee. This organization united individual clubs to the General Federation,

the largest volunteer women's organization in the world. Lucy Morris was the first president of WFWC. At the twentieth anniversary of the WFWC, she was given the title of honorary founder and, in 1918 was named honorary vice-president of the General Federation at its fourteenth biennial conference. She never missed a state convention or the biennial national meeting of the General Federation. Because of her devotion, she was affectionately known as "the little mother of the Federation."

Second only to her interest in the club movement was Lucy's interest in promotion of libraries. In 1896, Mrs. Morris was appointed to the Wisconsin Free Library Commission. For 20 years she helped establish traveling libraries throughout the state. These were especially valuable to country school teachers and small towns without free public libraries. A form of the traveling library continues in operation today.

Her list of accomplishments is long and reflects her dedication to her slogan "ability begets responsibility." Generous with her time and efforts, Lucy Smith Morris was admired and loved by people throughout Wisconsin. At the time of her death, May 29, 1935, the Tri-county News published a tribute written by Mabel Smith Brooks of Green Lake. "The women who knew her admired her and loved her; they depended on her but lost none of their self-reliance. She was a leader who never assumed command . . . The club women have lost a great leader, beloved advisor and a warm friend . . ."

(See Selected Honors, Accomplishments, Publications, page 311)

written by SR. MARGARET LORIMER, CSA

mother m. agnes hazotte

A year before Wisconsin became a state, on May 7, 1847, Anna Mary Hazotte was born in Buffalo, New York. This youngest of seven children was to become co-foundress of one of the earliest American religious societies for women, a pioneer educator and a leader in providing health care in Wisconsin.

Shortly after Anna Mary's birth, the Hazottes who had emigrated from France settled in the French community in Detroit, Michigan. While the little girl's early years were happy, from the time she was five, the family was shattered by a series of devastating losses. First, her 17-year-old brother died, followed in a few months by an older sister. The following year the family lost both father and oldest daughter. Despite the hardships, young Anna Mary was enrolled in St. Mary's School and given a good musical education. A picture taken

Above left:
Sketch of Mother Mary Hazotte by Sr. Julienne Rompf, CSA;
Left: Front view of original convent at Barton.

during this period shows a waif-like child with solemn and questioning eyes. When Anna Mary was 13, yet another tragedy struck—her mother died. The four remaining children were determined to stay together, supported by the two boys.

When Anna Mary was 15, a letter changed her life. She was invited to visit a neighborhood friend who had joined a newly-formed religious community in Barton (now part of West Bend), Wisconsin. Disregarding the strenuous objections of her sister and brothers, Anna Mary left for Wisconsin in January, 1863. She found in Barton a little group of poverty-stricken German and Irish women under the leadership of a zealous Austrian missionary, Father Casper Rehrl. The young women taught in public and Catholic schools. Their life was hard; preparation for their work was almost non-existent.

The enthusiastic Father Rehrl had been in charge of the missions on the east shore of Lake Winnebago since 1845. As he built churches from Milwaukee to Green Bay, his major concern was to preserve the Christian faith and to educate the children of the immigrants in the area. Schools were few and teachers were frequently incompetent, alcoholic or both. Rehrl believed that a religious community working along with him could provide both secular and religious education. He returned to Europe and begged for help. No one responded. Disheartened, he resolved to found a society of young women, a move truly audacious since other religious congregations had roots and rules from Europe. He named his Society after the young Roman martyr St. Agnes.

When Anna Mary Hazotte arrived, the Sisters were trying to farm 11 acres of land with almost no implements and teaching with little more skill. Anna Mary, talented and comparatively well-educated, was welcomed as a great gift. On July 2, 1863, she was admitted to the society and given the name of Mary Agnes. The following year when she was scarcely 18 years old, she became the first regularly elected Superior of the Society, a position she was to maintain until her death, 41 years later.

Sister Mary Agnes was soon teaching at St. Peter's in Washington County, as well as sharing with Father Rehrl responsibility for the Sisters. It wasn't long before the priest and the young woman were battling over the direction of the community. Father Rehrl, eager to establish schools, wanted the sisters in the classroom almost immediately. He himself led a life of exceptional austerity and hardship, and had little idea of the needs of young women. Sister Mary Agnes demanded for the women educational standards that were unusual for the period. The break finally came in 1870, when Sister Mary Agnes and the majority of the community, numbering 44, moved to Fond du Lac, where she had been preparing them for teaching in 15 Wisconsin schools, five public and ten Catholic.

The next few years were ones of crisis. The break from Barton had not been without suffering on both sides. Poor nutrition and austere living left the Sisters vulnerable to illness and death. In the decade after 1872, 13 young women died. Their average age was 24. Pneumonia, tuberculosis and cancer took the lives of these daughters of German and Irish immigrants. In their need, they begged for money to keep their work alive. Throughout it all, Sister Agnes' indomitable strength and calm sustained her Sisters through their struggles and suffering.

As the little community became better known, bishops and pastors began to request Sisters to

In Wisconsin alone, the Sisters are responsible today for a college, two hospitals, two high schools, 22 elementary schools and two nursing homes.

45

teach, to play the organ, to direct choirs—anything to help the overworked priests. In 1879, Mother Agnes sent her Sisters as far as Kansas and Texas. But it was not without cost.

The first two sisters sent to Kansas contracted typhoid fever. When one died, Agnes was torn between sending help to the remaining Sister and fear that those sent would also succumb. She wrote:

> *"Dear Sister, you must not think that we have forgotten you or that we do not care for you. I grieve to think that you are there alone and if it would be possible, I would go immediately to you myself . . . Dear Sister, I know it's hard for you to be alone, but . . . be resigned to the Holy Will of God . . ."*

In spite of the adversities young women kept coming, and the Sisters went out to schools in Wisconsin, Indiana, Illinois, Michigan, New York, Pennsylvania, Ohio and Kansas. They agreed to build and staff such institutions as Boyle Home for the aged, Boyle Hall, a sanitarium and St. Agnes Hospital in Fond du Lac. They undertook in 1889 the administration and management of Leo House in New York as a shelter where newly arrived immigrants could avoid the victimization that was common at the period. Schools were staffed and the Sisters made every effort to become licensed and educated beyond the requirements of the period. By 1880 the Society had become a recognized Congregation in the Catholic Church.

By the fall of 1904, Mother Mary Agnes was tired and ill. She was responsible for 206 Sisters and 79 missions, 39 in Wisconsin. On her final journey, she got no further than Kansas where the Sisters had been active since 1879. There, after some months of suffering, she died at the age of 58.

Today her Community still thrives.

(See Selected Honors, Accomplishments, Publications, page 309)

Mother Mary Agnes Hazotte.

written by KATHY VAN SISTINE &
JAMES KOLTES

ella wheeler wilcox

Once a girl was trained for sewing,
Spinning, knitting, nothing more
She must never think of knowing
Aught of things outside her door.
Now a girl is taught she's human
Brain and body, soul and heart—
All are needed by the woman
Who today should play her part.

Women's liberation was a daring idea in the Victorian age when Ella Wheeler Wilcox wrote these lines in 1892.

She delighted in her role, that of barefoot farm girl, who, through sheer persistence, became the best known poet ever to come from Wisconsin.

Ella was born November 5, 1850, in Johnstown, Rock County, Wisconsin, to parents who had left New England to find rich farmland in Wisconsin. When she was 18 months old, her family moved to Westport, north of Madison. The Wheelers were near-failures as farmers but had other talents. Her father and her sister were gifted musicians and her brother Marcus contributed articles to the *Wisconsin State Journal.* Ella was allowed to spend hours writing poetry much to the annoyance of the neighbors; she chafed at frontier customs demanding that females do only housework.

Ella's friend, Anne Fields of Token Creek, a skilled athlete, inspired the heroine of Ella's first novel, *Minnie Tighthand,* written at the age of ten. Anne encouraged Ella's childish pranks, and daringly they swam stripped to the buff in the Token Creek mill pond.

When Ella was 14, she used the *New York Mercury* as her guide to story writing. She was determined to trade some of her work for a free

Wisconsin's most famous poet, she was the first native verse writer to gain national attention.

"Though critics may bow to art, and
   I am its own true lover,
It is not art, but heart, which wins
   the wide world over."
                    ELLA WHEELER WILCOX

Left: (both photos)
Ella Wheeler Wilcox, leader
of the Milwaukee School
of Poetry in the 1880's.
(courtesy, State Historical
Society of Wisconsin)

subscription and it was not until her pieces appeared and an enormous roll of *Mercury* newspapers arrived that her family learned of her efforts.

Further inspiration for Ella's pen arrived when the Prohibition movement swept Wisconsin after the Civil War. She was active in creating anti-liquor sentiment among members of the Wisconsin Legislature, representing the Good Templar Lodge from Vienna Township, of which her family was a charter member. Fifty-six poems in support of total abstinence, *Drops of Water,* published by the National Temperance House in 1872, were reissued by a London company. The English press dubbed Ella ''Temperance Poet Laureate of Europe and America.''

Ella's story in verse, *Maurine,* was an attempt to write a best seller and escape the need to write for mercenary motives. It became so popular that babies all over the country were named for the heroine.

Congratulations poured in from her contemporaries, including the notable poet, James Whitcomb Riley, who praised her for all the good she was doing and arranged to meet Ella in Milwaukee. If he had visions of an Elizabeth Barrett-Robert Browning romance, it was not to be. He was shocked by her chic appearance and her love of dancing, believing a genius should be above such things. She demanded he return all their correspondence at once, as she ''did not want posterity to know that she had wasted so much time on an impossible person.''

Ella became notorious when a Milwaukee newspaper revealed that her *Poems of Passion* had been condemned as immoral by Charles Dana of the *New York Sun.* People wrote from all over the country asking where they could buy the book.

Ella Wheeler Wilcox
(courtesy, State Historical Society of Wisconsin)

Ella wrote a note of thanks to the critic for his novel way of advertising her book. The publicity lifted her forever out of obscurity.

Robert Wilcox, a representative of the International Silver Company, caught a glimpse of Ella one day in a Milwaukee jewelry store and asked who she was. He wrote to her and asked to be presented when he would again be in Milwaukee. They began a correspondence. Ella's friends warned her not to let Robert see her farm home or he might lose interest in her, but when he did visit, they discovered a mutual interest in spiritualism. After a Milwaukee wedding, exchanging vows that did not include the word ''obey'', they settled in Meriden, Connecticut, in 1884. Their only child died shortly after birth.

When they moved to New York City, they became frequent guests at parties given by Ella's publisher, Mrs. Frank Leslie. Here Ella got her first taste of high society. Many men were ready to flirt with the author of *Poems of Passion.* According to Jenny Ballou, her biographer, men who pursued her discovered ''you cannot talk ten minutes with her before she bumps you up against a two hundred-pound husband with whom she seems to be ridiculously enamored."

Both Robert and Ella were influenced by the ideas of the famous Hindu philosopher Vivekananda: the unity of all religions and humanitarian service. They also believed in life after life. A year after Robert Wilcox died in May, 1916, Ella received a message she felt sure was from him, and life was once again worth living. In response to his message, she went to France during World War I. She visited soldiers and lectured them on sex problems.

Ella's belief in the unlimited powers of the human spirit has given her words their distinctive life. She has expressed herself not only in poetry and prose, but also in opinions on controversial issues, such as abortion, divorce, female equality and venereal disease. *Cosmopolitan* magazine was her pulpit for nearly 40 years.

In 1919, Ella Wheeler Wilcox was hospitalized in Bath, England, with a malignancy that did not respond to treatment. Upon her return to the United States, she was carried off the ship on a stretcher and taken by ambulance to her home. She died there on October 30. The odyssey of the Wisconsin farm girl who became a woman of the world and an international celebrity was completed.

Her most famous lines express her upbeat approach to life:

> *Laugh and the world laughs with you;*
> *Weep, and you weep alone.*

(See Selected Honors, Accomplishments, Publications, page 314)

Ella Wheeler Wilcox (courtesy, State Historical Society of Wisconsin)

elizabeth peckham

Slightly over five feet tall and remembered as "the little woman with the vigorous voice," Elizabeth Gifford Peckham was not a squeamish lady. Indeed, she was a distinguished taxonomist who, with her husband, spent more than twenty years studying and publishing scientific works on wasps and jumping spiders.

In 1883, they published their first book. In 1889 and 1890, the Peckhams published papers on sexual selection and protective resemblances in spiders. Their major work, *The Instincts and Habits of Solitary Wasps,* was published in 1898 and is considered an authoritative work and a masterpiece of writing in its clearness, aptness and simplicity.

By 1909, the Peckhams had produced 31 publications, 25 of them dealing with the eight-eyed, eight-legged jumping spiders. The newsletter, *Peckhamia,* is circulated in New Zealand, Canada, Argentina and Poland as well as the United States. Fellow taxonomists also named a genus of spider *peckhamia.*

The Peckhams' collection of 4,000 specimens and their personal library were donated to the Milwaukee Public Museum.

Elizabeth Gifford was born in Milwaukee in 1854 and spent her childhood years at Rosebank, a picturesque estate on Spring Street (now Wisconsin Avenue). Her father, Charles Gifford, was an English landscape gardener. Her mother, Mary Child, was a native of Delafield. After her father's death, her mother remarried, and Swedish-born Dr. Charles Leuthstrom, who came to Milwaukee in 1862, became Elizabeth's stepfather.

She attended Vassar and, after her graduation in 1876, worked for a short time at the Milwaukee public library. Elizabeth took a job as research assistant to George Peckham, a high school biology teacher and pioneer in the use of laboratory methods in teaching. (He later became in turn,

Left: Mrs. George W. Peckham
Right: Sketch of Elizabeth Peckham, taken from later photo in a French book, "Bibliographia Araneorum" by Pierre Bonnet, Toulouse, France, 1945.

Superintendent of Milwaukee Schools and City Librarian. Peckham High School is named in his honor.)

In 1880, Elizabeth Gifford and George Peckham were married at Inter-lachen, a spacious home built by her stepfather, Dr. Leuthstrom, on Pine Lake near Hartford. They spent weekends and holidays there, collaborating in scientific research.

In 1894, Elizabeth Peckham was a prime mover in the organization of the Milwaukee Branch of the Association of Collegiate Women, which later became the American Association of University Women. She recalled, ''There was nothing formal about the organization of the College Club. Mrs. George Noyes sat on the piano stool in the living room of our home, Mrs. Perry Williams, decorous in the arm chair, and I perched on the edge of the table, while we talked about the need for some sort of a club here in the city which would encourage women to go to college.''

The three friends gathered five other college women enthusiastic about the idea, and this was the nucleus of the Milwaukee Branch of AAUW. Elizabeth was its first president, 1894 to 1895. The Milwaukee Branch functioned in a statewide capacity until 1908, when the Madison Branch was founded.

Members met in private homes until 1919, when a house at 236 Oneida Street was acquired. The old Patrick Cudahy mansion on Prospect Avenue overlooking Lake Michigan was purchased in 1922. Built in 1880, it was one of the finest mansions to grace Milwaukee's Gold Coast. The property was sold to the Layton School of Art in 1961, and later demolished for a freeway that was never built. The site of the Peckham home, two blocks west, is now part of the Hotel Astor parking lot. One block south is the handsome landmark College Women's Club at 1119 North Marshall Street. On the second floor in History Hall is a picture of petite, demure, Elizabeth Peckham with black bonnet, bustle, and tiny parasol.

(See Selected Honors, Accomplishments, Publications, page 312)

Elizabeth Peckham organized and became president of what was to become the first branch of the American Association of University Women in Wisconsin.

written by MARIA BODE

belle case la follette

Belle Case La Follette is often remembered as the wife and mother of the three famous Wisconsin La Follettes, founders and supporters of political activism in Wisconsin known as Progressivism. Her husband was Robert, Sr. (Fighting Bob), her sons Robert, Jr. and Philip.

But she was more. Her sound political judgment was considered one of the most valuable family assets. She wrote and spoke on issues of concern to her—female suffrage, race discrimination, protective legislation for working women, child labor law reform, peace, disarmament—and was often more radical then her husband, advocating causes long before they became popular.

Thus, it is an incomplete evaluation of her contribution to the heritage of this state and nation to remember her primarily as a wife and mother.

Short, of fair complexion, with small features and blue eyes, Belle Case La Follette was considered charming with a bubbly personality. She had a quiet, sympathetic manner which she used to effectively draw people out.

She was born in Summit, Juneau County, Wisconsin, on April 21, 1859. Her parents, Mary Nesbit and Anson T. Case came to Wisconsin shortly after they were married in 1854, before Belle and her six brothers and sisters were born. From her parents, she inherited robust physical

Belle Case LaFollette, formal portrait taken about 1905.
(courtesy, State Historical Society of Wisconsin)

Robert M. LaFollette with his family about 1917.

health, independence of mind, and self-reliance. One of her favorite people was her grandmother who taught her much common sense knowledge about survival.

When Belle was three, the family moved to a farm outside of Baraboo where she and her two surviving brothers grew up. In 1875, at 16, she moved to Madison to enter the University of Wisconsin. Of three courses available to her—classical, science, and modern classical—she chose the latter.

Belle Case met Bob La Follette in their freshman year at the University. Although he had been attracted to her from the first, she kept their relationship light-hearted until the end of their junior year, when they became engaged. Since they had no money, they decided to wait to get married and, upon graduation, pursued separate careers. Belle went to Spring Green to teach and serve as assistant principal.

A year later, in 1880, she moved back to Baraboo and taught seventh graders in the school she had attended. One of her students was John Ringling of the famous circus family.

"... when John read a long acount—interrupted with giggles from the school—of the side shows he and

Robert M. LaFollette, Sr. and family seated around a radio presumably listening to election returns, 1924. (Belle was in Washington, DC and Bob, Sr. in Madison at election time.) The persons in the photo, left to right: Isabel LaFollette (Philip's wife); Belle; Bob, Sr., seated; Philip behind the radio, Governor John Blaine, Robert, Jr. at extreme right standing.
(courtesy, State Historical Society of Wisconsin)

A leader in Wisconsin Progressivism, she was the first woman graduate of the University of Wisconsin Law School.

other boys had been giving every night, I lectured him and drew the moral that if John would put his mind on his lessons as he did on side shows, he might yet become a scholar. Fortunately the scolding had no effect."

While Belle Case was teaching, Bob La Follette obtained a law degree at the University of Wisconsin, and in 1881 was elected district attorney of Dane County. They decided they could now afford to marry. At Belle's request the word "obey" was omitted from the marriage ceremony which took place in her parents' home December 31, 1881. They made their home in Madison with his mother and sister in a house on what is now Broom Street.

In 1882, Fola, their first child, was born. At the time of her birth, Belle was very happy for she believed "the supreme experience in life is motherhood . . . Yet I am sure there is no inherent

conflict in a mother's taking good care of her children, developing her talents, and continuing to work along lines adapted to motherhood and homemaking." Fola remained an only child for 12 years as Belle expanded her interests beyond child-rearing.

Shortly after Fola was born, Belle enrolled in the Wisconsin College of Law, one of 19 students and the only woman, to study law for its "keenly enjoyable intellectual training." Two years later she became the first woman to graduate from the law school in Wisconsin. She was admitted to the State bar with the right to practice before the Wisconsin Supreme Court.

Belle never actually practiced law, but she advised La Follette for the next 40 years. He credits her with the brief which won him a case, broke new legal ground, and brought a compliment of the highest order from presiding Chief Justice William P. Lyon: "It is one of the best briefs submitted to the court in years, and in writing the opinion I quoted liberally from it because it was so admirably reasoned and so clearly stated."

In 1885, when Bob was elected to the United States House of Representatives, the family moved to Washington, DC, opening a new life for Belle. She was Bob's secretary and administrative assistant. Her experience in Washington, DC enlarged her views on opportunities for women and gave her an understanding of politics. She attended all important debates in the House and participated in most of La Follette's important policy conferences.

Following La Follette's defeat for a third term in 1890, they returned to Madison and a decade of private life. During this period, Belle began to develop her independent social and political views on such issues as physical education, dress reform, co-education, and women's suffrage. They decided it was time to complete the family they had planned. Bob, Jr., was born in 1895, Philip in 1897, and Mary in 1899.

But this was not the end of her political activism. With Belle campaigning at his side, LaFollette won the governorship of Wisconsin in 1900. He consistently referred to his years in the executive mansion as "when *we* were governor." Belle's outspoken views on issues, plus her early strong support of unpopular causes like female suffrage, took political and personal courage, for people often referred to her as notoriety-seeking.

La Follette served as governor of Wisconsin until he was elected to the United States Senate in 1905. Shortly afterward the family moved back to Washington, DC.

Belle and her husband launched the *La Follette Weekly Magazine* to disseminate ideas of Progressivism. Belle was devoted to this enterprise and worked long and hard to keep the magazine alive.

She wrote articles in support of improved working conditions for mothers, child labor reform, and race relations. When the federal government under President Wilson sought to reinstitute segregation in the Bureau of Engraving and Printing, she spoke out against discrimination, even going to the President himself. She also argued against Jim Crow streetcars.

But the cause with which she felt the closest identification was achieving the vote for women.

Initially Belle worked actively in the 1911-12 Wisconsin campaign to obtain the vote with other leaders like Ada James.

When Belle realized that achieving the vote on the state level was not effective, she turned to working for a constitutional amendment. In April of 1913, she appeared before the Senate Committee on Woman Suffrage, with other prominent speakers. The Senate committee unanimously recommended passage of the constitutional amendment but seven more years passed before final ratification in time for women to vote in the 1920 presidential election.

In the meantime, the United States had been involved in World War I. A determined pacifist, Belle spoke out against the United States entering the war, and after the war, she took up the cause for amnesty for political prisoners, and disarmament.

She was untiring and when in 1924, Belle's attention was once more drawn to her husband's political career while he ran for the Presidency of the United States as an independent candidate on the Progressive ticket, she actively campaigned for him. Less than a year after his defeat, "Fighting Bob" was dead.

Immediately, labor unions, women's groups, members of the Progressive party, and Wisconsin legislators petitioned Belle to run for his vacant seat in the Senate. Although mindful of the importance that her election might hold in paving the way for other women, she declined to run. She knew the demands of a public career, but had never at any time in her life felt inclined to choose one for herself.

At the time of her death, on August 18, 1931, *The New York Times* called her "probably the least known yet most influential of all the American women who had to do with public affairs in this country." She was much more than a wife and mother of famous men.

(See Selected Honors, Accomplishments, Publications, page 310)

Mrs. LaFollette speaks to farmers, Blue Mounds, 1915.
(courtesy, State Historical Society of Wisconsin)

written by GRACE DRAXLER

helen thompson

For more than a quarter of a century Park Falls in Price County was blessed with the ability, charm and sound judgment of Helen F. Thompson. She was one of the first women in Wisconsin to be elected as County Superintendent of Schools and one of the first to serve in the State Legislature. Representing Price County in the State Assembly bid, she defeated her opponent in the 1924 election by a margin of 3,088 to 1,663 votes.

Helen Thompson came to Price County from Menasha, where she was born into an Irish family. With her keen mind and her sense of humor, she quickly became a leader and influential citizen in the community. After teaching for several years, she purchased the Park Hotel, then called the Central Hotel. Under her management, it became the leading lodging and dining center for travelers, especially business and political leaders, and the social center of the community.

Her wide range of interests led her into other activities which later culminated in campaign for public office. The *Stevens Point Journal* (January 25, 1925) commended her, "Our hearty approval goes out to Miss Helen F. Thompson, a Park Falls schoolteacher elected to the Assembly, who announced on her arrival that she had 'no promises, no slogans, no platform. I'm going to proceed cautiously and hear the pro's and con's before I cast my vote.' . . . This is positively refreshing. It is restful occasionally to find a

Helen F. Thompson (courtesy, Park Falls Public Library)

statesman who does not claim a prophetic vision, an inspiration, a divinely appointed call to lead the public in new ways. She is just a well-educated, level-headed young woman."

In the Assembly, she introduced a bill relating to Forest Administration that was passed in 1925. This measure permits the Conservation Commission (now the Department of Natural Resources) to exchange state lands for private lands in order to build up some of the areas in the state. It is of special interest and benefit to Price and Sawyer counties and counties in the Northern Lakes region.

Thompson appreciated the courtesy the men in the State Legislature showed the three women members and wrote them a note, "I was decidedly pleased with the welcome the men of the Legislature extended us." (Madison *Capital Times,* February, 1925)

Thompson favored a semi-annual tax payment to ease the taxpayers' load. When she voted against annual payment of taxes, she received a note of congratulation from the *Park Falls Herald,* (April, 1925), "We congratulate Miss Thompson upon her ability to read the writing of the people."

This author remembers Helen Thompson, personally, not only as an outstanding teacher, but also as a friend, a neighbor, a person interested in people. She could promote lively conversation with humor on almost any subject, but politics was her favorite. She was well versed in history, government, literature, and religion. She could converse with laborer, merchant, educator.

She passed away February 15, 1935 after many years of devoted service to the church, the community, and the state. Funeral services were held at St. Anthony's church which she helped build, and the church was filled with those who loved and respected her. In her honor, the United States flag was carried in the funeral procession by a military honor guard.

Helen Thompson was considered Park Falls' best loved and respected citizen.

(See Selected Honors, Accomplishments, Publications, page 314)

*She was one of the
first women members of the e
Wisconsin State Assembly.*

*A staunch Republican, she
ran on a simple ticket —
"No Slogan, No Promises
and No Platform."*

written by MARGARET LAMOREAUX MACFARLANE

mary spellman

Mary Spellman gave a lifetime of service to her community. For nearly 50 years she taught in Beaver Dam public schools. At age 70, she was elected mayor of the city.

Beaver Dam had been incorporated for only eight years when Mary Ann Spellman was born on September 4, 1864. Her parents, Phillip and Ann Duff Spellman, had emigrated from Ireland, met in Beaver Dam and were married there in 1856.

Through hard work and frugality the Spellmans managed to own the little farm on which Mary was reared. They nurtured Mary's strong sense of duty and service. Mary was the youngest child, the only girl, in their family of four.

After graduating from high school in 1882, Miss Spellman began teaching in a one-room schoolhouse in Trenton with only two pupils. In

Mayor Spellman met the challenge of her office during the Depression so courageously that she was elected to a second term in 1936.

1884 she was hired to teach in the Beaver Dam public schools. During the ensuing half-century, Mary taught in several elementary schools spending the last twenty years teaching junior high arithmetic.

"What made Mary Spellman a great teacher was her sincerity, her unusual ability to teach in a dynamic way and her ingenuity in making the pupils believe that they were learning something which was necessary to a productive life," said Professor L.R. Creutz, former superintendent of Beaver Dam schools.

Miss Spellman taught as many as three generations in some families. Annually a large bronze plaque is given in her honor to the eighth grade student with the highest average in arithmetic. In 1981 the plaque contained 48 names, 27 boys and 21 girls, including the names of a father and son.

Less than a year after her retirement, at age 70, and after considerable persuasion by a group of former students, "her boys and girls" as she called them, Mary consented to become a candidate for mayor of Beaver Dam. She conditioned her acceptance of the candidacy on "No speeches, campaigning or politicking!"

It was 1934, the most difficult depression year for Beaver Dam which then had a population of nearly 10,000 residents. The city was disastrously affected by labor strife; industries were closing with the National Guard called in to quell the violence. Controversy was raging in the city's government.

In this chaotic atmosphere, without any personal campaigning, Mary Spellman was overwhelmingly elected mayor. The voters' mandate was clearly for new leadership and for a restoration of integrity in city government.

The day that Mary Spellman was inaugurated mayor, several thousand friends led a torch-light parade with bands and marchers through downtown Beaver Dam to the high school gymnasium where city officials and civic leaders gathered. In her inaugural address Mary pledged fiscal constraints except for expenditures needed to keep the city of Beaver Dam growing.

Mary Spellman was at city hall bright and early the next morning. During her administration many worthwhile work projects were carried out; painting the public schools, the addition of

Left: Mary Spellman, first woman mayor of Beaver Dam; Near Left: Mayor Spellman and Council.

sidewalks, installation of a band concert shell in Swan city park and development of a sanitary storm sewer system. As a former teacher, Mary added her support for some much needed athletic

fields so that the local "youth under God's blue sky can develop healthy bodies."

Near the end of her second term Miss Spellman was interviewed by a Milwaukee newspaper reporter who noted she was busily knitting at her desk. She told the reporter it would be foolish for a woman of her age to be just sitting there trying to look official and important when there was no immediate city business.

Miss Spellman knitted all her life—sweaters for the World War I doughboys, mittens and socks for nephews and great nephews and afghans for her niece, Margaret, who lived with her in the family home.

The Beaver Dam Women's Club was co-founded in 1898 by Mary Spellman and Caroline Beule. This club was responsible for the introduction of manual training and domestic science courses in the public schools. During Mary's term as mayor, a fund-raising campaign was undertaken to build a 50-room hospital. St. Joseph's Hospital was completed in 1939. Miss Spellman became first president of its service club.

Mary Spellman continued to be active and interested in the youth and citizens of Beaver Dam until a fall resulted in a broken hip, precipitating her death at age 80 on April 4, 1945.

The entire community mourned her death. Mary's legacy to Beaver Dam was a half-century of dedicated service as an educator, two terms as mayor and a lifetime of community service.

(See Selected Honors, Accomplishments, Publications, page 313)

Civic leader Mary Spellman established the acceptance of future women on the Common Council.

written by DOROTHY & LEE NEWCOMER

jessie jack hooper

Jessie Jack Hooper's frailty early in life belied her later role as a state and national feminist leader for more than a quarter of a century.

Born in rural Iowa in 1865 Jessie Jack was educated by governesses except for a single year of art study at Colman College in Des Moines.

In 1887, while visiting her married sister in Oshkosh, Wisconsin, she met a young lawyer, Ben Hooper. The couple married the next year and were blessed with a daughter, Lorna.

Ben encouraged his wife to become active in the community and soon Jessie said "one thing led to

Above: Jessie Jack Hooper, 1890.
Right: Mr. and Mrs. Ben Hooper and daughter Lorna, 1892.
(courtesy, State Historical Society of Wisconsin)

another.''

Jessie Jack Hooper's activity in woman's suffrage began in 1911, the year before Wisconsin held a state referendum on suffrage. She joined Ada James' Political Equality League. In Oshkosh its members rang doorbells, held a mock election and conducted speaking tours. In spite of statewide efforts, the suffrage referendum lost.

In the next few years as a lobbyist for the Wisconsin Woman Suffrage Association Hooper had "presence" and a remarkable self-control; her disposition was such that, as an opponent said, she smiled even when she lost. Carrie Chapman Catt, head of the National Woman Suffrage Association, called her to Washington often, and she became Catt's "right-hand man"; the push now was for a suffrage amendment to the US Constitution. Catt and Hooper tramped in many a suffrage parade together including the memorable 1916 Chicago march to the Republican National Convention in the rain. Jessie, her daughter, Lorna, and two nieces, their white dresses wet and streaked with yellow from their suffrage tunics, never left the line of march.

When the war came in 1917 Hooper volunteered for work under the state's Council for National Defense. In Washington Mrs. Catt called for a petition drive to enlist 224,000 potential voters, men and women, to support the national amendment. "Attend to the petitions with your greatest earnestness in addition to war work."

On the day the Nineteenth Amendment finally passed Congress Ben Hooper wired his wife, "Hooray. Congratulations." After Wisconsin ratified, the first state to do so, the legislature voted its thanks to Jessie Jack Hooper. "That wasn't because her hair was marcelled," observed a reporter, "it was because she had won a difficult political victory."

In 1920 the National Woman Suffrage Association transformed itself into the League of Women Voters. With Hooper as its first president, the Wisconsin League adopted the practice of sending questionnaires to candidates for public office and supporting bills but remaining officially non-partisan. At League workshops throughout the state, the message according to a Superior headline was, "Women Urged to Learn Politics; Protect Family."

Early in the afternoon of June 27, 1922, a telephone call from the Democratic state convention in Milwaukee offered her the nomination for the United States Senate to oppose the Republican incumbent, Senator Robert M. LaFollette. She accepted the nomination believing that women should not only vote but run for office.

Hooper immediately resigned the League of Women Voters presidency. Since LaFollette had opposed entry into the World War, she stressed the Americanism issue, "the right and justice of our cause in the war." In contrast to LaFollette's isolation, she called for international cooperation and participation in the World Court. Her platform also included support of a federal department of education, a child labor amendment and prohibition.

Although Hooper polled more votes in the primary than any man on the state ticket, none

1922 Campaign Staff, US Senate Race, Jessie Jack Hooper, middle. Surrounding her are (clockwise behind her) Ella Sweeney, Ella Treat, Liba Peshakova, Gertrude Watkins, Mrs. Bemis.

She lobbied in Washington, DC for the suffrage amendment and then, back in Wisconsin began a campaign to insure that Wisconsin would be the first to ratify.

65

received the 25 percent to get on the ballot as Democrats in the general election. All had to run as Independents.

Hooper hired two women organizers to help her get to every woman in the state, in every walk of life. "For five weeks," she said later, "I spoke from one to four times a day, indoors and out, in big opera houses and in small halls."

No one expected her to win. On election day LaFollette rolled up 83 percent of the vote and carried every county. The day after the election employees at her husband's wholesale grocery firm placed a liquor bottle tied with ribbon on her desk. Jessie enjoyed the prank.

For the rest of her life, Jessie Jack Hooper worked for world peace. She pressed for an organization to give overall direction to women's groups in the peace campaign. The Conference on the Cause and Cure of War was formed with Mrs. Catt as chairman.

In 1928 Hooper submitted to the Conference a comprehensive plan for peace. It included the outlawing of war, arbitration, entry into the World Court, and no arms sales to warring powers.

Senate ratification in 1929 of the Kellogg-Briand Pact of Paris for the renunciation of war was due in large part to zealous effort by Conference leaders. "I wish I could be in every place at once," Hooper wrote, "my whole heart is in this work." Later she continued to work for American entry into the World Court.

After one of her speaking tours she returned home to nurse her granddaughter, Lois, who had scarlet fever. She sat out the quarantine in her granddaughter's room, for as she wrote Mrs. Catt, "I did not have the heart to turn the little tot over to a strange nurse."

Hooper ran for the Wisconsin State Senate in 1934 to speak "from the inside" for legislation that women wanted. Often accompanied by her granddaughter, she would drive in her "spiffy" Franklin motor car campaigning around the district. She was defeated in the primary. One month later this woman who had fought diabetes for years learned that she had cancer.

She remained at home among family and friends, and she continued her correspondence with Mrs. Catt until her death, May 8, 1935. Woman and pragmatist, Jessie Jack Hooper set about accomplishing specific needed reforms. There are no improvements in government, she maintained, when "women are at politics zero."

(See Selected Honors, Accomplishments, Publications, page 309)

She never quibbled. She either "firmly believed" or was "wholly and unequivocably opposed."

Her rare and fine collection of antique glass paperweights placed the Bergstrom Art Center and Mahler Glass Museum in the front ranks of centers housing important American collections.

evangeline bergstrom

A young girl's fascination with the beauty of a glass paperweight later became a collection ranked among the finest in the world.

Evangeline Hoysradt Bergstrom was born May 23, 1872, in Ithaca, New York, the only child of Dr. and Mrs. George W. Hoysradt. She attended the Anne Brown School for Girls in Ithaca and met John Nelson Bergstrom while he was a student at Cornell University.

The couple was married in 1901 and moved to DePere. In 1904 they moved to Neenah where Bergstrom joined his father, D.W. Bergstrom, in founding the Bergstrom Paper Company. They had no children.

Small of stature but possessing a vital personality, Mrs. Bergstrom was described as religious, strong-willed, outspoken and shrewd. She gained the respect of all who dealt with her. She had another requisite for an interest such as hers, a supportive spouse.

She began her paperweight collection in the 1930's, but it was as a young girl she developed her love for the smooth glass half globes. Her grandmother had allowed her to hold and study a colorful weight.

"That paperweight was of the millefiori type . . . it amused me by the hour to try to find two similar florets. Years later at an antique show I found a weight like that one I had loved as a child. It had a 'B' with the date 1847 . . . I bought it after much deliberation and also another which took my fancy. The first proved to be a Baccarat and the second an American weight made in Fowlerton, Indiana.

"I started with one French and one American and have been intrigued by them ever since. They have a sparkle and brilliancy resembling precious jewels to me," she said.

From the 1930's to the early 1950's Mrs. Bergstrom continued to gather paperweights. She read all the available information about them.

Evelyn Campbell Cloak was the first curator of the Bergstrom glass paperweight collection. She wrote and published the book, "Glass Paperweights of the Bergstrom Art Center."

Mrs. Cloak wrote, "There is something truly remarkable in the fact that this woman in Middle West America, not only brought together such an amazing collection, but delved so deeply into the history and techniques of making paperweights and the factory sources of the specimens of her collection.

"It is even more astonishing that as early as 1940 Mrs. Bergstrom had the temerity to publish the result of her scholarly work in the handsome book, *Old Glass Paperweights.*"

The collector also wrote several articles for magazines. One titled, "Pinchbeck but Precious," printed in *The American Collector,* is ranked "The best piece written on the subject" by Paul Holister, New York glass paperweight expert.

John Bergstrom bequeathed the Tudor style home in Neenah to be used as a museum. Before her death in 1958 at the age of 86, Mrs. Bergstrom willed her extensive glass paperweight collection to

Evangeline H. Bergstrom (courtesy, John Nelson Bergstrom Art Center, Neenah, Wisconsin)

the museum and provided the housing of the collection in the home.

All paperweights are carefully catalogued giving descriptions, date of acquisition, source (French, English, Scottish, American or whatever), designer-creator and other pertinent facts about the weight.

At the time of her death, Mrs. Bergstrom's glass paperweight collection numbered around 700 pieces. With the endowment, gifts from other collectors and special gifts presented directly to the museum, more weights have been added, now numbering over 1400.

When announcements of a commemorative glass paperweight enclosing the likeness of Mrs. Bergstrom were sent out in 1973, return orders brought with them letters telling of her influence on other collectors.

Wrote one, "My collection began with the weights my uncle gave me with help in selection from Mrs. Bergstrom, a longtime friend."

Another told of assistance offered by Mrs. Bergstrom in identifying several glass paperweights, a lift she gave to several others as she shared her pleasure in the beauty of the weights.

The collection, a permanent part of the John Nelson Bergstrom Art Center and Mahler Glass Museum, is a continuing memorial to the woman whose fondness for them inspired a gift of beauty to future generations.

(See Selected Honors, Accomplishments, Publications, page 306)

B

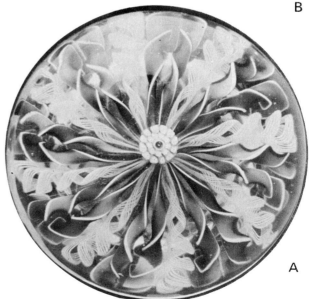

A

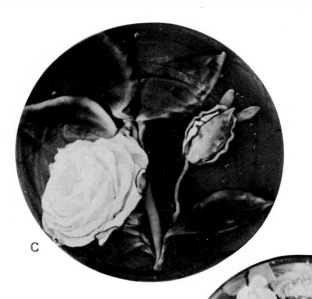

C

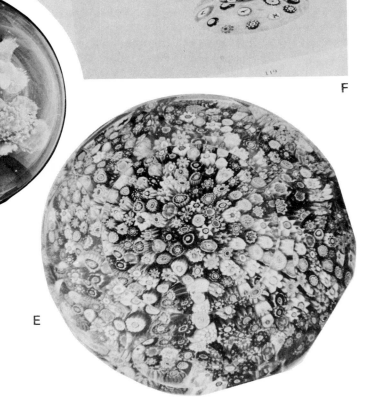

F

Selections from
Evangeline Bergstrom's
glass paperweight
collection:
(Courtesy, Bergstrom Art
Center and Museum)
Clockwise beginning at
lower left:
(A) St. Louis (French)
mid-19th century.
Crown weight.
Alternating red/blue/
white twists and white
filigree form medallion

D

at Millefiori cane apex. (B) Baccarats (French), mid-19th
century. Top left: Sulphide portrait of Romanesque head
of Napoleon with star overhead on transparent turquoise
over opaque white. Top right: Sulphide portrait of George
Washington. Below left: Floating flat bouquet. Below
right: Floating flat bouquet, white clematis, red/white
primrose. (C) French, probably Pantin, ca. 1878. Full-
blown, lemon yellow rosebud with sepals, green leaves,
stem on translucent cobalt blue ground. (D) Mt. Washington Glass Works, New Bedford, MA, ca. 1869-94.
Lampwork motif of red strawberries, white blossoms, pale
green leaves. Rare. (E) Clichy (French) ca. 1845. Probably
an early Clichy close millefiori. Motif includes at least 25
Clichy roses in varying shades of pink. (F) Baccarat
(French) mid-19th century. Patterned millefiori in three
tiers; rare.

E

Zona Gale on her graduation from the University of Wisconsin, 1895, and, right, In the backyard of her home on the Wisconsin River.

zona gale

Zona Gale is remembered today as a feminist, pacifist, political activist. Her impressive literary achievements, culminating in the Pulitzer prize for drama in 1921, have been overshadowed by her activities as an ardent reformer.

She was born in Portage, August 26, 1874, the only child of Eliza Beers and Charles Franklin Gale. Her close attachment to her parents was a major influence in her life. As a child, her health was delicate. She had a quiet grave manner and a tendency to drift off into a world of her own populated by imaginary playmates. She wrote her first book at seven, and submitted a novel for publication when she was 13, which was promptly rejected.

"I inherited predominant elements of character from both parents," she once stated. "From my mother imagination and initiative; from my father reflection and meditation."

While a student at the University of Wisconsin-Madison from 1891 to 1895, she took courses in literature and wrote sentimental poetry. Her stories and poems appeared in the *Aegis,* a campus publication. After graduation she became one of the first woman newspaper reporters in Milwaukee.

After receiving her masters degree from UW in 1901, she moved to New York where she worked for the *Evening World.* Her assignments were mainly social events.

Then she fell in love with Ridgely Torrence. Torn between her love for him and her devotion to her parents who warned her of the consequences of entanglements, she endured two torturous years of inner conflict. "I can't bear anything that gives them pain," she said and finally fled New York and returned to Portage to her parents' home.

She buried herself in her work. Her first successful novel, *Romance Island,* was published two years later. Proceeds from the sale of the book financed the stately home she built for her parents on Edgewater Street. It is now owned by the

Women's Civic League, an organization she founded.

Although it was a financial success, *Romance Island* did not impress the critics. "Occasional moments of suspense fail to relieve the cloying sentimentality."

Her world was one of neighborly kindness and friendly concern. The first collection of *Friendship Village* stories appeared in 1908. Portage was portrayed as an idyllic, romantic place.

The declaration of war in 1917 propelled her into the real world. She was an ardent pacifist and her attitude was considered close to treason by many local persons. Charles Gale bought Liberty bonds in her name to squelch the controversy.

However romance and beauty faded from her work. *Birth*, published in 1918, represented the

Below (left to right):
Zona Gale with her parents, Eliza
Beers Gale and Charles Franklin Gale;
Zona at the time of her marriage,
October, 1928; portrait (courtesy,
State Historical Society of Wisconsin);
last photograph taken at the
Green Bay Peace Conference,
October 1938.

emergence of serious realism in her writing. A newspaper critic applauded the new style, "*Friendship Village* made you want to bolt to the delicatessen for a pickle and *Birth* supplies the pickle."

In 1920, Zona Gale published *Miss Lulu Bett* acclaimed as "the best fictional study of the unmarried sister, the poor relation who has become the indentured slave of well-to-do relatives." The book shared honors with Sinclair Lewis's *Main Street* as the best selling novel that year. She won the Pulitzer prize for drama when she adapted *Miss Lulu Bett* for the stage a year later.

Zona Gale equated injustice with sin which she defined as anything that prevents or delays growth in body, mind, and spirit. She advocated Prohibition. She joined the Sacco-Vanzetti movement and the American Civil Liberties Union. She helped write the 1921 Wisconsin Equal Rights Law prohibiting discrimination against women. She was a staunch LaFollette supporter and campaigned actively for him during his 1924 bid for the Presidency.

When her mother died in 1923, she lost her anchor in life. Zona Gale's writing went beyond realism. *Preface to a Life* published in 1926 reflected her preoccupation with the occult. Later "Bridal Pond" was her most successful effort to explore the regions of insanity.

She became an ardent follower of Robert LaFollette and his Progressivism —an enthusiastic pacifist and advocate of social reform.

Zona Gale (1874-1938)

When she was 54, Zona Gale married William Llewelyn Breese, Portage industrialist and lifelong friend. She continued to sign her maiden name and she wore no wedding ring. Breese had a daughter, Juliette, from a previous marriage who lived with them. The couple soon adopted a three-year-old girl, Leslyn, and Zona enjoyed what she often called the happiest days of her life.

She died of pneumonia December 27, 1938. The Winnebago women clad in native garb who stood outside the church on the day of her funeral testified to her benevolence for them—the grocery bills paid, mortgages never foreclosed because of her intervention.

Biographer Harold Simonson captured her presence with these words:

"From these Wisconsin books more than a novelist, a reformer, or a Portage Citizen emerges, for whomever comes to them comes to Zona Gale, the woman."

(See Selected Honors, Accomplishments, Publications, page 308)

lillie rosa minoka-hill

Lillie Minoka was born on August 30, 1876, on the St. Regis reservation in New York, where her Mohawk mother, according to a family legend, died shortly after childbirth. When Lillie was five years old, her father, Joshua G. Allen, a Philadelphia physician, sent for her. Years later, she described her arrival in Philadelphia as feeling like a "little wooden Indian who hardly dared look to right or left." Allen renamed her Rosa, because he thought she was "too dark to be a lily," and enrolled her in the Graham Institute, a Quaker

Dr. Lillie Rosa Minoka-Hill practicing in her "kitchen-clinic" 1947. (courtesy, Milwaukee Journal, October 19, 1947)

boarding school. There she received the training of a proper Quaker girl, graduating from high school in 1895.

Imbued with the Quaker precept to "do good," Minoka planned to enter nursing, but her family considered medical school more appropriate for an educated woman. Since she was still quite young for medical training, Allen sent her to Quebec to live in a convent where she studied French. This Canadian visit reawakened her memories of Catholic rites at St. Regis, and the sisters of the convent and their works profoundly impressed her. She decided to convert to Catholicism, and her father accepted her decision.

On her return to Philadelphia, she eagerly attended the Woman's Medical College of Pennsylvania from which she graduated in 1899. Following an internship at the Woman's Hospital in Philadelphia, she and a former classmate, Frances Tyson, established a private practice in the city and also attended indigent immigrant women at the Woman's Clinic, a dispensary connected with the Woman's Medical College. In addition Minoka worked at the Lincoln Institute, a government boarding school for Native Americans. There she met Anna Hill, an Oneida student, who introduced Minoka to her brother, Charles Abram Hill, a graduate of Carlisle Institute. In 1905 Minoka and Hill were married. She understood that he wished to return to his farm in Oneida, Wisconsin, and that he wanted her to be a farmer's wife, not a doctor. She agreed.

Compared to the city life she had known, farm life in Oneida was primitive. Minoka-Hill (after marriage she always hyphenated her name) moved into a small house with no running water. She had to learn to prime a pump, to cook on a wood-burning stove, and to help with the farm chores.

During the next nine years she bore six children.

She did not, however, abandon her interest in medicine. She talked with tribal medicine men and women and added their herbal remedies to her medical school knowledge of botanics. Slowly, relatives and neighbors who distrusted the only licensed physician in Oneida began to seek out Minoka-Hill's medical services. Many years later, this unpretentious woman recalled, "At first I administered only to those who beat a path to my door. But the more I served, the more came, and the more asked me to come. So I started visiting." Local Brown County physicians encouraged her to serve the people of Oneida and soon Hill proudly accepted his wife's unofficial medical practice.

When her husband suddenly died in 1916, Minoka-Hill was left with six children, ranging in age from five months to nine years, a mortgaged farm with no running water or electricity, and a few farm animals. Though Philadelphia friends urged her to return East, she refused. "While in college, I resolved to spend some time and effort to help needy Indians," she explained later. "In Wisconsin, I found my work."

Shortly after Hill's death, the only other doctor in Oneida left the area. From then on Minoka-Hill's "kitchen-clinic" became the focal point of medical practice in the community. She stocked this office with herbals and medicines she bought or received from physicians in nearby Green Bay and from her old friend Tyson. In addition to her kitchen-clinic, Minoka-Hill's practice included housecalls, a large proportion of them obstetrical cases. Over the years this indefatigable woman traveled many difficult miles, often in the worst weather, to serve her patients. Not limiting herself to curative medicine, she also taught her patients the rudiments of nutrition and sanitation.

On the whole, the residents of Oneida were poor. Recognizing this fact and also believing that "If I charged too much, I wouldn't have a very good chance of going to heaven," Minoka-Hill charged her clients only what she felt they could afford. When a case required a drug, this empathetic clinician did not send the patient to a pharmacy with a prescription; the family probably did not have enough money to pay the druggist. Instead, Minoka-Hill supplied the medicine herself and charged what she thought was appropriate for

Though faced with numerous physical and financial hardships, Minoka-Hill attended her patients both in her kitchen-clinic and in their homes.
And the people for whom this unstinting healer worked regarded her with admiration and affection.

the family's circumstances. Moreover, she did not insist on cash payment. Her patients paid with money, when they had cash, but they also gave her supplies and worked on her farm in return for medical services. Her idiosyncratic fee schedule is apparent from her few extant case notes. For example, to pay for one obstetrical case in February, 1931, the family gave her $15 in May and sent her two chickens in July. In May of the same year, a delivery and postnatal care consisting of 14 visits earned her $2 in July, $2 in August, and $5 in November. Similarly, for her attendance at a July birth, she was paid $5 in cash and in November received $5 worth of "pole wood."

When the depression temporarily wiped out the small trust fund left Minoka-Hill by her father, her already precarious financial situation was severely weakened. The federal government established a Relief Office in Oneida, but it could not direct patients to her nor reimburse her for services rendered because she was not a licensed Wisconsin physician. Furthermore, without a license, she was not permitted to admit her patients to the hospital and instead had to refer those needing such services to licensed Brown County practitioners. Physician friends encouraged Minoka-Hill to apply for the license and even loaned her the $100 application fee. After four months of study, she sat for the two-day examination in 1934. At the age of 58, thirty-five years after her medical school graduation, Minoka-Hill received her Wisconsin license. She continued to practice in Oneida. Though a heart attack in 1946 forced her to curtail some of her medical activities (she no longer made house calls), she did serve her patients in the kitchen-clinic until the early 1950's.

Minoka-Hill was modest in appraising her life in Oneida. "It has been a privilege to be helpful to those in need of help. . .(as) cheerfully and as promptly as I could," she explained in 1949, "because I felt it was the Master's work, assigned to me, and that I must be a willing worker."

Despite her diffidence, others recognized the significance of this dedicated woman's work among the people of Oneida. Probably her most prized honor came in 1947 when the Oneidas adopted her with the name "You-da-gent" (she who serves). Two years later, a testimonial from the University of Wisconsin College of Agriculture described her as "Inspiring homemaker and mother, untiring builder of health, unselfish servant of the public, and deserving bearer of the tribal title 'she who serves'."

Dr. Lillie Rosa Minoka-Hill died in a Fond du Lac hospital on March 18, 1952. Outside Oneida, her grateful patients erected a monument in her honor. The memorial reads: "Physician, good samaritan, and friend to all religions in this community, erected to her memory by the Indians and white people. 'I was sick and you visited me.' "

(See Selected Honors, Accomplishments, Publications, page 311)

written by JANE NEE MARR

Ada James, leader in Women's Rights and Suffrage movements in Wisconsin.

ada james

"Votes for Women!" This became a battle cry throughout the United States after the first suffrage conference in Seneca Falls, New York, in 1848. Ada James was a leader in the fight for women's right to vote. She grew up with the movement.

Ada James was born in Richland Center in 1876 into a political family that had been fighting for women's rights for many years. Her mother, Laura Briggs James, organized the local Women's Club in 1882 to promote women's suffrage. Susan B. Anthony was a guest at the James' home when she spoke in Richland Center in the fall of 1886. Ada, a young girl at the time, was destined to become Wisconsin's outspoken advocate for women's rights.

To an Oshkosh editor, Ada James wrote, "A professor in a German university held that women should never be allowed to have any broad interests because the size and weight of her brain showed her to be unable to cope with anything outside of her 'Kinder, Küche, and Kirche' interests. When this opinionated professor died and his brain was weighed by colleagues, it was found to weigh less than the average woman's. No doubt it was the tenacious holding of his idea about women which shriveled and shrank his brain."

She organized the Political Equality Club for young women of high school age. In 1911, she helped form the Political Equality League of Wisconsin and was president for two years.

Ada James and the Political Equality League canvassed the state. Speeches were made from automobiles, in parks, and on street corners. During the month of August, outdoor meetings

Ada James at work in her Milwaukee office, and left, in center with ribbon. Campaign for Woman's Suffrage, 1911-12. (courtesy, State Historical Society of Wisconsin)

were held. An aviator was hired to drop literature at county fairs. Speakers of national and international fame were engaged—Belle Case LaFollette, Reverend Olympia Brown, and Sylvia Pankhurst. The press committee published a weekly bulletin mailed to more than 500 newspapers in the state.

Despite this exhausting work, a crushing defeat came in 1912 when suffrage was defeated by 90,000 votes. The common feeling was that the liquor lobbies had defeated the referendum, as breweries felt women's votes would give political power to the temperance movement.

In March, 1913, Ada James and her father appeared before a State Senate committee advocating the resubmission of women's suffrage to the electorate. Parades and marches were held throughout the country and Ada James was in Chicago marching during the 1916 National Republican Convention. The following year she became a member of the National Women's Party.

The movement took a different turn during World War I as women streamed into factories and fields to do jobs previously held by men. Protest intensified as suffragettes were outraged that they were still not allowed to vote in such times.

As the war came to an end, pressure for a constitutional amendment intensified. After Congress approved the amendment, Ada James worked for ratification. In Richland Center, women and children marched in the streets.

The Wisconsin legislature ratified the 19th Amendment about 11 a.m. on June 10, 1919. Word was received that Illinois was also voting. The excitement of that day was the culmination of Ada James' tireless work on behalf of women. In her diary, she wrote, "We wanted our legislature to ratify first, but Illinois telegraphed that they had ratified. Our chairman did not give up. . .A committee of women went to see the governor and he appointed Dad special messenger. Illinois had their papers sent special delivery. We got very much excited in getting Dad off. I pinned my belongings into a newspaper and gave Dad my grip." He carried the ratification document to Washington personally by train, arriving early on the morning of June 13 to secure the proper papers from the office of the Secretary of State. His efforts made history—Wisconsin was the first state to officially ratify the 19th Amendment.

This victory did not end Ada James' political or community life. Always an active social reformer, she worked with poor and underprivileged children in Richland County, providing financial help or taking them into her home. She was a prime force in the founding of the Children's Board, the first of its kind in the state. She administered the David C. James Memorial Fund giving financial aid to children who needed medical or psychological care.

Her concern for neglected and abused children spurred her activity in the birth control movement during the 1920's. She served as vice chairman of the Republican State Committee and president of the Wisconsin Women's Progressive Association.

Ada James throughout her life devoted herself to those who needed help and counsel. "It was familiarity with existing conditions—municipal, state, and national, that made woman's enfranchisement a religion with me", she explained.

Women throughout the state and the nation are grateful for her fight.

(See Selected Honors, Accomplishments, Publications, page 310)

written by GERI NIKOLAI
submitted by MARIAN SEAGREN HALL

Above: Fay Crow with a friend from India.
Below: Miss Crow (right) with Clara Sodke (left) on WIAN, Alaska Airline from Fairbanks to Barrow. It was the second time the airline had taken passengers.

fay crow

Although she has friends across the nation and the world, her own determination may be the truest friend Fay Crow has ever had.

It was what enabled her to get a college degree in 1916 when there was no money in the family for education, land her dream job as an executive with the Young Women's Christian Association, survive the 1937 Johnstown, Pennsylvania flood, and later a tornado in Illinois, not to mention the wrath of Oklahoma Southern Baptists, travel to nearly every major country in the world, and get financial backing for the Marathon County Commission on Aging.

Raised in Bellaire, Ohio, she came under the influence of her grandfather, a veteran of the German potato famine and a believer in improving oneself.

"He had the usual German zeal for education and loaned me money to attend Hiram College in northern Ohio," she recalled. After one year, her grandfather died, and she taught for two years to earn money to go back to college.

In high school, Miss Crow had a teacher whose relative held a high position in the national YWCA. In college, she was active in a strong student YW. Miss Crow decided that's how she wanted to make a living. But the YWCA job required extra training and that cost money. So Miss Crow took several other jobs until 1922 when she received a scholarship for the training needed to be a YWCA executive.

Her first YW executive job was in the oil field country of Ardmore, Oklahoma. "I was considered a radical, as well as a damn Yankee, by some of the Southern Baptists in Ardmore," says Miss Crow.

Founder of the Marathon County Commission on Aging and past executive director of the YWCA, she was a longtime volunteer worker.

83

After two years, they were reluctant to renew her contract, and she didn't argue. Her next job was a seven year stint on Ottumwa, Iowa.

Miss Crow returned to Union Theological and Columbia University in New York following her stay in Ottumwa to earn a master's degree in Christian education. Then she took a YWCA job that provided one of her most memorable experiences.

It was in Johnstown, Pennsylvania, where Miss Crow one day received a call to come to the YW office. Heavy rains and melting snow were threatening to flood the building.

Before she could walk the few blocks to the office, mobility was stopped by the flood. Returning to her apartment, she found water up to the front door. Miss Crow measured how fast the water was rising, and soon decided that valuables better be moved to the third floor.

"We sat through the night on the third floor, listening to the waters recede," said Miss Crow. "It was a night of terror."

After Johnstown, Miss Crow found herself working for a YMCA in New Rochelle, NY. The YW, feeling the effects of the Great Depression, had few openings, so she accepted a job in what was to be a combined YW and YMCA.

"It was a real experience," said Miss Crow, but not one of her favorites. Women's programs at the Y were almost non-existent, she said, and the organization was involved in shaky financial dealings.

After overseeing a YWCA building program in Lockport, NY, Miss Crow moved to Quincy, Ill. where she one day asked the board why the Y carried tornado insurance. A short time later, she found out. A tornado struck, taking the roofs off the YWCA and nearby buildings. Miss Crow was becoming an expert in rebuilding.

Fortunately, that's a job she didn't have to tackle in Wausau, where she came to work for the YWCA in 1952. She retired nine years later.

Trips were interspersed throughout and after her YW career. "I grew up with an interest in the rest of the world, partly because of my grandfather, and because of the people I met," said Miss Crow.

Miss Crow traveled to most of the world. She visited many places, including the Soviet Union twice. She also corresponded regularly with people she met all over the world. "Once you've made a friend in another country, that country isn't very far away anymore," she said.

Upon retirement, Miss Crow was active in programs for older citizens in the Wausau area. She pushed hard for a commission on aging, but the City Council remained unconvinced it was a priority for funds. Miss Crow and others finally secured an office and—at first unpaid—director for the commission, and urged that one of its first projects be a shop where older people could sell handmade items.

According to a longtime friend, "Fay was a hard worker and enjoyed every minute of the time that she spent on her work, her clubs, and her church."

The last day of her life she said to a friend, "Take my hand, hold it tight; but when one goes, one must go alone."

(See Selected Honors, Accomplishments, Publications, page 307)

emma duerrwaechter

Christmas 1881 was special for immigrant, Philip G. Duerrwaechter, father of three sons. His only daughter, Emma, was born on December 26. She soon became the apple of her father's eye and he encouraged her steadily saying often, "You can do anything anyone else can do!"

Banker Philip nurtured Emma's natural interest in his profession. Her bank experience began at the bottom rung of the ladder. After school she frequently cleaned and serviced the bank's oil lamps. By 12 Emma checked bank entries, posted the ledgers and acted as messenger girl while also helping with maintenance.

Upon completing grammar school, Emma Duerrwaechter briefly left the family's green shuttered, white frame home and ventured to Chicago to undertake a short course in Mechano Therapy, a natural method of healing. Emma's younger brother, John, was subject to seizures and she sought help for him. After five weeks she received a "doctor's degree" and returned to Germantown and to banking.

Emma's interest in banking expanded. She desired a broader knowledge and applied herself diligently to correspondence courses offered by the American Institute of Banking and to banking courses offered by the University of Wisconsin. Emma studied with Washington County banking groups as their only woman member. Her keen interest, efficiency, knowledge and progressiveness made her a valuable asset within the banking community. She earned the respected and affectionate title, Miss D.

In 1923 Emma's father died. At 42 Miss D was voted director and president of the bank which her father had spent a lifetime guiding. Undaunted by the tremendous responsibility so suddenly thrust upon her and despite her mother's remonstrances, Emma readily accepted her new position.

Thus began the period of Emma the professional. She had lived in her father's shadow for many years, and now she was soloing. Before she was seen by others as petite, frail, cheerful, well-dressed and friendly. Gradually and steadily Emma emerged as a respected, cooperative, practical, powerful and efficient executive. She functioned and was accepted as a woman in a man's position. Emma acted as silent diplomat in her small rural community, keeping her hand always on the pulse of the times. When many believed that a woman's place was in the home, Miss D became a pioneer in the struggle for equal women's rights, respected and sought out as a community leader.

Emma skillfully guided the bank through the Great Depression. She dreamed of innovative banking practices. Emma was cautious but steadfastly determined. She was the first Wisconsin woman to join the National Association of Bank Women which then was made up only of women from New York State. Emma was also an energetic member of the Wisconsin Bankers Association and its Fifty Year Club. A year after her retirement they named her Wisconsin's First Lady of Banking.

Miss D retired from the presidency of the bank in 1959. Throughout her lifetime Emma was devoted to her community. During two world wars she was active in the Women's Society of World Service and was recognized for outstanding war bond sales. Miss D donated $30,000 to establish

Wisconsin's "First Lady of Banking," she was highly respected.
She was bank president in Germantown for 36 years.

and support Germantown's village library.

Throughout her life Emma supported her younger brother, John, and provided a home and an education for her godchild whose mother had died.

Humane, understanding and helpful to family, community and profession, Emma Duerrwaechter used the vantage point of success to benefit others. At age 87 she died at Milwaukee's Mill Road Nursing Home on October 9, 1969. Wisconsin's First Lady of Banking was first in the hearts of her family and her community.

(See Selected Honors, Accomplishments, Publications, page 308)

She had lived in the shadow of
her father for many years, and then
suddenly became "Emma the professional"

Emma Duerrwaechter (courtesy, Cleveland Photography, Menomonee Falls, WI)

written by *SHIRLEY WHIPPLE HINDS*

elma spaulding schuele

Long before the goals of the women's movement were articulated by the Gloria Steinems and Betty Friedans in the 1960's, Elma Spaulding Schuele of Oconomowoc, Wisconsin, was a pioneer in the demand for social justice for all. Elma Schuele was a liberated woman from the time she was left motherless at 12, with several younger sisters to look after, until she died in 1969.

A contemporary, illustrating why Elma was able

"She was tireless in her many efforts to modernize, beautify, educate, organize or clean-up whatever upset her high standards—absolutely fearless."
—MARGARET HAEGG, Daughter

to accomplish so much in her lifetime, said, "She makes the snowballs and tosses them to us. Then we have to work fast!" It is an imaginative description of a woman who did not insist on being in charge but who initiated projects in such a manner that those who supported her cause would close ranks and work together before the enthusiasm melted away.

Elma was born in 1883 in the Pacific Northwest where independence was a way of life and self-reliance second nature. Her family was of moderate means, and a college education could not be guaranteed. But since higher education was considered a necessity for a fruitful life, the answer for Elma was to attend Pullman State College (now Washington State University) in her hometown. Elma considered her degree in modern languages from Pullman to be a gift because she had the good fortune to live in a college community. It was a gift she gave back in kind.

Her grades were the highest and her involvement in college life total. In speaking of her mother, Margaret Schuele Haegg says, "There was nothing else but all A's to be considered. She settled for nothing less than perfection. That was the way she carried on her life with her family and with the groups with which she was involved." On the occasion of the fiftieth anniversary of her graduation from Pullman, she was elected to Phi Beta Kappa which did not exist at the time she was a student.

Elma met her husband while both were students

Left to right: Elma C. Spaulding and Charles Schuele, sparking in 1905; Elma in 1909; with baby son David (1913); daughter Margaret, son David and Jean Grindnod in Oconomowoc, about 1919; with daughter Margaret, about 1921. Above: Mr. and Mrs. Charles Schuele in 1942 in their lake front yard with grandchilren.

at Pullman. It has been said that while they were undergraduates, they ran the school. When Carnation moved its headquarters to Oconomowoc, Charles Schuele, a company chemist, was transferred there. Elma Schuele set about "making snowballs" to involve her community in crucial causes.

One of Elma's earliest recollections was being paid ten cents a day to sit on a hill overlooking an approach to downtown Pullman to yell support for a presidential candidate. It was inevitable that she would become politically active. During her years in Oconomowoc she attended School Board and City Council meetings regularly and was often embroiled in controversy. On occasion, her quiet, peace-loving husband returned home from work to ask, "Well, are you still alive?"

Elma worked hard to secure women's right to vote, and in 1920, after the adoption of the 19th Amendment, she helped establish the Oconomowoc chapter of the League of Women Voters. At the first meetings, new members were taught the fundamental knowledge of city, state, and national government that would help them understand their new duties as active participants in American democracy. In 1923, Elma helped found the American Association of University Women in Oconomowoc and introduced graduate women to the politics of education as well.

Several years before the formation of the LWV and the AAUW, the Women's Christian Temperance Union, with Elma's guidance, started the Waukesha County Humane Society. Today, the Society is concerned with animal welfare, but in 1915, its main objective was the welfare of children. Programs to aid dependent children and protect them from abuse did not exist in the county at that time.

"I still remember coming home one day to find my father absolutely stunned. He had just learned that my mother had slapped the mayor for his insolence to a group of community concerned women. I remember Dad saying he might be sued for everything he had — which wasn't much. We were all properly scared!"
MARGARET HAEGG, Daughter

Long before schools had federal hot lunch programs, Oconomowoc was serving hot lunches to school children because of Elma's determination and ingenuity. She suggested the idea to the local School Board and was told the school had no room for such a program. After locking horns with the administration, Elma went home one day, cooked up a ten-gallon milk can of vegetable soup, carted it to school in her son David's little red wagon, announced that hot soup was available, and served it to the children in the main corridor. Soon after that, Oconomowoc began a hot lunch program in its schools.

Fowler Park, one of the city's most popular recreation spots, owes its existence to Elma's Garden Club. Thanks to Elma and her associates, the trees in the park were saved from developers' bulldozers. When children play in the park's winter wonderland, they do not realize how symbolic are the snowballs they toss, how Elma's determination made their world a better place in which to grow up.

She was always the power behind the throne—aggressive promoter, expert organizer, fearless fighter, and uncompromising dreamer . . . "snowball tosser par excellence!"

(See Selected Honors, Accomplishments, Publications, page 313)

written by BEVERLY PRIETO

edna ferber

Edna Ferber was known for her multi-generation regional novels crammed with vigorous descriptions, action and colorful characters.

Author of such successful novels as *Show Boat* and *Giant,* winner of a Pulitzer Prize, collaborator with George S. Kaufman of hit Broadway plays, and member of the legendary Algonquin Round Table, Edna Ferber began her writing career earning $3 a week as a newspaper reporter in Appleton, Wisconsin.

Born in Kalamazoo, Michigan, on August 15, 1885, Edna grew up in small midwestern towns spending her adolescent years in Appleton. Her father, Jacob Ferber, had emigrated from Hungary to America to get away from the farm. Her mother, Julia Neumann Ferber, was from a spirited Chicago family. Julia with daughters, Fannie and Edna, followed Jacob Ferber from one small town to the next as he started dry goods and general stores. They shared his misfortunes and cared for him as his health failed. When he began to go blind, Julia took over the business, "My Store," on Appleton's College Avenue.

As Jacob became an invalid and Julia revitalized the family business, Edna attended Ryan High School. She remembers those years in glowing terms in *A Peculiar Treasure.* Edna belonged to the Forum, a debating and literary society. She gave recitations, sang in the chorus, wrote for the school newspaper and belonged to a social club called the Lucky Twelve. According to a school newspaper account, "she imitated the 'Bowery Tough' with ease and ability," in a dramatic presentation.

Edna had her heart set on being an actress; her

Edna Ferber in her Appleton years. (courtesy, Outagamie County Historical Society)

plan was to go to Northwestern University's School of Elocution. The Ferbers always loved the theater and saw every play that came to town. It was often the bright spot during the family's struggling years. Edna was shocked when she was told she could not go. The family just couldn't afford it. There was a fierce family argument and Edna stormed the offices of the local newspaper, *The Crescent.* She got a job as Appleton's first girl reporter.

Edna was welcomed with glowing words: "One of the brightest young women of this city, Miss Edna Jessica Ferber, gives promise of becoming one of the best newspaper women in the state." She worked as a reporter for about one and a half years and described herself in retrospect as pretty obnoxious in her zeal and determination to get the story she was after. Third down on a totem pole of three, Edna got the crumbs, but she made the most of them. Her stories ranged from pieces on the Poor Farm to behind the scenes at the Barnum & Bailey circus to an interview with Lillian Russell.

Edna had thrown herself heart and soul into her new career. She wholeheartedly embraced the role of girl reporter. When she was abruptly fired by a new city editor, she was devastated. Fortunately the *Milwaukee Journal* hired her and put her right to work covering the big scandal of the day, the Schandein trial.

Edna credited her four years with this Milwaukee newspaper as a wonderful training ground and her "college education." She learned to write tight, clear copy, to meet deadlines and to type very fast with two fingers. Exhausted and anemic, Edna fainted one day getting ready to go to work. Julia Ferber fetched her daughter home to Appleton.

While recuperating under her mother's watchful eye, Edna began her first novel. She threw her Milwaukee newspaper life, its people and places, into the novel.

Edna was soon addicted to writing and began doing short stories which sold immediately. Jacob Ferber died, and within a year, Julia sold the store and the house and the three Ferber women moved to Chicago. The year was 1910 and Edna Ferber, author, was on her way to fame, fortune and a career that spanned over sixty years.

National recognition came first for a series of short stories about Mrs. Emma McChesney, a traveling saleswoman for the T.A. Buck Featherloom Petticoat Company. Edna had created a new character in fiction, the American businesswoman.

Emma McChesney was smart, hardworking and virtuous. She was divorced from her no-good husband so she had to work to support herself and her young son, who grew up to be too good looking, with too much easy charm and a crooked streak inherited from his father. Edna drew on her own experiences, as she did in most of her early novels and stories. Appleton, Julia Ferber, "My Store," and Edna were liberally mixed into background and characters. The public loved Emma McChesney. The President of the United States, upon meeting Edna Ferber, advised her that

She was a great advocate of the working woman and her Emma McChesney stories were the first about the modern businesswoman.

91

Emma ought to get married.

Not all Edna's readers were fans. As she developed her regional novels on the Northeast, Texas and Oklahoma, cries of outrage as well as praise greeted the books, particularly *American Beauty, Giant* and *Show Boat.* Unfazed, she continued to write as she chose.

Theater-going was a vital part of Edna's life, and she was now in a position to be actively involved. Two of her short stories were produced as plays. Ethel Barrymore starred as Emma McChesney. Edna wrote six plays for Broadway with George S. Kaufman. Most of her books were made into movies.

When she died in New York on April 16, 1968, at the age of 82, Edna Ferber left behind a written legacy of which she was proud: twelve novels, eleven volumes of short stories, six major plays and two autobiographies.

(See Selected Honors, Accomplishments, Publications, page 308)

Edna Ferber, novelist and war correspondent.
(courtesy, State Historical Society of Wisconsin)

marguerite davis

Marguerite Davis is ranked by the *Encyclopedia Britannica* with Edward Verner McCollum for the discovery of the fat soluble vitamin A and water soluble vitamin B. Truly a pioneer in the field, Miss Davis worked with McCollum at the University of Wisconsin in the second decade of this century.

Born in Racine on September 16, 1887, to Dr. John Jefferson Davis and Anna Margaret Snyder Davis, she came naturally by her scientific and scholarly interests.

Marguerite's father was one of the first graduates of the University of Illinois. He practiced medicine in Racine from 1876 to 1911 and then became curator of the herbarium at the University of Wisconsin, most of whose specimens he had collected himself. It was regarded as one of the best in the Middle West and, the parasitic fungi section, the best in the nation.

Marguerite was an independent, spirited child. Unknown to her own mother, she satisfied requirements for confirmation at St. Luke's Church. And long before slacks were acceptable attire for women, she strode about town in her brother's trousers or wore ankle socks with her earth shoes.

She attended the University of Chicago and the University of Wisconsin, but graduated from the University of California at Berkeley in 1909. That summer she returned to Madison to assist Dr. McCollum in his experiments with white rats.

Because they eat the same kinds of food as humans and respond in like manner to different diets, white rats became popular laboratory animals early in the 20th century. Intrigued by the experiments and such a correlation, Marguerite

*Truly a pioneer in her field, she is ranked with Edward Verner McCollum
for the discovery of vitamins A and B.*

worked as a volunteer, feeding and watching the rats for five years.

In 1913 she and Dr. McCollum excitedly published jointly their findings on Vitamin A, the first to be identified. Many revisions and future findings ensued. Dr. McCollum, who went on to extensive work in nutrition, is also credited with originating the letter system of naming vitamins. Of Marguerite, he says, "Without her cooperation it would have been impossible for me to have carried on so extensive an experimental program as we did together." From this partnership grew her lifelong interest in nutrition.

She went on to organize the School of Pharmacy at Rutgers University, New Jersey; she worked in the Squibb Pharmaceutical Laboratory, and she founded the Nutrition Laboratory at the University of Wisconsin-Madison.

In 1940 she retired to Racine to care for her crippled brother Archie. They occupied their grandmother's house which Marguerite restored to its near original state in 1956. Racine became her home.

Refusing to drink the city water, she had a tank for special water installed in her house. A home economist was startled once to be met at the door by Miss Davis wearing a copper wire twisted about her neck. Observing this reaction, Marguerite said she hoped to inspire others to do likewise. Apparently she did not regard the copper cure for arthritis as an old wives' tale.

James Molbeck, of a family grocery store, remembers her walking miles across the city to procure unusual vitamins from him. He attributes to her demands, the installation of a line of health foods which the store has increasingly enlarged.

To her friends Miss Davis often gave expensive Christmas baskets containing these health foods which Mr. Molbeck said were not always received gratefully. Now some of those early scoffers have turned disciples.

A memorable character, Marguerite Davis was generous and active in the communty; public concerns were also hers. Leaving no survivors nor close relatives, she died on September 17, 1967. She did leave, however, an impression upon those whose lives she had touched.

The Marguerite Davis Hall of Natural History and Ecology in the Racine County Historical Museum stands today as a record of man's effect on the ecosystem and a tribute to the woman whose concern it exemplifies.

(See Selected Honors, Accomplishments, Publications, page 307)

*Of slight build, Marguerite
had sparkle and
abundant humor as
well as many eccentricities.*

rosalie ganz

Miss Ganz? Yes, I remember her. She always looked like a mother hen with her chicks when she was walking down the street with her children from the Model Room. It was necessary for children to make an appointment to hold her hand on the way home at noon.

Rosalie Ganz was born on September 28, 1888 in a "teacherage." It was the custom in Swiss communities for the teacher to live on the second floor of the schoolhouse. Her father, E.F. Ganz, the teacher in Waumandee, Buffalo County, Wisconsin, lived there with his wife Kunigunde Wald Ganz.

Rosalie spent 27 years as an educator. Her last teaching position was at Buffalo County Normal School, later known as Buffalo County Teachers College, first as a teacher, then as principal. Finally, she became County Superintendent of Schools for Buffalo County. She was one of the first of a small number of women who became county superintendents in Wisconsin. She held this position until she retired in 1941.

Her work at the Normal School was a special family affair. Her father, a teacher for 14 years, and editor of the *Buffalo County Journal* from 1890 to 1913, was primarily responsible for the formation of the school. He used the pages of the newspaper to advocate that a teacher training school be located in Buffalo County. In 1902 it became the fourth such school in Wisconsin.

In 1907, Rosalie graduated from the one-year course, and her younger sister, Olga, taught domestic science for a time there. After graduation, Rosalie lived with Grandmother Wald's family for five years while she taught at Mill Creek School.

During World War I, she finished the year as a second grade teacher, then responded to a call for the Army Nurse Training Corps. With her sister Olga and a friend, she was sent to Camp Grant, Illinois. Here, these volunteers helped care for thousands of patients during the height of the flu epidemic.

After the war, Rosalie furthered her education at La Crosse Normal School, now University of Wisconsin-LaCrosse. After completing work there, she became principal of Viroqua Junior High School and then Supervisor of Rural Schools in Juneau County.

Her Swiss ancestry was evident in many ways. The family owned a city home on Second Street in Alma and a 360-acre farm on a bluff about 500 feet above the city's main street. Her grandparents came to the area in the 1850's from Parpan and Zurich, Switzerland. It is said that the hills reminded them of their homeland. Local residents agree and add, "We've been climbing ever since." While at the normal school, Rosalie lived on the farm and walked up and down the steep bluff every day except in winter.

Miss Ganz is known statewide as one of the founders of Delta Kappa Gamma in Sigma State. She helped organize Theta chapter in La Crosse and remained active until her retirement in 1941.

Rosalie lived at Buena Vista Farm with her sister Olga and brother Armin until her death on October 31, 1974.

Out of thoughtfulness and concern for their ancestry and as a memorial to their parents, Rosalie with her sisters and brother gave the city of

Known throughout the state as a founder of Delta Kappa Gamma, she spent 27 years as an educator.

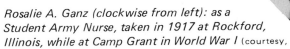

Rosalie A. Ganz (clockwise from left): as a Student Army Nurse, taken in 1917 at Rockford, Illinois, while at Camp Grant in World War I (courtesy, Reynold's Studio); *as a baby, age 2* (courtesy, Gerhardt Gesell); *as an adult on front lawn; as graduate from Alma High School, 1906.* (courtesy, J. Keller).

Alma a parcel of land on the bluff above the city to be known as Buena Vista Park. Today this lovely park overlooks the Mississippi River with a panoramic view of Minnesota across the river. A monument at the site bears these words: "Such scenes have power to quiet the restless pulse of care."

(See Selected Honors, Accomplishments, Publications, page 309)

written by CATHERINE KRUEGER

georgia o'keeffe

"I have picked flowers where I found them—have picked up sea shells and rocks and pieces of wood...that I liked...When I found the beautiful white bones on the desert I picked them up and took them home too...I have used these things to say what is to me the wideness and wonder of the world as I live in it.

"Where I was born and where and how I have lived is unimportant. It is what I have done with where I have been that should be of interest."

Above and right:
Wisconsin born artist Georgia O'Keeffe.

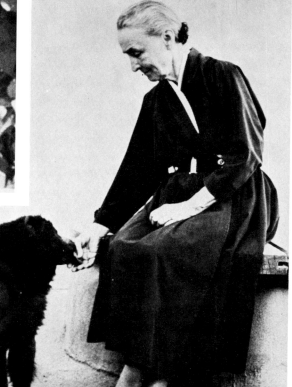

She is one of the world's great artists. Her work is represented in the permanent collections of the major museums in this country and in many private collections. She has had retrospective exhibitions in all the major art galleries in the United States. She has received honorary degrees from the University of Wisconsin, Harvard, Columbia, and many other universities. She is Georgia O'Keeffe.

Although her work is extravagantly praised, she is not impressed by what others say. "I get out my work and have a show for myself before I have it publicly. I make up my own mind about it—how good or bad or indifferent it is. After that, the critics can write what they please. I have already settled it for myself so flattery and criticism go down the same drain and I am quite free."

She followed her own way of thinking, her own way of painting with her skyscrapers of New York, her flowers, the crosses, barns, and clean white bones, clouds, the desert hills and the cliffs, and in every period, abstractions. Her inspiration comes from the world of nature.

Georgia O'Keeffe was born in 1887 on a farm near Sun Prairie, Wisconsin, the daughter of an Irish father and a Hungarian mother, the second of seven children. She says, "I always feel I was very fortunate to have grown up on a farm. I had a very pleasant childhood, though I was somewhat of a rebel."

By the time she finished eighth grade, she had made up her mind to be an artist. "I hadn't any desire to make anything like the pictures I had seen. But in one of my mother's books I had found a drawing of a girl that I thought very beautiful . . . For me, it just happened to be something special . . . that picture started something moving in me that kept on going and has had to do with the everlasting urge that makes me keep on painting."

At 13, she attended Sacred Heart Academy, a boarding school on the outskirts of Madison now known as Edgewood High School. The Sister in charge of art classes criticized her first studio drawing saying it was too small and too black. Georgia thought she had been terribly scolded and

She leads her life exactly as she chooses, undaunted by the demands and modes of society.

"It's as if my mind creates shapes that I don't know about."
—GEORGIA O'KEEFFE

never drew another heavy black line that year. She spent the next year at Central High School in Madison where her art teacher encouraged her to look carefully at the details, outline, and color of growing things.

Because the harsh Wisconsin winters were undermining her father's health, the family moved to Williamsburg, Virginia, and Georgia was sent to Chatham Episcopal Institute. The students took many afternoon walks across the hills and woods, in a line headed by a teacher. "I loved the country and always on the horizon far away was the line of the Blue Ridge mountains—calling—as the distance has always been calling me. . . . Those walks over the Virginia hills and through the woods were the best things that happened for me in those years—because I never did like school."

When she was 18, O'Keeffe studied at the Chicago Art Institute. Here she learned the fundamentals and looked forward to the lectures of John Vanderpoel on drawing the human figure. She remembers him as one of her few real teachers.

In 1907, she entered the Art Students League in New York where she studied with William Chase. Along with other students, she made her first visit to the Alfred Stieglitz Gallery "291" to view the Rodin exhibition.

Texas had always been a far away dream of hers. "When we were children mother read to us every evening and on Sunday afternoons . . . I had listened for many hours . . . all the Leatherstocking Tales, stories of the Wild West, of Texas, Kit Carson, and Billy the Kid. It had always seemed to me that the West must be wonderful—there was no place I would rather go—so when I had a chance to teach there—off I went to Texas."

She became Supervisor of Art in the Amarillo public schools. After two years, she headed the Art Department at West Texas State Normal College at Canyon, Texas. She liked everything about Texas and did not mind the dust, hot sun, or harsh winds. At this time, her sister was living with her and they often took walks miles away from town in the late afternoon to watch the sunset. "There were no paved roads and no fences—no trees—it was like the ocean but it was wide, wide land. The evening star would be high in the sunset sky when it was still daylight. That evening star fascinated me . . . Ten watercolors were made from that star."

But it was Arthur Dow who helped her find something of her own. In 1915, while teaching at Columbia College, South Carolina, she suddenly realized that everything she had been taught was of little value.

"I had been taught to work like others and wasn't going to spend my life doing what had already been done. I have things in my head that are not like what anyone has taught me, shapes and ideas so near to me, so natural to my way of being and thinking that it hadn't occurred to me to put them down. I decided to start anew, to strip away what I had been taught, to accept and trust my own way of thinking. This was one of the best times of my life. No one around to look at what I was doing, no one to satisfy but myself, alone and free working on my own."

She began with charcoal and decided not to use color until she could not do what she wanted to do in black and white. She sent some of these drawings to a friend in New York with instructions to show them to no one. But her friend, much excited, took the drawings to Alfred Stieglitz who was so interested that he exhibited them. These drawings were private for O'Keeffe and the idea of them being hung on a wall was just too much for her. She went to "291", Stieglitz' gallery, and demanded that he take them down. They argued and, though she did not like it, the drawings stayed on the wall. It was hard to win an argument with Stieglitz.

Stieglitz and O'Keeffe corresponded during the next year, and in the spring of 1917, he gave another show of her watercolors and drawings that she had sent to him rolled up in newspapers. Hearing that "291" was closing and the building to be torn down, O'Keeffe went to New York to see the final show. It had been dismantled, but Stieglitz put it back on the wall for her. The first of his hundreds of photographs of O'Keeffe were made at this time. Encouraged by him, she gave up teaching and returned to New York in 1918 to devote full time to painting. He held yearly exhibitions of her work from 1923 until 1946.

Her relationship with Stieglitz was of great significance in her life though he was a people person whereas O'Keeffe was a private person. They were married in 1924. What held them together was their genuine interest in each other's work.

The first of her famous flower paintings appeared in 1926. Explaining this phase of her work, O'Keeffe says, "A flower is relatively small . . . it is so small—we haven't time—and to see takes time like to have a friend takes time . . . I'll paint what I see . . . but I'll paint it big and they will be surprised into taking time to look at it—I will make even busy New Yorkers take time to see what I see of flowers."

Later, she wrote, "Well—I made you take time to look at what I saw and when you took time to really notice my flower you hung all your own associations with flowers on my flower as if I think and see what you think and see of the flower—and I don't."

She always wears white or black and all her dresses look exactly the same.

She spent the summer of 1929 in the high wild desert country of New Mexico. There she felt close to something she had been trying to reach in her painting. "The color up there—the blue-green of the sage, and the mountains, and the wild flowers—is a different kind of color from anything I'd ever seen." Often she saw crosses in unexpected places. The Indians had put them where someone had been killed. O'Keeffe painted the crosses as a way of painting the country. When it was time to return East in the fall, she took a barrel of bones she had collected, her way of taking a part of the country with her.

Her second summer in New Mexico she discovered the Rio Grande Valley, the country to the west. The shape of the hills fascinated her, "The reddish sand hills with the dark mesas behind them. It seemed as though no matter how far you walked you could never get into those dark hills."

Every fall, O'Keeffe returned to New York to Stieglitz who remained very much the center of her life. After his death in 1945 she spent three more winters in New York settling his estate, then moved to New Mexico permanently in 1949.

Her first western home was on the Ghost Ranch, which is surrounded by spectacularly beautiful high cliffs, where one can see for miles across the vast country. The Pedernal, which she calls her private mountain, rises in the distance beyond her sage-filled patio. The air is very clear and fresh in this high country and at night it seems one can almost reach up and touch the stars. Her house is sparsely furnished and here she spends the summers. It is her part of the world.

As the ranch is too remote for winter living, she bought a house in Abiquiu in 1945. It was in ruins when she first saw it, roofless and crumbling to dust. Pigs were kept in one part, but in the patio, along one wall, was a black double door. It was the door that made her buy the house. She has made many paintings of that door. It took three years to rebuild the house. There is a high wall around her garden. She grows most of her own fruits and vegetables and her studio has a view of the Chama River Valley, and the surrounding hills and mountains.

In 1977, she allowed PBS cameras a rare glimpse of her world. An hour documentary, "The Originals", women in art, was made for television. This was an extensive film portrait of O'Keeffe who was 90 at the time. After the film was shown at the Elvehjem Art Museum in Madison, University students who filled the auditorium gave her a standing ovation.

Her work speaks to all ages.

(See Selected Honors, Accomplishments, Publications, page 312)

written by DIANA MARGOTTO

emily cowles

Emily Cone Harris Murphy Cowles is a Wisconsin woman with roots in the Green Bay area, where she spent all of her 79 years. She was a member of one of Green Bay's first families. Her maternal great-grandmother was Mary Catherine Irwin Mitchell. Born in 1821, she was the first white girl born in what is now Wisconsin. The Cone Harris surnames from her mother's family can be

Left and above: Emily Cone Harris Murphy Cowles.

traced back to 1737.

Frank Murphy, Emily's father, was a member of a wealthy lumbering family that came to Green Bay in the 1880's. As a young girl, Emily drove for her invalid father. She said she was the first woman in Wisconsin to have a driver's license.

Emily was a graduate of Green Bay East High School. She exhibited her singing and acting talents in hometown musical productions, often in the leading roles. She sang in her church choir for many years.

On February 19, 1917, Emily married Dr. Robert Lewis Cowles, an obstetrician-gynecologist. The couple had three children—Frank, Emily Ann, and Robert, Jr. The mother of three was active in many organizations. She was a charter member of the Sewing Club, organizer and first president of the Neighborly Club, member of the Euchre Club and the Green Bay Woman's Club. She was indefatigable as volunteer, wife, mother, and friend. She was an excellent seamstress and made many of her children's clothes.

For more than half a century, Emily lived at Braebourne, a country home on Riverside Drive, built by her father in the early 1920's. Situated on a four-acre estate, Braebourne was the scene of many meetings of civic groups and gala social events.

With her husband, she was a firm supporter of many organizations—the Salvation Army, St. Mary's Hospital, St. Vincent's Hospital, the Door County Hospital in Sturgeon Bay—and many others. Dr. and Mrs. Cowles contributed more funds for civic betterment than they were ever willing to acknowledge publicly.

An outstanding example of Emily's endeavors is the Green Bay-DePere YWCA building. For many years she served the YWCA as board member, finance chairman, chairman of the New Building Fund, and representative at national conventions. She was directly responsible for the site of the present YWCA. Her donation of this property provided the impetus for the construction of a new building. Later, she and her husband gave $180,000 towards the New Building Fund. The Cowles Auditorium is named in her honor.

A practising Christian with a caring attitude toward all persons, Emily Cone Harris Murphy Cowles provided leadership in advancing the condition of women. She shared her abilities, talents, and financial resources to advance community interests.

She was dedicated to working for the solution of social and civic problems, and had a lifelong love affair with her community.

(See Selected Honors, Accomplishments, Publications, page 307)

*Left: Four generations, great-great-grandmother Hannah Irwin,
grandmother Jessie Harris, mother Emily Murphy and great-
grandmother Mary Catherine Mitchell;*
*Above: Pope-Hartford automobile belonging to Frank Murphy
which incorporated all of the "standard" features of the day—
right-hand drive, hand crank starting, high-pressure tires,
kerosene side and tail lights, gas headlights (fed by a carbide
generator), outside shift-lever, and even some kind of a bar
resembling a bumper! The fair chauffeur in this instance is Miss
Emily Murphy (Cowles).* (courtesy, Neville Public Museum)
Below: Braebourne, 1920's, the home of Dr. and Mrs. Cowles.

written by MARGARET JANE PARK

Above: Peg Bradley, and right, her favorite painting "Woman with Cat," by Kees Van Dongen. Gift of Mrs. Bradley, 1975, to Milwaukee Art Center.

peg bradley

Quixotic, determined, possessed of a tenacious Irish nature, Peg Bradley knew what she liked. Typically she might buy a painting on sight, enjoy it in her home or place of business and then give it away. Her giving began with her collecting.

Peg Bradley was one of the foremost collectors

of 20th century painting and sculpture in Wisconsin. After acquiring a major private art collection, inspired by a deeply rooted desire to share it, she gave much of it to the Milwaukee Art Center (now the Milwaukee Art Museum). Her generosity and that of her family were major factors in building both the Bradley Wing of the Milwaukee Art Museum and the Bradley Art Pavilion of the Milwaukee Performing Arts Center.

Tracy Atkinson, director of the Milwaukee Art Museum, says, "The significance and quality of its major pieces are certainly equal to any museum in the world. Like all truly superb art collections, it is a real expression of the enthusiasm, commitments, even the whims of the collector."

Peg Bradley's interest in painting and sculpture was inspired by the fine art collection of Charles Zadok, former manager of Milwaukee's Gimbel Department Store. Her first purchase was "In Drydock" by French artist, George Brach.

Most of her purchases were made, not by careful study, but by what attracted her interest in color or by a spontaneous reaction to the painting. Atkinson noted that, "Mrs. Bradley is an instinctive collector. She can afford to be. She has a flawless eye for quality which is unerring."

Peg Bradley collected the posters and lithographs of Toulouse-Lautrec. She was captivated by German expressionists such as Willi Baumeister, Hans Hartung, Fritz Winter and August Macke, the founder of the Blaue Reiter movement. Wisconsin artists, Karl Priebe, Guido Brink, Edmund Lewandowski, Carl Peter and John Wilde, drew her attention.

In 1963 Peg and Harry Bradley gave 22 major works, valued at $100,000, to the Art Center, including paintings by Oskar Kokoschka, Alexej Jawlensky, Rufino Tamayo and Raoul Dufy. In September 1975 the pair gave $1 million to the Milwaukee Art Museum for a new wing to house the collection then valued at $13 million. Peg Bradley helped supervise the construction and later the placement of the paintings.

Peg was born Margaret Blakney on March 5, 1894 in Milwaukee, the only daughter of Mr. and Mrs. John S. Blakney. She attended grade school on Milwaukee's East side and in 1912 graduated from Riverside High School. Margaret attended National Park Seminary in Washington, DC for two years.

She was married in her early 20's to Dwight Sullivan and their only child, Jane, was born on October 29, 1918. The marriage ended in divorce. For a time, Peg worked as a stenographer at the North Avenue State Bank.

In 1926 Peg married Harry Lynde Bradley, vice-president and treasurer of the Allen Bradley Company. With his brother, Bradley founded the company, which specialized in the manufacturing of industrial control equipment.

Harry Bradley was a traditional man who believed that old family portraits should be hung in the home. Gradually as Peg Bradley's enthusiasm grew, family portraits were taken down.
At one time Mr. Bradley rebelled and they went back on the walls.
Mrs. Bradley was not a woman to accept this return to the past. With her inexhaustible energy and determination the modern paintings remained.

In the early 1930's, when the nation faced the Great Depression, Peg Bradley, unable to pay a large clothing bill at the Zita Shop, offered to work to pay it. During the two-year commitment, she discovered her talent as a businesswoman. She continued working at the shop, frequently accompanying owner Gertrude Zohrlaut Lee to New York for fashion shows and buying trips. Peg was intrigued with marketing women's clothing and enjoyed meeting famous designers and couturiers. She was described by fashion designer, Bill Blass, as "a terrific and unique, ageless woman with vitality and interest in everything."

When Mrs. Lee became ill in 1941, Peg was asked to assume responsibility of management. Early in 1949 she bought control of the shop, eventually developing four Zita Shops in Milwaukee and in Naples, Florida.

Two years after their marriage, the Bradleys purchased the 40 acre farm "Lynden" on the Brown Deer Road. Eventually this natural setting became the site for the Bradley Family Foundation sculpture gardens.

Peg Bradley supervised the placement of each piece of sculpture. Included in the collection is the massive 1966 sculpture, "Ursa Major" in Cor-Ten steel by William Underhill. There are works by Henry Moore, Alexander Calder, Alexander Liberman, Sorel Etrog and Barbara Epworth.

Peg Bradley, who had "accumulated paintings faster than she could hang them," died February 1, 1978. She left a legacy of painting and sculpture to enrich the cultural life of her community, her state and the whole country.

Edith Heidner of West Bend.

(See Selected Honors, Accomplishments, Publications, page 306)

edith heidner

Edith Heidner was a pioneer in the teaching of local history. Her enthusiasm inspired appreciation of a precious heritage and helped to perserve it.

She was a prime mover in the successful effort to save the old courthouse tower, a local landmark, from demolition. Largely because of her efforts, the Washington County Historical Society, housed in the old County Jail, has an outstanding collection of materials documenting the history of Washington County.

She was born in Ozaukee County in 1891, and the Heidner family moved to West Bend when Edith was four years old. It was a community of

A dedicated historian, she was a pioneer in incorporating local history into high school curriculum.

*Left:
1937 High
School
Museum,
Miss Heidner,
second from
left.*

first and second generation Germans, Yankees from New England, Irish, and French. These pioneers brought with them the stamina, basic education, and skills needed to succeed in their struggle to establish homes in the Wisconsin wilderness.

Edith Heidner attended elementary and high school in West Bend, and attended Milwaukee-Downer College for two years. She transferred to the University of Wisconsin-Madison where she earned a bachelor's degree in 1913, with a major in history and minor in German. Later she attended summer sessions at the University, and at Columbia, New York, the University of Chicago, and American University, Washington, DC.

After teaching high school in Mazomanie, Edgerton, and Oconomowoc for several years, she came back to West Bend High School where she taught American History from 1919 to 1955. She was a pioneer in the integration of local history into the curriculum at both the high school and adult level.

The study of the westward movement in the United States, which involved her own ancestors, along with research for a pageant celebrating the 50th anniversary of West Bend's city charter, aroused her interest in local history.

Most high school courses ignored local history close to the lives of the students and their families. Her course recognized the way local happenings fit into the national course of events.

Students in Edith Heidner's classes studied the history of Washington County, researched family history, histories of local business and industry, farms, schools, churches, civic organizations, local government, famous persons, cemetery markers. They learned about daily life and old time customs—housecleaning procedures, church suppers, weddings—anything of special interest. They conducted interviews, did original research in records, documents, newspaper files. Their written reports were edited for accuracy and form and rewritten. The papers are on file for reference at the Washington County Historical Library and Museum in West Bend and are a valuable part of the local archives.

The Historical Library and Museum grew from a single display case in the American history classroom to twelve cases in an adjoining room, with a well-catalogued collection of books, manuscripts, official records and documents, maps, photographs, and miscellaneous artifacts. The library was moved to the old jail in 1962.

Upon her retirement, the West Bend Education Association recognized her years of service. She received the State Historical Society's Local History Award of Merit in 1965, and awards from the Washington County Historical Society in 1967 and 1972. A special award was presented by the Washington County Environmental Council on November 15, 1972, for saving the old county jail threatened with demolition, and the tower of the old courthouse. The latter, now restored, remains the most striking downtown landmark in the City of West Bend, a memorial to the contribution of a remarkable woman to her community.

Edith Heidner quietly passed away on November 27, 1981.

(See Selected Honors, Accomplishments, Publications, page 309)

written by E. FRANKIE DREYFUS

clare dreyfus

When Clare Bluett Dreyfus was proclaimed Wisconsin Mother of the Year in 1951, Governor Walter J. Kohler wrote, "Your long and glowing record of service to your community, your state and your nation is something in which you should take great pride."

Governor Lee Sherman Dreyfus remembers his mother as "a woman of incredible strength and great dignity, with a sense of purpose and mission in life." She believed that the Lord put us here for a reason and that our task is to discover that reason. Her philosophy was that we each have an obligation to tithe our most precious possessions. She tithed her time and talents.

As a homemaker-volunteer, her wide ranging community service included the Lutheran church, mental health, American Red Cross, the Parent-Teacher Association, radio and television, and twenty years of membership on the Milwaukee School Board.

Clare Emma Henrietta Bluett was born March 24, 1894, in Milwaukee, the eldest of five children of Thomas and Matilda Bluett. Her philanthropic inclinations became evident at an early age when she brought her first grade teacher and classmates home for lunch without forewarning her mother. (She told them it was her birthday, except that it was not.) On another occasion, she distributed the contents of her mother's jewelry box to passersby.

After graduating from Second Avenue School as valedictorian of her eighth grade class, she attended South Division High School, but family circumstances forced her to drop out before graduation. After her father's death in 1909, she assumed partial responsibility for supporting the

Clare Bluett Dreyfus and husband Woods Orlow Dreyfus.

For Clare Dreyfus,
no job was too difficult,
no distance too far.
She was always available
for any effort if the
project could ultimately
help children.

family. She worked in turn as department store clerk, artist, and dental hygienist.

One of her earliest volunteer projects was working with the American Red Cross during the influenza epidemic of 1918. Clare was a lifelong member of that organization.

She married Woods Orlow Dreyfus on July 3, 1920. The couple had three sons: Woods Bluett, Neal Thomas, and Lee Sherman. Homemaking responsibilities were complicated by an illness of the eldest son that lasted two years. Her devoted care led to complete recovery, although doctors had despaired of his survival.

Clare Dreyfus' involvement with the Parent Teacher Association began while Woods was in first grade. He insisted she attend an evening meeting at his school because "All the mothers will be there." She became president of the Townsend School PTA, president of the Milwaukee City Council of PTA and eventually state president. She edited the *Wisconsin Parent Teacher* from 1951 to 1965. She earned the title "Mrs. PTA of Wisconsin." The Milwaukee PTA Council established the Clare Dreyfus Scholarship Fund in her honor in 1951.

The family home was often shared with relatives and friends during the depression years. She was matriarch of a closely knit clan. "We are blessed, we are happy to share," she often said.

Governor Dreyfus recalls accompanying his mother during the 1930's when she undertook a door-to-door campaign to convince parents their children should be immunized against smallpox and other infectious diseases. She rolled up her son's jacket sleeve to show the vaccination scars.

All three Dreyfus sons served overseas during World War II. Clare worked as air raid warden for Civil Defense in the Milwaukee area, and undertook the sensitive task of delivering "killed in action" notices to bereaved parents and offering them her support and consolation. A telegraph announcing that her son Neal was missing in action in the China-Burma theater remained unopened for several days in a stack of mail. Clare assumed it was intended for someone else. The delay shortened the agonizing interval of 43 days that elapsed before his safe return was reported.

It was during this tense period that 17-year-old Lee Sherman, the youngest son, asked her to sign his Navy enlistment papers. She agreed, on condition that he first complete high school.

After the war, President Harry Truman appointed Clare to the White House Committee on Children and Youth. Under President Eisenhower, she served a four-year term on the White House Conference on Education. She was on a national commission to improve standards of comic books for children and received a special award from the Save The Children Federation in 1961.

Clare Dreyfus commanded the respect of people in all walks of life. She dedicated herself to the service of her family and her community. She died November 6, 1971 at the Milwaukee Home for Aged Lutherans, which she had served for many years as Board member. The eulogy at the memorial service proclaimed the central theme of her life, "She daily called upon her inner source of strength to give and share with any and all of her fellow human beings . . . no greater words of praise can be given to anyone."

(See Selected Honors, Accomplishments, Publications, page 308)

1933 Family photo, sons in front — Neal Thomas, Lee Sherman, Woods Bluett

112

The standards she developed to teach public school students discrimination in judging radio and TV programs brought her national recognition.

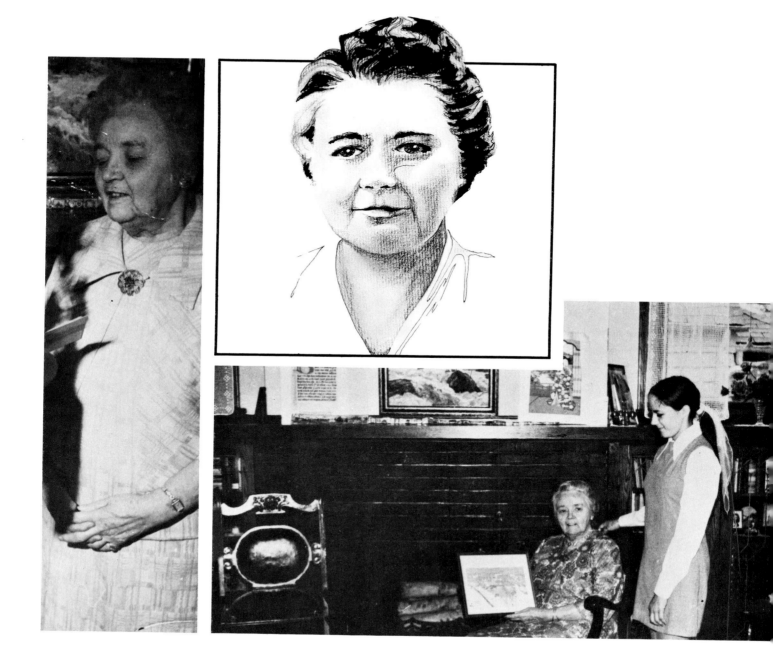

greta celia lagro potter

Greta Lagro Potter often asserted that the most important thing she learned in high school was, "If you don't want to be criticized, say nothing, do nothing, be nothing." She also believed that "Most critics are never wrong because they say nothing original and never make mistakes because they do nothing original." In her long life she feared neither critics, criticism, nor criticizing and said much, did much, became much. A creative thinker and doer in several fields, she was a librarian and professor of library science for many years; but perhaps her greatest influence was exerted through her leadership role in the formation of the American Council for Better Broadcasts and her subsequent support, through writing and lecturing, of the cause for better radio and television broadcasting.

Greta Celia Lagro was born May 26, 1894, in West Superior, Wisconsin, the only child of Charles and Celia Lagro. Her father, born in Norway and educated at the University of Christiania (now Oslo), came to Duluth in 1881 and moved to Superior in 1885. He married Celia Swenson, daughter of a Swedish immigrant in 1880.

While returning from a trip west, Lagro contracted pneumonia when his train was delayed for five days by an avalanche, and died June 17, 1894, at Wenatchee, Washington. He never saw his daughter.

Greta Lagro's only tangible inheritance from her father was his library, for her widowed mother was obliged to sell the family home and work as an itinerant nurse, leaving the child with her maternal grandparents in Superior. Greta helped deliver milk from her grandfather's farm and spent many summers in the homes of the affluent people who employed her mother. Through them, she was introduced to opera, the theater and museums.

Her most vivid childhood memory is of President McKinley, who campaigned in Superior in 1899. "He was in a great roped-in circle near the station. I ran away from Grandmother, under the rope; he shook my hand and spoke gently. I wept when my President was shot."

Greta was graduated from Superior High School in 1911. The school publication, *The Echo,* records her as valedictorian with the nickname "Gretchen" and the motto *Dux femina facti.* The quotation, from Virgil, refers to the valor of Queen Dido, "A woman, the leader in the deed".

She earned a BA in mathematics at the University of Minnesota in 1915. After working for a year as a substitute teacher, she taught at Superior High School at a salary of three dollars a day during the spring semester of 1917. That summer, she studied library science at the University of Minnesota to prepare for her subsequent positions of teacher-librarian in Minnesota and North Dakota schools.

In 1922, when gasoline was eleven cents a gallon, she drove an open Model T to Boston and New York. She recalled, "In New York, a policeman said he had never seen a small car from so far away."

After serving as Head Librarian at the Superior Public Library in 1926 and 1927, she traveled from

Greta Lagro Potter

Scotland to Italy and visited great libraries everywhere. Back in New York, she earned a bachelor's degree in library science at Columbia University in 1928. From 1929 to 1931, she was associate professor of library science at Alabama College, now the University of Montevallo, where she organized the department and developed the curriculum. There she became interested in radio, and broadcast a series of book reviews and programs about libraries over Station WAPI, Birmingham. A year later she earned her MS degree in Library Science from Columbia and in 1937 she began her doctoral studies at the University of Chicago. She was professor of library science at Clarion State Teacher's College, Clarion, Pennsylvania, from 1938 to 1941.

Greta Lagro married Dr. Alden H. Potter, an osteopath, September 30, 1933 in Minneapolis. He died in Ashland, Wisconsin, three years later. There were no children.

During her academic career, Professor Potter published articles in many periodicals. Her speciality was medieval paleography and early printing. One of her major articles, "An Appreciation of Sir Emery Walker", *Library Quarterly,* (July, 1939), gave recognition to the man responsible for the renascence of fine printing. In demand as a speaker, she assembled a collection of Bible leaves, dating from AD 1121, to illustrate her lectures.

In the summer of 1941, her academic career was abruptly terminated at its height. The death of an aunt left her responsible for the care of three elderly relatives. She decided to make her home in Superior at their residence, and devote herself to writing, lecturing, and civic work.

It was then that she became involved in a campaign for better radio programs and became chairman of Better Broadcasts for northwestern Wisconsin. She was the speaker when the American Council for Better Broadcasts was founded in 1953, as an expansion of the Wisconsin Association.

With her friend, Dr. Mary Leslie Spence, then president of ACBB, she traveled to the west coast to organize Better Broadcasting groups from San Diego to Seattle. In 1958, she was elected to national office as Chairman of the Policy Committee of ACBB.

Her efforts to improve the quality of radio and television programming were largely responsible for the establishment of educational television in Duluth. The techniques she developed to teach discrimination in judging radio and television programs brought her national recognition.

Greta Potter always regretted that she was forced to terminate her career as teacher of library science. In 1979, she donated $1,500 to Columbia University for scholarships in library science. The funds came from the sale of her manuscript collection. Intellectually active throughout her life, she published *Forever Real: Chequamegon View Hilltop and Other Poems* in 1977, when she was 83. She died in Superior on August 22, 1981.

She exemplifies the person who does not accept that enforced withdrawal from a profession means the end of a useful life.

(See Selected Honors, Accomplishments, Publications, page 312)

Performances of her orchestral works include two with the Chicago Symphony at the Pabst Theater under Dr. Frederick Stock and Desire DeFauw.

edna frida pietsch

It's curtain time . . . the house lights dim . . . listen and hear the sounds of the night . . . in flute, harp, piano, muted strings, then kettledrum and bassoon creating the rhythm and the mood. . .the many fantasies, miniatures of life.

Her "uniqueness lies in the fact that she is not only a good composer but a good woman composer, of whom there are few even nationally. Her works have just enough of the modern idiom to make them interesting to the average listener and still remain definitely romantic," says Joseph Skornika, for many years the conductor of the civic orchestra in Milwaukee. She is one of a very few local composers who have had the privilege to have their compositions performed by the Chicago Symphony Orchestra.

She is Edna Frida Pietsch. For half a century she has been called the "dean of Milwaukee composers." She is still radiant and charming at 87.

On May 7, 1894, Edna Frida Pietsch was born in Milwaukee to Ferdinand and Ida Pietsch. She shares her birthday with Brahms and Tschaikovsky.

Miss Pietsch grew up in a home on Kilbourn

Left to right: The Edna Frida Pietsch home built by her grandfather Louis Hildebrandt, well over 100 years ago. "This picture was taken when I was about 10 or 11 years of age. My father owned the horse and buggy in the driveway and also the carriage in front of the house. However, he rented the two black horses for several weeks while my aunt and her three children visited us. That enabled my family and relatives to go out driving on Sundays together. In this picture, I am standing in front, next to the fence."
Insert: Edna Frida Pietsch at eight years of age, 1902.
Near left: Miss Pietsch in her garden, September 1966. (courtesy, Milwaukee Journal)

Avenue where she still lives. It is a large house that her grandfather built over 100 years ago. Her father was a structural and ornamental iron contractor. His work can be seen in many Milwaukee buildings and homes.

Miss Pietsch loves flowers and still takes care of the English garden along the fence that extends to the rear of the house. The composer believes that to write beautiful melody, one has to have the capacity to love many things. "I love my flowers and animals—and I have a lot of friends."

Long before she began school Miss Pietsch was playing the piano and improvising melodies. When her older sister practiced on the piano she listened and in a short time was playing the same melodies by ear.

When she was eight years old she began her piano instruction with Ida Schroeder and continued with her for over 20 years. Miss Pietsch was earnest in her efforts to learn. The understanding and encouragement of her parents and teachers helped to lay the foundation of her lifelong career.

She attended Story School, West Division High School and the Wisconsin Conservatory of Music. She learned harmony, composition and theory with Wilhelm Middelchulte, Carl Eppert, Rudolph Kopp and Dr. Bernard Dieter, dean of the Chicago Conservatory. To understand stringed instruments she took violin lessons from Pearl Brice.

The composer whose music most influenced her in her early years was Edward MacDowell. Over the years her favorite composer has been Tchaikovsky. "His music is so emotional, full of long lined melody." This is also characteristic of her music.

Her inspiration has come from many things. "One day years ago I had a beautiful bunch of lavender lilacs," she told. "It sat there on the piano in a lovely vase and as I looked at it, inhaling the beautiful fragrance, I wondered if I could capture that feeling in music."

Some of her works have been published and many have been performed. This includes over 30 songs, a full symphony, concerti, chamber music, piano solos, duo piano numbers plus many piano teaching pieces.

Miss Pietsch became both composer and teacher to generations of piano students. She received numerous awards and won the acclaim of critics and friends. Her scrapbooks are filled to capacity.

She still teaches about ten students twice a

On one occasion she recalled she was trying so hard to concentrate on her music that everything seemed to distract her and, even the motion and tick of the clock she had to stop.
She was about to strike a chord when she heard a tap, tap.
Her father was in the basement shelling nuts. When she asked him to move to another part of the basement, he grumbled, "This is still my house," as he picked up and moved along.

week. There is no limit to their age; five years or older, they are all a challenge to her. Her fees are minimal.

For those who have a special interest in music, she advises, "Get a good background in the old composers; take lessons twice a week if at all possible. Music demands patience and concentration. In anything worthwhile, you have to work. You don't get anything for nothing and there are no short cuts in music."

Why is she so dedicated to this art?

"I suppose it's because when I leave this world I'd like to leave something worthwhile behind. And if I've done that in giving my students a feeling for music, and if my compositions have inspired other people, then I think I haven't lived in vain. If my name lives at all, it will be through my compositions, my brain children."

Editor's Note: Edna Frida Pietsch died Friday, July 16, 1982. She suffered a heart attack while visiting relatives in Eagle River, WI.

(See Selected Honors, Accomplishments, Publications, page 312)

*Maestro Kenneth Schermerhorn and Edna Frida Pietsch.
Taken after Schermerhorn conducted her
"Five Oriental Impressions" in Uihlein Hall
of the Performing Arts Center after the April 4, 1978,
Senior Citizen Concert.*

gladys mollart

Gladys Mollart was born in Watertown on January 11, 1895, the daughter of Lobegott and Minna Mollart. Except for her college years (she is a graduate of Vassar), and a few years in New York during World War I, she has always lived in Watertown.

Gladys's father sensed his daughter's talents for leadership and human relations when she was quite young. "He suggested I go into the mission field," Miss Mollart relates. "It seemed to him I had leanings that would equip me for that type of work." But she chose service nearer home. She often

Right: Gladys Mollart in gown of Victorian Era awaits guests on the porch of the Octagon House.
Below: Miss Mollart was honored with the Outstanding Citizenship Award by the Jefferson County Chapter of the Reserve Officers Association of the United States.

The preservation of the historic Octagon House and the first kindergarten in Watertown was largely the work of Miss Mollart.

121

speaks of her family and chuckles at one of her first accomplishments. An older brother taught her the cake walk, and she won prizes for this achievement.

Several Watertown organizations are indebted to Gladys Mollart for years of volunteer service. Leading the list is the local historical society. The history of the Watertown Historical Society, founded in 1933, is part of the history of Gladys Mollart.

The famous Octagon House designed and built in the 1850's, was deeded to the Society in 1938. Gladys Mollart played no small role in the transaction. "My interest in the preservation of the house appealed to my sense of the love of old Watertown. We were very grateful to the Richards family for the fabulous offer. We accepted the house with great joy, knowing that there would be much to be accomplished. But we had the courage to accept the challenge, which was immense— $800 in the treasury for a starter, in the spirit of adventure." From 1945 to 1978, she was volunteer curator and still serves as society historian.

"My additional interest was the original kindergarten building which was moved from North Second and Jones streets to the Octagon House grounds. It was necessary to raise money for the moving—more than $3000."

"Now she and the other members of the Society have in mind an administration building," said publisher John Clifford in 1969. "Rest assured there will be an administration building. She'll see to that."

The new administration building opened within a year and was dedicated in September, 1970. In the dedication speech, Lee Block, then president of the Society, stated, "It is my pleasure . . . to dedicate this building and name it in honor of the single person who has been most responsible for the successful operation of the Society, the restoration of the first kindergarten and the pioneer barn . . . By proclamation, this building will hereafter be known as the Gladys Mollart Tour Center."

Miss Mollart found time for other community services. She was chairman of the Home Service Committee of the Watertown Area Red Cross. She directed the activities of the Watertown Family Welfare for several years. Her concern for child welfare resulted in an appointment as a delegate to a 1960 youth conference in Washington, DC which developed recommendations for citizen action youth programs.

Miss Mollart is a charter member of the Watertown Branch of AAUW. She helped organize the branch and the first meeting was held in her home. She is also a member of the Wisconsin Antiquarian Society, the State Historical Society Women's Auxiliary, and the Saturday Club, local affiliate of the Wisconsin Federation of Women's Clubs. She enlisted the services of the Saturday Club to erect five historical markers in the city.

Despite all her awards and accomplishments, Miss Mollart seeks no credit or praise. She refers to those who have worked with her on her projects as "tremendous assets" and adds, "Besides, I've enjoyed every minute of it."

(See Selected Honors, Accomplishments, Publications, page 311)

written by HAZEL MC GRATH

helen c. white

Helen C. White (courtesy, UW-Madison Archives)

No more fitting monument to one of its most eminent scholars could have been built by the University of Wisconsin than Helen C. White Hall, the solidly handsome, seven-storied building overlooking Lake Mendota at the foot of the Madison campus.

Opened in September of 1971, it houses the English department, moved down the hill from Bascom Hall where Miss White spent more than 40 years of her professional life. It also contains the college—or undergraduate—library, where part of her bequest to the University of more than 4000 volumes found a home.

Miss White came to Wisconsin in the fall of 1919, with BA and MA degrees earned at Radcliffe College and two years of teaching experience at Smith. She intended to stay one year.

Settling into a room at 211 W. Gilman Street, she wrote her mother, "Do you know, mama, that I've been 'tigered' twice? The other day I came in to my huge overflow class of 90—mostly men—to be greeted by an awful hissing. I was frightened and terribly worried. Then such a yell—and 'Miss White!' It was the 'tiger' and said to be a great honor and very seldom given to newcomers. Of course, I didn't know then and I felt so queer, but I got it again . . . "

The "tiger," later called the "sky-rocket," began with "SSSSSS", continued with a loud "Boom" followed by "Ah" and ended with the name of the honored teacher.

In those days Miss White devoted every Saturday morning to tutoring whoever came to her office, "almost to the neglect of my own graduate work.

Her novels are amazing for the brilliance of the characterization,
the intricacies of plot and the deep religious feeling pervading them.

123

But I felt compelled to do what I could to get the boys (veterans of World War I) on their feet. Their English is incredible,'' she confided to her mother.

The honors and awards accumulated in her lifetime began early. Her first book, "The Mysticism of William Blake," was published by the University of Wisconsin Press in 1927, and was followed by other scholarly works. She also wrote several religious novels inspired by her devotion to the Roman Catholic Church.

Her talents and energy were quickly recognized. She became the first woman to hold a full professorship in Letters and Science at the University of Wisconsin and twice she was chairman of the English Department.

Miss White, who described herself as "the large woman in purple," explained her addiction to garments of this color, "I simplify my wardrobe by wearing purple because it's practical and becoming. When I fly off for a weekend engagement, everything matches automatically."

"I have four desks in my apartment," she once said. "One is for personal correspondence; that is hopelessly littered and I never can find a thing in it. The second one is for the notes for my books that I haven't gotten around to writing yet. The third is for the work that must be cleaned up immediately, and the fourth is for typing."

Sister Mary Paynter expounded upon this filing system. "One seminar I took from her in the early 1950's met in her apartment. She intended to return someone's seminar paper and calmly began sorting through the immense piles of journals, mail,

papers, books, etc., that covered every inch of table, bookshelf, open space. Finally, she opened the refrigerator door, musing to herself, 'Now I know it's here somewhere . . . ' and there it was!"

As national president of the American Association of University Women from 1941 to 1947, Miss White was called on to lecture to

Helen C. White as a wide-eyed babe.
(courtesy, UW-Madison Archives)

branches across the country as well as to write for its national publication. In 1949, she was given the AAUW $2,500 achievement award for "professional and literary achievements, and for her international work in humanities in serving as US delegate to the preparatory commission for UNESCO in 1946, as member of the education mission to Germany that year, and as member of the US delegation to the second UNESCO conference in Mexico City in 1947." She was also the first woman to be elected president of the American Association of University Professors. In 1958, Queen Elizabeth named her "Honorable Officer of the Order of the British Empire" for her eminence in the field of 16th and 17th Century English literature.

About her collection of honorary degrees, she remarked that Catholic colleges gave her honorary degrees because she was a Catholic and a woman, and Protestant colleges to show how liberal they were, adding: "Think how many I would have if I were also black!"

The light side of her personality was equally matched with intellectual insight. "There is no better assurance of a student's respect," she said, "than the confidence that the teacher really knows what he is talking about . . . Essential though it is to keep one's specialty in constant repair, the specialist would do well to lift his eyes from his own preoccupations and take advantage of the breadth of the milieu in which he finds himself . . . The creative imagination is found in physics or education as in painting or criticism."

Miss White's long career came to an end suddenly, after 47 active years. On June 7, 1967, she died.

At a Memorial Service in St. Paul's University Chapel in Madison, on May 19, 1968, her old

Above and right: Helen White, student, author, scholar.
(courtesy, UW-Madison Archives)

friend Mark Ingraham said: "I am glad that this service, a ritual she loved, in a Church she affectionately supported, comes so long after her death that we sense our gratitude more than our grief and realize how short a shadow is cast by the sadness of her last year in the light of her luminous and lofty career—for now we may smile at her foibles, admire her achievements, and rejoice that she was our friend."

(See Selected Honors, Accomplishments, Publications, page 314)

*Occasionally a character I've about decided
to eliminate entirely
pops up in the second chapter, and he's there
to stay, no matter how hard I try to oust him.
When the story is finished,
a good deal of the plot is found to hinge
on this recalcitrant personality."*
—HELEN C. WHITE

written by MAXINE ELLIS

breta luther griem

"Breta Griem was everybody's favorite grandmother."

Although that is not Breta Luther Griem's only claim to fame, thousands of Milwaukee area people may have felt this way about the lady who came into their homes in the 1950's on her WTMJ-TV program "What's New in the Kitchen." She was of the best known cooks in all of Wisconsin. Her program was one of the first television cooking shows in the United States and one of the longest

Milwaukee's first local TV stars in the early 1950's included Breta Griem demonstrating recipes in her "What's New In the Kitchen" show.

running.

In 1949 Mrs. Griem started her show as a twice a week, 15-minute segment of Nancy Gray's "What's New in the Home." When Mrs. Gray left the program, Breta's segment was extended until it eventually had a 60-minute format, six days a week. It ended in 1962 when it was part of the "Women's World" TV program.

Breta Luther was a 1919 graduate of the University of Wisconsin-Madison in home economics specializing in dietetics and nutrition. She worked in areas dealing with food all during her long career, enthusiastically committed to spreading words about good nutrition.

She successfully combined career and marriage in a time when this was the exception. She married Milton E. Griem, a research chemist whom she had met in college classes at Madison. They had two children, a son Melvin and daughter Margaret.

"I encouraged both my daughter and daughter-in-law to establish themselves well enough in a profession so that if anything did happen they would not be without resources."

The success of her show stemmed mainly from her awareness of the needs of her audience, its love of food and its budget consciousness. "I do all my own shopping for the show. That way I get to know prices. And I watch the baskets that women push around the markets, which tells me what they are buying so I can keep the show timely," she once said.

The early show kitchen consisted only of an electric stove with limited power. If she ran the oven, she could not use the big top burner at the same time. The cupboards and sink were make-believe. Breta had a terrible time keeping guests from using the sink during the show, so a bucket was placed under the sink to catch liquid that guests would pour down the non-functional drain. "Our source of water was the sink in a janitor's closet down the hall. That was quite a relay." Later the studio kitchen grew into one of the best equipped in the country.

From left: Connie Daniels and Breta Griem about 1951, WTMJ-TV; with parents; on the set with mother Lulu Luther, husband Milton and daughter Margaret Williamson; Breta, about 1970-73.

A major part of her show was to present tips on shopping wisely and using practical methods to fix tasty, good-looking dishes which she referred to as "Cinderella Meals."

Once a month a member of the Wisconsin Restaurant Association told his story of the growth of his restaurant. Often the chefs shared a favorite recipe or demonstrated how to fix a special dish. Breta was an honorary member of the Wisconsin Restaurant Association and was awarded a lifetime membership upon her retirement.

Breta also wrote articles on nutrition for restaurant trade publications and a regular column in the *Milwaukee Journal* for a number of years. Another of her concerns was the CARE program (Cooperation for American Relief Everywhere). Starting in 1954, Breta competed with Milwaukee's WTMJ personality John Drury to raise money for the CARE program. Between 1954 and 1961, the Griem-Drury team raised $212,499 for this worthy cause.

After her retirement Breta organized her collection of cookbooks numbering between 4,000 and 4,500 volumes. In 1966 she gave over 3,000 volumes to the Milwaukee Library, including many books she had gathered during her world travels. The oldest book was published in Italian in 1669 on parchment, written by a royal chef. Many are from famous Milwaukee hostesses and cooks of the 1880's.

Even in her 70's, Breta taught classes in elderly nutrition for Milwaukee Area Technical College and continued to write and do service work, especially as it related to her interest in nutrition.

Breta Griem died on April 5, 1980. "Everybody's favorite grandmother" was a woman ahead of her times.

(See Selected Honors, Accomplishments, Publications, page 309)

Above: Harriet Harmon Dexter
Right: Mrs. Dexter and Charles Penn as she holds a small replica of Northland College Seal. Dedication of stained glass window in Wheeler Hall, 1976.

She was the first woman to hold the post of Acting President at Northland College.

harriet harmon dexter

Harriet Harmon Dexter's influence was felt from northern Wisconsin to China and Lebanon. In her lifetime of 82 years, she never faltered in the strong Christian beliefs she joyously preached.

Harriet Harmon was born December 21, 1897, in St. Paul, Minnesota, the second of four children. Her father, Dr. Andrew Davidson Harmon, was then pastor of the Disciples of Christ Church. Her mother, Alice Gadd Harmon, was an ordained minister. Through them she found her solid commitment to religious ideals.

Much of Harriet's childhood was spent in Cable, Wisconsin where her parents had a summer home on the lake. There she learned to love the out-of-doors. Her knowledge of plant life was phenomenal. The happy days spent at the cottage were a great joy then and in later years.

Graduating from Cable High School in 1915, she entered Cotner College at Lincoln, Nebraska, earning a bachelor of arts degree in 1920. Determined to immerse herself in matters of religious concern, she went to New York and worked as editor of Congregational church publications for two years. By 1925 she had earned a masters degree in religious education at Transylvania University of Lexington, Kentucky.

The next year, Harriet responded to a call from China to teach for a year in a government normal school for boys at Luchowfu, Anwhei, China. It was a mission that left a lasting impression. She maintained a lifelong correspondence with many of her students.

Returning home, she joined the faculty at Northland College in Ashland as Dean of Women. When she married Professor Nathaniel Beech Dexter on June 16, 1923, she lost her job. The college did not allow both husband and wife to be faculty members.

As a faculty wife, Harriet continued an active interest in college affairs, and was constantly in demand as a speaker. She was the organist and choir director at both the Ashland and Cable churches the Dexters attended, playing on a reed organ that had to be pumped.

Two children, Ray and Betty, were adopted in 1933. That same year, the Dexters left Northland. Nathaniel became a company commander in the Civilian Conservation Corps and Harriet, the first editor of an interdenominational journal for United Church Women.

She served in this position until her return to Northland in 1942, as admissions counselor and English teacher. For 25 years she taught with enthusiasm.

In 1950-61 she took a leave to teach at the American University in Beirut, Lebanon. For several months in 1971 she served as Acting President of Northland College. In addition to teaching, she even found time to write four books.

John Bobb of Sturgeon Bay, a former student, recalls, "In the classroom, in simple conversation, in major projects, she had the ability to involve people, including the shy, the reticent, the reserved, and, in the process, make them feel good about themselves and what they were doing." In the pulpit or at the rostrum, she was articulate, perceptive, comprehensive, inspiring.

In her waning years, she fought vigorously to combat cancer. When the battle·could not be won, comforted by her deep religious faith, she planned her own memorial services. She died February 12, 1980.

Harriet Harmon Dexter left a legacy of love and enriched all whose lives she touched.

(See Selected Honors, Accomplishments, Publications, page 308)

maurie applegate clack

Mauree Applegate Clack was fired from her first teaching job. At age 17, a rural Iowa school board dismissed her. "They told me I couldn't handle children," she later recalled. "Some of the students were nearly as old as I was."

She went on to a teaching career that spanned 54 years. Her career was built around preparing other teachers to handle and get the most out of children.

Mauree Applegate was born November 11, 1897 at Atlanta, Illinois, later moving to Washington, Iowa, where she completed high school. She continued at the Washington County teacher training department through 1916, then started to teach. After being dismissed, she moved to Wisconsin where she received a diploma from Platteville State Teachers College. Mauree continued study at the University of Wisconsin-Madison and at Northwestern University, Evanston, Illinois where she received bachelor's and master's degrees.

Her Wisconsin teaching career was in rural schools where she served as both teacher and principal. In 1934 Mauree was named Rock County Superintendent of Schools remaining through 1941 when she became City Supervisor of Schools in Neenah.

In the fall of 1945 Mauree Applegate joined the faculty of then LaCrosse State Teachers College, staying for the rest of her teaching career. When she retired in 1966 she was given the title of Professor Emeritus of Elementary Education.

Besides teaching Mauree Applegate wrote books on teaching. She believed firmly in keeping language simple. "If you can't make a thing simple,

Maurell Clark

For 12 years her radio program "Let's Write" reached more than 60,000 grade school children throughout Wisconsin.

Her words are like a box of colors that can stimulate the imagination and open a whole new world of expression.

you don't understand it yourself," she wrote. "I have tried to keep my writing at a level at which an eighth grader can understand it."

Beginning in 1952 Mauree Applegate started her radio program, "Let's Write," on the Wisconsin School of the Air. She continued for 12 years reaching more than 60,000 grade school children throughout Wisconsin. She stressed the importance of children learning to express themselves even if they do not do it perfectly the first time. "Teach writing as you teach art. You can't scold a child who draws a man higher than a house when he first learns to draw. Why treat mistakes in his first writing any differently?" she said.

Once while leading a group of children in a discussion about a rabbit, Mrs. Clack said a little boy told her, 'The farmer chased the rabbit with a hay-picker-up thing, and the rabbit ran out of the garden." Important to her was that the lad did not strangle his idea by having to think of the correct word before he expressed it.

In December 1955 Mauree Appletate married Willis Charles Clack. He died less than a year later. Strengthened by the tragedy she continued to fill her life with educational pursuits.

In mid-career Mauree wrote, "I am very interested in making schools natural places for children to live in. It seems to me that school is taught the hard way. We as teachers know how children learn but we do not know how they feel and think . . . If each teacher in her own way follows a vision of what a school can really be like, she grows and develops with her children."

In addition to her teaching, writing and radio program, Mauree Applegate was nationally known as a lecturer and workshop leader until her retirement in 1966.

Collecting Wedgwood English china was a favorite hobby. Mrs. Clack also liked to write poetry in what she called her "poor verse." Birthday cards and other special greetings were not usually cards purchased at shops but a "Mauree Applegate" special. For nearly 13 years friends looked forward to her Christmas card—a beautiful Wedgwood cover printed on a booklet of her own poetry.

When urged to publish her verse, Mrs. Clack would shrug it off assuring her friends her poems were only for sharing.

A La Crosse reporter once said of Mrs. Clack that her words are like a box of colors or paints that can stimulate the imagination and open a whole new world of expression. Through her books, cross country lecture tours, radio program and teaching duties, Mrs. Clack kept up her life work of sharing her ideas with countless children and teachers. Words came to life under her pen.

Mauree Applegate Clack died July 11, 1969 at the age of 79.

Her last "poor verse" booklet ended with this:

AGRICULTURAL PRONOUNCEMENT
From sending cards—a long vacation—
Life customs, too, need crop rotation.
From fallow years, new richness born,
So be it, friends, next year, no corn.

(See Selected Honors, Accomplishments, Publications, page 306)

written by DOLLY STOKES

ruth west

In 1932, a young Manitowoc man who had just graduated from Cornell University in Ithaca, New York, asked Ruth St. John to become his bride. He brought her home to Wisconsin.

Ruth Cronk was born in a Quaker community in Schuyler County, New York, in 1898, the oldest of five girls. She attended a two-year county normal school and taught first grade through first year high school for two years in a rural school.

Left: Ruth West and Tommy (courtesy, Daryl Cornick)
Left below: Tulip Tea (courtesy, John D. West)
Below: Ruth and her tulips (courtesy, Milwaukee Journal)

In 1919, Ruth married Morgan St. John, a tax attorney and a nationally recognized authority on the game of bridge. They lived in Ithaca, New York, where Morgan, handicapped by polio, had an extra office and studio in their home.

In 1929 Morgan St. John died, and Ruth rented the former office area to students from Cornell University. It happened that John D. West, a student from Manitowoc, Wisconsin, came to stay at the St. John home. Because John seldom traveled home for holidays, Ruth would often invite him for dinner. Perhaps it was her cooking, perhaps her characteristic hospitality, but in 1932 Ruth St. John and John D. West were married. After graduation, they moved to Manitowoc, where he became involved in the family business. the Manitowoc Shipbuilding Company.

In her meanderings around her new home town with the trained German Shepherd dog she brought from Ithaca, New York, Ruth soon came upon six acres of quack grass and thistle. The land lay just within the northern city limits of Manitowoc, bounded on the east by Lake Michigan. Ruth acquired this land to the amazement of many townspeople who did not perceive the piece as desirable.

In 1934 a team of dapple grey horses pulled the plow that turned the first furrow on the long, narrow strip of land. Thus began Ruth West's 47 years of dedication to gardening. With no previous knowledge of horticulture or landscape design, and without professional assistance of any kind, Bill Mueller, a native German farmer, and Ruth started the task of developing "West of the Lake." Bill spaded the entire acreage by hand, while Ruth, following along on her hands and knees, and dressed in an old mink coat in cold weather, shook out the matted roots of quack grass and thistle. It took nine years to complete the lawns.

Eugene Burish was hired in 1945 to help with the necessary but uninteresting garden chores. In 1969 Bill Mueller died and Gene inherited the responsibility for planting and maintaining the six acre plot called "West of the Lake". Except for a student helper during summer vacation to assist with the lawnmowing Gene and Mrs. West have handled the entire project for 36 years.

The garden is now considered one of the most comprehensive private gardens in Wisconsin. The gates are always open to visitors and hundreds come to see and enjoy Ruth's gardens each year. One visitor called her trip to the gardens "A

"West of the Lake" Gardens (courtesy, Green Bay Press Gazette)

pilgrimage to a shrine of beauty. Love and patience are evident everywhere."

During the years of the Tulip Tea, an annual event held from 1936 to 1966 for the benefit of her church and the Manitowoc garden clubs, visitors saw as many as 30,000 tulips blooming on the grounds. In 1967 the tulip was adopted as the official flower of Manitowoc in recognition of the fame brought to the city by the "West of the Lake" tulip teas.

The summer garden features 800 rose plants, and many perennials and annuals. "A glimpse of heaven on Earth" is the way a sister of a religious order described the West gardens, with their decorative stone beds, meditation areas, floral paths, and varieties of exotic orchids nurtured in the green houses.

The West interests widened to include the visual arts. "My more recent and exciting interest in art was a natural outgrowth of my garden work, where I learned through the planning phase of this project the practical application of art principles. I began by collecting Wisconsin art in 1966, my preference being abstract art. Collecting is an incurable disease." In 1975, the Wests funded an addition to what is now known as the Rahr-West Museum and Civic Center.

As chairman of the Rahr-West Museum and Civic Center board, Mrs. West was successful in having the old Rahr Mansion placed on the National Register of Historic Sites. This was followed by a complete restoration of the exterior of the mansion undertaken by the city of Manitowoc. For the past five years, Mrs. West has personally renovated and restored every room in the mansion except the Rahr parlor.

"I am a very lucky person that I have been generously endowed with an imagination and given the health and strength to do its bidding. Of course, at age 83, I keep my fingers crossed! Another asset is that I have a compatible, successful and generous husband who has shared my life for 49 years. His influence and confidence in me has made it possible to develop my dreams in my own way." West is also the "Official Photographer" of the West Gardens, and has recorded the beauty of many seasons.

Ruth West is understandably in demand as a speaker. In 1965 she was to lecture to the DePere Women's Club. While setting up her equipment, she fell and broke her wrist. She went on with the lecture, and when she finished she had her wrist put in a cast and a sling. Her reaction? "I have 750 pansy plants to set out!" And set them out she did!

(See Selected Honors, Accomplishments, Publications, page 314)

"I believe I have an obligation to share everything I have with others.
This urge to share has provided the impetus and the long years of dedication to my garden and the community in which we live."
—RUTH WEST

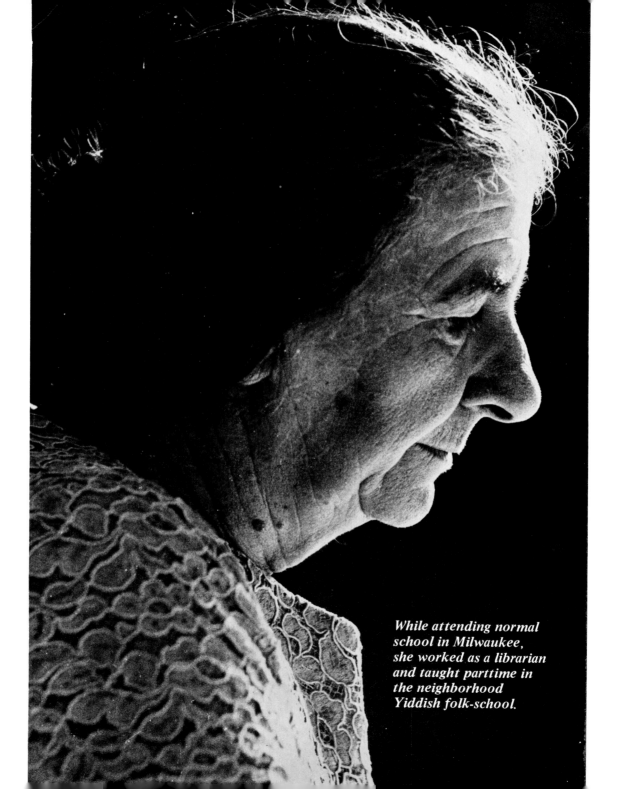

While attending normal school in Milwaukee, she worked as a librarian and taught parttime in the neighborhood Yiddish folk-school.

golda meir

Golda Meir, Israel's first woman prime minister would have been a rare woman in any circumstances. Wife, mother, grandmother, and the heroine of Jewish national independence, she was elected to power in the fruition of unique talents.

Golda was born to a Jewish carpenter, Moshe Mabovich, and his wife, Bluma, on May 3, 1898, in Kiev, Russia. The second oldest of three surviving daughters, Golda knew both poverty and oppression. In Czarist Russia, Jews existed under anti-semitic laws, heavy economic and social discrimination and the terror of pogroms.

In an indelible early memory she watched her father nail heavy boards over doors and windows to protect his home and family from the feared pogrom onslaught. At four she witnessed a mob of Cossacks and peasants surge through Kiev, looting, beating and stabbing every unwary Jew that could be found. Years later Golda spoke of that fearful, trembling child hiding helplessly behind boarded doors waiting for the violence of the mob. Such was the probable origin of her lifelong rebellion against passive suffering.

When Golda was five, Moshe left Russia for the promise of America. Bluma Mabovich and her daughters moved to Pinsk where Golda heard of the establishment of a homeland for the Jewish people in Palestine.

In 1907 Golda's papa sent for his family from Milwaukee, Wisconsin, where he and they would settle. The family's first American home was but

two rooms and a kitchen in the rear of a small store on the corner of 6th and Walnut Streets, a poor Jewish section of ethnic Milwaukee. As the family's needs grew, Golda's mother entered the grocery store business. Golda and her younger sister enrolled at the Fourth Street Grade School, located in a fortress-like building near the Joseph Schlitz brewery. Though Golda loved school, she seldom arrived on time, being required to work in the family grocery store until what her mother optimistically termed the "morning rush" was over.

Golda quickly mastered English and within two years she stood at the head of her class. When she graduated from 8th grade, Golda had held a part-time job for more than a year as a messenger girl at the Boston Store. Every Saturday she wrapped packages and made deliveries from 9 a.m. to 9 p.m. She was paid a dollar a day. The following summer she worked full time and saved enough money to buy a winter coat, the first purchased with her own earnings.

Golda entered North Division High School in the fall of 1912, but her stay was brief. Believing that "teaching was the noblest and most satisfying profession of all," she hoped to enter that profession. Golda's mother had other ideas. Bluma learned that married women were not permitted to teach in Wisconsin schools and, not wanting her daughter to be a spinster, she insisted that Golda quit school and go to work, or transfer to business school and learn skills which would not interfere with marriage. Golda's father agreed.

The final blow came when Golda's mother began to negotiate a marriage for her daughter with a

Golda Meir (courtesy, Milwaukee Journal)

prosperous real estate man in his thirties, who regularly patronized the family store. Golda was outraged and in November of 1912 ran away to live with her older sister and brother-in-law in Denver, Colorado.

There Golda attended high school and helped out in her brother-in-law's dry cleaning business. In her free time she listened with fascination to the young Socialists and Zionists who congregated at her sister's home. It was at one of these gatherings that she met Morris Meyerson, a gentle, soft-spoken young man who worked sporadically as a sign painter. They soon fell in love.

After two years in Denver, Golda reconciled with her parents when Papa wrote begging her to come home. He assured her that she might finish high school and even go to normal school.

Back in Milwaukee, Golda made up for lost time and in less than two years graduated from high school and enrolled at the Milwaukee Teachers' Training College. Meanwhile her interest in Socialism and Zionism grew and crystallized. In 1915 Golda joined the Paole-Zion, a small party of labor Zionists which called for the building of a cooperative commonwealth in Palestine. Golda was soon speaking on street corners for the Zionist cause.

In 1917, instead of pursuing a career as a teacher, she became a full-time staff member of Paole-Zion at a salary of $15 a week. The future was now clear. Golda determined to go to Palestine and, as a condition for marrying Morris Meyerson, who had followed her to Milwaukee, she insisted that he promise to emigrate to Palestine with her. With considerably more enthusiasm for Golda than for the prospects of building a life in Palestine, Morris agreed and the couple married on December 24, 1917.

Four years later, Golda persuaded her husband to go with her to Palestine where they joined a kibbutz near Nazareth. The area was marshy and malaria ridden. Life on the kibbutz was difficult and physically demanding. In 1924, exhausted by the strenuous agricultural work, which did not seem to tire his wife, Morris Meyerson insisted that they leave the kibbutz, move to a city and start a family. Reluctantly, Golda agreed. For the next four years, the couple lived in abject poverty in

After nearly 50 years of service to her country she was recognized universally as an astute politician who advocated strength and military determinism, tempered by compassion for her adversaries.

139

Tel Aviv and later in Jerusalem. During this period, Golda and Morris became the parents of two children, first a son and then a daughter.

Life as a full-time homemaker hardly tested Golda's driving energy and desire to contribute actively to the building of a labor-Zionist state. In 1928 she returned to work and was soon appointed executive secretary of the Women's Labor Council. In the early 1930's she worked in the United States as a representative of the Pioneer Women's Organization. Like many husbands, Morris Meyerson disapproved of his wife's dedication to work and her absence from home. The couple finally separated, but never divorced.

The dynamic Golda rose rapidly in the Palestinian labor movement and in the world Zionist campaign. During World War II she worked days for the Allied war effort and secretly worked nights for the Mossad, smuggling into Palestine Jews emerging from the holocaust of Europe. After the war, in the struggle to establish a Jewish homeland, Golda sided with David Ben-Gurion's activist faction. When the State of Israel was established in 1948 by edict of the United Nations, Golda was a signer of the Proclamation of Independence.

From then on with her drive and an unsquelchable enthusiasm for Israel's welfare, it was merely a matter of time before Ben-Gurion was to refer to her as the "best man in my cabinet." He also urged her to adopt a Hebrew name and Golda Meyerson became Golda Meir.

In 1969 at age 70, Golda Meir became the fourth Prime Minister of Israel, leading a nation demoralized by economic problems and constant war. Until her death in December 1978, she continued to be a strong voice in the Israeli Labor Party.

"Someday when peace comes," she once said, "we may forgive the Arabs for having killed our sons, but it will be harder for us to forgive them for having forced us to kill their sons."

(See Selected Honors, Accomplishments, Publications, page 311)

written by JANE HUELSKAMP

maren christine pedersen

When Maren Christine Pedersen entered first grade, she could speak only Danish. Her parents told her that the teacher would ask her name, and that she should reply, "Maren Christine Pedersen." When the teacher asked that question and many others, the reply was always the same, "Maren Christine Pedersen." The bewildered teacher apparently garnered one word, "Christine" and she has been Christine ever since.

Her parents, Laura Smith and Peder Pedersen, came to the United States from Denmark. Shortly after their marriage, they purchased a small farm, their home for the rest of their lives, on the South Fork of the Kinnickinnic River, commonly known as Pete's Creek. With the exception of the first, all of their 12 children were born on this farm. Peder Pedersen planted a tree to commemorate the birth of each child. The second in the row of trees was planted March 1, 1900, the day Christine was born. Some of these trees still shade a part of the University of Wisconsin-River Falls campus. The Pedersen farm was acquired by the State of Wisconsin in 1962, and added to the campus.

The family business was a dairy farm, and for many years, Pedersen had a milk route, making two deliveries daily with a horse and buggy. Milk sold at a nickel a quart. One of his helpers was Christine. She remembers vividly trying to complete the route by the time the curfew sounded at nine o'clock. Along with other members of the family, she helped milk the cows and operate the hand-powered separator.

Though the dairy farm was their means of support and involved long hours of labor, the

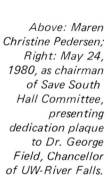

Above: Maren Christine Pedersen; Right: May 24, 1980, as chairman of Save South Hall Committee, presenting dedication plaque to Dr. George Field, Chancellor of UW-River Falls.

She has always loved library work—she organized a student librarian's workshop in 1963, the first of its kind in western Wisconsin.

141

education of the children was the chief concern of their parents. The farm adjoined the campus of what was then the Normal School. As they reached school age, each of the Pedersen children trudged off to the Training School. Nine of them, Christine included, are graduates of the Normal School-State Teachers College, a record number from one family.

While in school, she worked in the library for 10 cents an hour. This experience kindled her interest in becoming a librarian. She received her certificate to teach primary grades in 1919, and taught kindergarten and first grade in North Menomonie the next fall in a two-story wooden structure with outside toilet facilities. Her salary was $75 a month. Since she would be 60 miles away, there was no chance of going home weekends. Thanksgiving, Christmas, and Easter were the only vacations, and she experienced many lonely hours away from her family.

Acquiring enough money to purchase a trunk and a wardrobe needed before starting her job was a problem solved by a calf-raising project. The year before graduation, each of the older children was given a calf to be sold at the time of leaving home for the first position. Christine learned one of life's lessons the hard way. She was out to "get rich quick" with disastrous results. At feeding time, when no one was looking, she held her pail under the cream spout of the separator for short periods of time. Her calf grew sleek and fat. Encouraged by success, the proud owner started holding the pail under the cream spout for longer and longer periods. The calf's "mysterious" death shattered her dream.

Although she enjoyed teaching primary grades, Christine was anxious to move into library work. An opening in the River Falls High School Library was her chance to fulfill that wish and also move back home. To qualify as a librarian, she attended summer school at River Falls and the University of Minnesota, completing the work in 1932. Her duties were by no means confined to those of a librarian. She had charge of attendance records, was treasurer of school activities, coached girls' basketball, and organized a school lunch program for rural students. Her day lasted from 7:30 a.m. until 5:00 p.m. or later, and on Saturday mornings she supervised the study hall to which students were sentenced for chewing gum and other misdemeanors.

In 1932 she became librarian at Wisconsin Rapids Senior High School, where she stayed for 18 years. The last 15 years of her long career as a teacher and librarian were spent in Eau Claire—first in the Junior High and finally in the newly-built North High School, for which she helped plan the library.

Christine Pedersen's retirement in 1965 marked the end of one career and the beginning of another. She moved back to her beloved River Falls and immediately plunged into volunteer activities and untiring community service.

Daughter of a pioneer, Christine Pedersen has been a pioneer in her profession of Library Science. She has influenced and continues to influence many people. Her unselfish concern for others, her keen wit, common sense, enthusiasm, and willingness to work are well known. She is inspiring, combining the best qualities of teacher, citizen, and Christian.

At 82, she is still going strong.

(See Selected Honors, Accomplishments, Publications, page 312)

One of the highlights of her life was "to go into the practice of family medicine" where she stayed for half a century.

frances cline

After retirement from a career in public health and general medicine, Dr. Frances Almeda Cline of Rhinelander developed a new method of service when she was nearly 80 years old. She established a chapter of I-ACT (International Association for Clear Thinking), a non-profit organization that inspires individuals to help themselves.

I-Act is an association of self-help groups that study and practise rational self-counseling. Its purpose is to teach members to reduce painful emotions such as anxiety, guilt, anger, and depression, and to increase positive emotions such as serenity, joy, love, and enthusiasm.

Dr. Cline closed her medical office February 29, 1980 and in April began her new project.

Frances Cline was born May 25, 1900 on a farm near Calhoun, Illinois, the oldest of five children of George and Julia Harpster Cline. She attended a one-room rural school and Olney Township High School. Impressed by the town's medical center, Frances, along with three of her 48 classmates, decided to study medicine.

Her father, thinking medicine was not a fit career for a girl, suggested home economics and offered to help her financially. But she had had home economics in high school and did not want any more of it.

Instead she took a course in "pedagogy" in high school. This enabled her to become schoolmistress at the one-room country school her mother had attended. The salary was $45 a month. After a year, she went to the State University at Normal for the summer session.

Learning that the grass was greener in the black corn belt, she was accepted as teacher at Holder, a one-room school, at $120 a month. She taught for two years and saved "every nickel" for medical school. Then followed two years of premedical studies at the State University at Urbana and four years at the University of Illinois College of Medicine.

"When I started med school in Chicago, there were 120 in my class, including eight women... We were in the Class of 1929, but they wouldn't give us our MD until we had put in one year of a rotating internship."

Finding a good internship that would take

women was difficult. "These were the days after the stock market crashed." Dr. Cline found one at Memorial Hospital in Worcester, Massachusetts, staffed by women interns, and she finally earned that long sought-after degree.

But there was no money to set up a practice. So she took a position as a resident at the Tuberculosis League in Pittsburgh. The previous resident was in surgery having her phrenic nerve pulled. She had developed TB while working with the patients. "I didn't contract TB while I was there, even though it was rampant all across the

Above: Frances Cline, MD (courtesy Tom Michele, "Our Town");
Left to right: On her 80th birthday (courtesy, Phyllis Prek) *and seated in her consulting room.* (courtesy, Tom Michele, "Our Town")

Dr. Frances Cline in her examining room. (courtesy, Tom Michele, "Our Town")

country."

It was the State Board of Health in Madison that drew her permanently to Wisconsin. They needed a woman physician in the Bureau of Maternal and Child Welfare. The Board had established baby centers around the state.

"The first clinic was held in the Rhinelander City Hall on January 20, 1932. I came by train on the North Western sleeper. I worked out of Madison until 1937 when the Board was decentralized."

Then she came to Rhinelander as Maternal and Child Health Physician under Dr. Frisbee, the district health officer until he died in 1938. "I did both jobs until the following spring. The Board wanted a man in the job and said, 'We've never had a woman before, but we will try you.' I got the job and held it until June 15, 1954."

But she had studied medicine to practice medicine, so Dr. Cline joined Dr. Kate Newcomb at Lakeland Memorial Hospital in Woodruff.

In 1955, Dr. Cline realized her dream—a practice of her own. On January 1, she opened an office in her home at 123 North Stevens Street, Rhinelander. She was part-time city health officer at $50 a month, for she was concerned about meeting the mortgage payments. She still holds the health officer position.

For 25 years, Dr. Cline practiced family medicine, one of those rare individuals who made house calls. A special kind of devotion characterized her practice. Meals, even Sunday and holiday dinners, had to fit around her patients' needs. At times, guests had to tend the dinner.

In 1972, at age 72, she was certified by the Board of Family Practice. A friend commented, "It is remarkable that Dr. Cline could pass the rigorous examinations for family practice at a time of life when most of us have retired to an easier life style."

Her life has been dedicated to helping people. Dr. Cline believes as I-ACT teaches, that "we are all fallible human beings. No one is perfect, but . . . we can change and be what we choose. It takes persistent hard work."

(See Selected Honors, Accomplishments, Publications, page 307)

written by BETSY HODSON

bernice scott

Bernice Scott's heritage is education. Her mother, two aunts, and two uncles were educators. There was never a question about her career choice—she would be a teacher. Forty-three years of her life have been devoted to this profession.

Her philosophy is, "In general, don't generalize. At no time must we do anything to lower the youngster's opinion of himself." She has been a battler for the right of each young person to be an individual in the face of pressure.

This pioneer in the field of guidance has been the confidante of thousands of young people who have talked things over with her.

Howard Vieth, assistant principal of North High says of her, "She was a counselor to young people before counselor became a position in the schools . . . the type of teacher paraphrased in the *Education of Henry Adams.* 'A teacher affects eternity: she can never tell where her influence stops.' "

When she retired in 1967, Sheboygan North High School celebrated "This is Miss Scott Day." Huge posters were put on the walls, students wore stickers reading "Thank you, Miss Scott." The North High Student Council called it a "labor of love." An editorial in the student newspaper said she should not be forced to retire at 65, her outstanding skills were still needed.

What kind of person could command such devotion and esteem? Only an extraordinary teacher sensitive to their needs and devoted to bringing out the best in her students.

Bernice Scott was born August 4, 1902 in Cambridge, Wisconsin, one of four children. Her father, Daniel Scott, was a farmer and owner

Bernice M. Scott at John Michael Kohler Arts Center
(courtesy, Sheboygan Press)

of the Cambridge Flour and Feed Mill. Her mother, Luvenia Potter Scott was a rural school teacher.

"My mother influenced me the most," Bernice states. "She was an energetic, caring woman with high standards who followed through in what she believed. I marched with her and my aunts in the Fourth of July Parade in 1912, wearing banners which supported women's right to vote.

"When I brought home my report card, she

would ask, 'Is this the best you can do?' If I said it was, it was fine with her, as nothing but the best was acceptable to her. She set goals for us and expected us to live up to them.'' This standard of excellence was the hallmark of Scott's life—nothing but her best would do.

In high school, Bernice Scott took every course that was offered. ''My mother made me,'' she commented. ''She believed in keeping children busy, then they couldn't get into mischief. I even played interscholastic basketball in high school. The bloomers we wore had to be wide enough to look like skirts. Our games were played before the boys' varsity game.''

Her first teaching job was in a small high school in Medford, Wisconsin, from 1924 to 1927. Her parents were not too happy about her going up into the ''north woods''. Her father asked how

She joined AAUW in 1928, became very active on the branch level, and served
on the Wisconsin State Division Board for 30 years.

147

much she would be paid. She told him, $1400 a year. "Take it quick", he advised her. In 1924, that was a lot of money.

After three years at Medford, she moved to Marinette where she taught for six years, except for a semester leave to do graduate work. She received a master's degree in political science from the University of Wisconsin-Madison in 1933 and moved to Sheboygan that fall. She earned her master's degree in Educational Guidance in 1952.

Bernice Scott joined the American Association of University Women in 1928 as an organizer and charter member of the Marinette-Menominee Branch. She has been very active in the Sheboygan Branch and has held many responsible positions at the Branch and State Division level.

Kathryn Hill, former State Division President and long time friend, declares "Bernice was 'Miss AAUW'. She certainly knew more about the organization than almost anyone in the state."

In 1975, the Wisconsin State Division established the Bernice M. Scott Endowed American Fellowship, in honor of her outstanding service to AAUW, her 43 years as administrator and educator, and her contributions to the community and the state. Over $75,000 has been raised by Wisconsin branches for this fund, granted to American women scholars at the doctoral and post-doctoral level.

In 1980, to commemorate AAUW's centennial, branch members from all over the state constructed a quilt recognizing outstanding Wisconsin women. Sheboygan chose Bernice. Its square, designed by Nancy Schreiber, shows an outstretched hand, signifying the need to reach out beyond one's self to the community, to guide the young, and to work to improve the quality of life.

It is a true symbol of the life of Bernice Scott. At 80, her work is not done. As long as she is able, she will serve. There is no retirement for this educator, counselor, and community leader.

(See Selected Honors, Accomplishments, Publications, page 313)

*Her philosophy is
that study comes first,
and then action,
but always that both
are needed
to move forward.*
—NANCY Z. SCHREIBER

Bernice M. Scott (courtesy, Sheboygan Press); *Cambridge High School girls basketball team, 1919, Bernice in center with basketball; With two North High students on the day she retired.* (courtesy, Sheboygan Press)

148

*Above: Lois Almon as a small child;
Top right: High school graduation; Right: Lois
seated at the Almon Recreation Area that
she established in July 1967.*

She was a dedicated naturalist, conservationist and teacher

lois almon

A barbed wire fence was no barrier to this small, gray-haired woman on a nature walk. She would drop to the ground, roll under the wire, and bounce up on the other side. Lois Almon was a quiet, gentle person who eagerly shared her knowledge and love of the wonders of nature.

A native of Milwaukee, Dr. Almon spent many childhood days in the parks and public museum. Her college education was interrupted for two years while she worked for the Milwaukee Public Museum.

She graduated from the University of Wisconsin-Madison with a major in botany and minor in zoology. A year of teaching high school followed, prior to her return to the University for a master's degree and a doctorate in bacteriology and botany in 1932.

"My life really consisted of two careers, research and teaching." Teaching jobs were almost nonexistent during the depression years. She accepted a position with the State Laboratory of Hygiene, conducting research on pathogenic fungi. Later, she taught medical technology and was largely responsible for its development in the University curriculum. She worked for the State for 14 years, about half of that time in charge of the Branch Laboratory of Hygiene in Rhinelander.

Desiring new challenges, she accepted a teaching position at UW-Eau Claire. She spent a year as exchange teacher at Bishop Otter College in Chichester, England. Her vacations allowed time to visit Ireland, France, Denmark, and Switzerland.

She taught at North Dakota State before returning to nutrition research at the Mississippi State Experimental Station. Her mother's illness prompted her return to Milwaukee, and she taught medical technology at Mt. Sinai Hospital. Returning to the South, she taught at Miles College, a Black school in Birmingham, Alabama, until her retirement in 1966 at age 62.

There her activities included collecting plants for two college herbaria. She was active in the Congregational church, the American Association of University Women, American Civil Liberties Union, and served on the Alabama Council on Human Relations. For the next nine years, she divided her time between Mobile and northern Wisconsin.

Many years earlier, while employed in Rhinelander, she had purchased 156 acres of wild land. It had many different varieties of trees, several hundred feet of lake frontage, and swampy land and bogs, of which she was especially fond. A

Promptly at 8:00 a.m.
every Saturday morning
during "birding season,"
she would conduct
a nature walk at no charge.
She would be there
during an early
morning thunderstorm,
a cold, drizzly rain,
summer fog, bright
sunshine and even when
the mosquitoes were
out full force.

small frame house was on the property.

She once stated, "Wild land should belong to the public, if the public respects it and does not desecrate it." In 1968, she donated her property to Oneida County. The county developed its beautiful white sand beach and provided facilities, including rest rooms, shelter house, grills, picnic tables and parking area. Dr. Almon assisted in laying out two nature trails. The Almon Recreation area is enjoyed by thousands of persons each year.

At the dedication ceremony, Dr. Almon said, "I hope this facility will help make a better world for the future. People naturally respond to the strength and placidity of an outdoor environment. As a result, they seem better equipped to solve their problems."

She was an active participant in annual Christmas and spring bird counts. From spring until fall, she led bird walks and nature hikes. A sign in the recreation area advertised her free services as a naturalist and gave directions to her home. Her expertise included flowers, trees, plants, shrubs, animals, and insects.

She loved the wildflowers and plants best. She explained the Latin names, history, reproductive process, identification hints, and told humorous anecdotes. "Teaching ecology to children and adults," she confided, "is what I most enjoyed doing all my life."

An avid gardener, she competed with marauding rabbits, deer, raccoons, and humans for the harvest. Fencing provided some protection, but she did not mind sharing her produce. In winter, she grew plants and flowers in a greenhouse and gave most of them away.

Her association with AAUW and IFUW (International Fellowship of University Women) was a major interest. She attended IFUW Conferences in Mexico, Japan, and Australia. Locally, she was chairperson of the international relations and religious study groups and vice president in charge of programs. She developed a Folk College, open to all in the community, as an annual AAUW project, using the Danish concept of adult education.

Dr. Almon's philosophy is explained best in her own words, "Preserved wilderness has no monetary value. How do you put value on the sun shining on pines evoking their special fragrance? What is the worth of a pond full of frogs in full chorus? How do you estimate income from a calm lake reflecting a sunset, with only a loon breaking the perfect upside down picture? Can you sell a family of young weasels, tumbling with each other in play among the rocks? Have you ever tried to put a carpet of anemones and violets into your bank account? These things have infinite value, and therefore, no monetary value . . . A walk in the woods or a meditation by a lake can lead to love, compassion, peace and creativity."

On March 9, 1981, Dr. Almon met her eternal peace.

(See Selected Honors, Accomplishments, Publications, page 305)

della madsen wendt

Small of size but a dynamo of energy and very much a woman of the present, Della Madsen Wendt is a model of her firm belief that "every one has a responsibility for the concerns and needs of one's community, and that this sharing together and working together is most stimulating."

Della was born July 31, 1903 on a farm near Stoughton. Her parents had emigrated from Norway as children. Life had not been easy for them and they instilled in their five children an appreciation of education and a sense of responsiblity.

"My father used to take us to the city library when we went to town for shopping. I always looked forward to that. I also remember his great effort to get us children to school one time during a heavy snowstorm. The storm was so severe that my father told us the horses just would not be able to get through the drifts. I began to cry over the idea of missing school, so he decided to try it anyway. My brothers, sister and I bundled up and we started out. The snow was so deep that each farmer along the road to school came out to shovel a path. We finally covered the two miles, the men opened the school by climbing in through a window, built a fire and left us to await the arrival of the teacher. She never made it. Eventually we ended up trudging those long miles back home through drifted snow."

After the country school, Della continued her education at Stoughton high school, graduating

The expressive faces of Della Wendt.

number one in her class.

"At the exercises I asked a classmate what she planned to do and she told me she was going to St. Olaf College in Northfield, Minnesota. There had been no counseling in high school so I had received no encouragement along this line. I went back to school and asked the principal if he thought I would be able to go to St. Olaf, also. He advised me it was very late to apply but he would do what he could to help."

Della majored in English at St. Olaf College,

Above: Della Wendt (courtesy, AAUW)*; Left: Restoring antique autos was a family interest in the Wendt household. Attired in her mother's duster, Della is being helped into their 1929 Franklin by husband Francis.*

She had enriched her community and state with the efforts of
53 years of active, dedicated and meaningful participation in civic affairs.

153

transferred to the University of Wisconsin-Madison and graduated with senior honors in 1924. Two years later she was teaching social studies at McKinley junior high school in Racine.

Della married Francis Wendt, a Racine lawyer, in 1935. At that time marriage meant the end to jobs outside the home for most women. Della's energy was such that this did not end her focus on community involvement. Active participation in the American Association of University Women and the YWCA flowered with many other related activities.

Even the birth of her two sons, John in 1936 and Richard in 1938, did not slow her civic activities. Their births came during her term as state division president of AAUW.

Della has boundless energy and good health which enables her to go from afternoon meeting to evening meeting with household chores sandwiched in between.

"Yes, it was rather hectic at times," Della recalled. "I am thankful for my Viking stamina. Sometimes I found myself working half the night to get my housework done and there would be tight schedules getting everybody off to meetings, lessons, etc. But as a mother I needed the stimulation from outside activities."

Della's family shared her regard for community and education. Her husband served as mayor and circuit judge. Her sons both graduated from the University of Wisconsin-Madison and hold PhD's.

The Wendts take pride in the progress of the many foreign students and teachers they have entertained in their home—young men and women from Korea, Hong Kong, Taiwan, Japan, India, Nigeria and Turkey. Two Chinese girls adopted them as "American parents" and asked them to announce their engagements in this country. Now the Wendts are "American grandparents" to six Chinese children.

Active in legislative affairs, Della worked tirelessly in 1976 to promote a change in Wisconsin rape and sexual assault laws. After determining that a special order of business would be required to bring the proposal to vote in the legislature, Della followed through with at least 50 letters to appropriate lawmakers and circulated petitions at women's meetings. Such effort was productive; the bill passed.

When Della tackles a project she does her homework and has the ability to look at an issue with fairness and concern for the greatest good of the most people. A part of her effectiveness is her innate friendliness. Her warm smile, her faith in others and her willingness to help elicit the best from her associates.

She has been active in supporting measures which abolish all forms of discrimination and in opposing bills and amendments which would interfere with "the right to individual choice in the determination of one's reproductive life" on both state and national levels. She is a staunch supporter of public education and legislation that improves the status of women.

(See Selected Honors, Accomplishments, Publications, page 314)

written by FRANK J. PRINCE

anita hankwitz kastner

Since her first piano lesson as a six-year-old, the primary interest of Anita Hankwitz Kastner has been music. Although she does admit to not being too overly ambitious in those early years, her father made certain she had a full education in music.

"My father was firm," she recollects proudly. "And because of this Germanic characteristic I was able to obtain a good education and an eventual professorship." Her parents' concern for her education was further demonstrated when she wanted to study in Europe.

They sent her abroad to earn diplomas in piano performance, teaching and music theory from the Conservatoire Americaine, Fountainbleau, France, and to study in Berlin and Vienna. Her teachers included some of the most honored in music, Isidor Philipp, piano, and Nadia Boulanger, theory (France); Leonid Kreutzer, Professor an der Hochschule fur Musik (Berlin); and

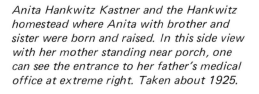

Anita Hankwitz Kastner and the Hankwitz homestead where Anita with brother and sister were born and raised. In this side view with her mother standing near porch, one can see the entrance to her father's medical office at extreme right. Taken about 1925.

She continues to be active as a pianist, accompanist, organist and ensemble performer as well as serving as adjudicator in music contests and auditions.

Dr. Paul Weingarten, Professor and der Hochscule fur Musik (Vienna).

Now professor emeritus, School of Fine Arts, Department of Music at the University of Wisconsin-Milwaukee, teacher, composer and musician Anita Hankwitz Kastner retired just over a dozen years ago and today still continues an active life, and she loves it.

Her teaching career began at the State Normal School, Natchitoches, Louisiana, in 1926 when she was 20. Later, after continued graduate study and teaching elsewhere, she made her home in Milwaukee in 1940 rejoining the University of Wisconsin system where she previously taught at the University of Wisconsin-Madison.

Mrs. Kastner taught music history, music literature, piano and theory of music. Her Music appreciation course—or as it was termed, "Music Aesthetics"—was a delight to her, but sometimes set her to wondering just how much the students benefited. She remembers one young man who did not receive the grade he expected and protested, "But I purchased 40 classical music albums during the semester!"

A composer as well as teacher, Anita Hankwitz Kastner wrote the marching song the Milwaukee State Teachers College used for many years before merging with the University of Wisconsin-Milwaukee. She has also written an original cantata, "The Lady of Shallot" and instrumental and vocal compositions as yet unpublished.

Her husband, the late William G. Kastner, shared those musical interests as a pianist and singer. Their courtship was a whirlwind event.

She met him when she was a 13-year-old and he was a faculty member who was introduced to freshmen during high school orientation. Later he was her botany teacher. Kastner was an educator

Matilda Steinbeck Hankwitz (1875-1953), a former Milwaukee school teacher who came from Mazomanie, and Paul G. Hankwitz, MD, (1871-1949), born in Reppen, Germany. They were married in 1903.

and principal in Milwaukee Public Schools from 1918 to 1959. When he retired, he left Milwaukee and later became a widower. But he did not forget his talented former pupil. On a visit to Milwaukee in 1965 he got in touch with her.

"Before he left that evening he proposed," Mrs. Kastner beams. "And do you know what I said? I said, 'This is so sudden!' " She goes on to describe their three-and-a-half year marriage as idyllic. "Every day revealed his inner beauty . . . we had fun together . . . he couldn't do enough for me," she recalls.

Anita Hankwitz Kastner is a past president of the Seven Arts Society of Milwaukee, in fact, its first woman president. She is a member of Sigma Alpha Iota—an international professional music fraternity for women, and is associated with many other cultural and professional organizations where she has held various offices and chairperson positions. She served for many years as organist and choir director in Milwaukee area churches and continues to play the Grand Avenue Congregational Church organ for the annual commencement ceremonies of Deaconess Hospital nurse graduates. She is also frequently called upon to serve as adjudicator in music auditions.

She continues to fill her days with the industry that built her reputation for excellence.

(See Selected Honors, Accomplishments, Publications, page 310)

ruth de young kohler

"I'm going to marry that girl!"

The occasion was the fourth annual Women's Congress, March 10-11, 1937, sponsored by the *Chicago Tribune,* arranged and presided over by Ruth De Young, the *Tribune* women's editor. Thousands of women attended the two-day meeting which featured in six sessions 44 noted national and international figures.

"Ruth De Young, in charge of the Congress and the only person to be on the platform for every session, had the women agog with her procession of clothes. She had a completely different outfit, from shoes to hat and flowers and furs, for each session, and how she ever found time to change . . . we can't see . . . But she managed it," reported the *Decatur Herald.*

Among those invited to address the Congress on behalf of industry was Walter J. Kohler, president of Kohler Company and former Wisconsin governor. Herbert V. Kohler, who accompanied his brother, was so impressed by Ruth De Young, to whom he had not yet been introduced, that he made a firm resolve to "marry that girl."

He did marry her three and one half months later on June 21, 1937.

Ruth Miriam De Young was born August 24, 1906, in Harvey, Illinois, daughter of Frederic Robert and Miriam Cornell De Young. Her father was Chief Justice of the Illinois Supreme Court.

At Thornton Township High School she was an excellent student and active in publications and

Ruth De Young Kohler, her favorite photo.

"*Each of us is a trustee of the past;
we have the important task of
living up to our inheritance and adding
something to it.*" —RUTH KOHLER

music groups. A member of Phi Beta Kappa, she graduated with honors from Smith College in 1928 with a bachelor's degree and a major in history.

After a year of study at the Sorbonne in Paris and the University of London, she joined the staff of the *Chicago Tribune* as reporter and, later, as women's editor.

After their marriage the couple lived in Kohler and raised three children, Herbert V. Jr., Ruth De Young II and Frederic Cornell. The family was the center of their lives, yet Ruth remained active. In 1940, she wrote a column for the *Tribune* and presented a weekly news commentary over WGN.

She became president of the Kohler Woman's Club in 1943 and the following year, inaugurated the "Distinguished Guest Series" that brought famous political and religious leaders, artists, writers and commentators to Kohler. Her list of activities grew numerous; her interests included education, history and women's concerns.

In conjunction with Wisconsin's centennial observance in 1948, she was chairman of the committee on Wisconsin women. Working with groups all over the state, the committee set up the Women's Building at the Centennial Exposition— 12 rooms depicting the history of family life in Wisconsin. Authentic furnishings and clothing worn by mannequins in each room were carefully assembled from throughout the state.

Several years later Milwaukee Sentinel reporter Dorothy Parnell recalled the opening day, "We remember well the months and months of work Ruth undertook for the Wisconsin Centennial Exposition here in August 1948 . . . and the day of the opening of the women's building . . . when two of her youngsters came down with a contagious disease. She drove from Milwaukee to Kohler to comfort and establish the ailing youngsters in an isolated part of the house and was back in Milwaukee to meet the public on time . . .

"She smiled composedly as the people walked into the Early American setting she had planned.

"She said, aside to me, 'The butterflies are churning in my tummy. I'm ready to drop, and all I can think of is those poor youngsters. We're all pretty sure of ourselves, we career women, but let something happen to our children, and we're just plain mothers.' "

By 1950 she was directing her attention to the restoration of Wade House, a stagecoach inn on

The young family of Ruth and Herbert Kohler. Children, left to right, are Frederick, Herbert, Jr., Ruth De Young II.

the old plank road between Fond du Lac and Sheboygan, built before the Civil War and operated by the Wade family for almost a century.

The Kohler Foundation purchased the property which included Butternut House, built in the 1850's by Charles Robinson, the Wades' son-in-law, and a blacksmith shop. Much restructuring was needed as the buildings had deteriorated badly. Many original furnishings still on the site were refurbished. Others were obtained from the Wade family. Ruth Kohler acquired additional artifacts of the period, many of them heirlooms contributed by friends.

Mrs. Kohler explained the personal significance of the Wade House project, "May I underline the belief that each of us is a trustee of the past . . . Let us always remember that there was a time in this country when even a whole day of life was not taken for granted; much less water, shelter, and a safe night's sleep . . . Perhaps they (the pioneers) had no thought for us; they were concerned with making *their* America. But what they made is what we have.

"To take this heritage unthinkingly for granted is a first step to losing it."

After three years of painstaking work the restoration was virtually complete and plans were being made for the dedication and transfer of the property to the State of Wisconsin in June, 1953. But Ruth De Young Kohler did not live to participate in the ceremony. She passed away suddenly March 7, 1953, at the age of 46.

(See Selected Honors, Accomplishments, Publications, page 310)

Ruth Kohler—her husband's favorite photo.

written by ALICE ZILLMER

hildegarde

"Sometimes when I look at a lighted marquee," Hildegarde says, "and see *Hildegarde—The Incomparable,* I think, Incomparable is right! Incomparable gumption! Without gumption, no one would ever have heard of me."

Born in Adell, Wisconsin, February 1, 1906, Hildegarde, daughter of Charles and Ida Sell, was raised with her two sisters in New Holstein. Her mother, a devoted Catholic and fine musician, began teaching her the piano when she was seven.

"Music transported me. Practicing devastated me. 'Hilde,' my mother used to bribe, 'If you'll practice I'll do the supper dishes.' Anything was preferable to doing dishes so I'd practice for exactly 30 minutes. It took me years and years to learn that only by diligent application would I ever get anywhere."

At her mother's insistence, the family finally moved to Milwaukee to provide the girls with parochial schooling. The need for money in those trying days prompted her mother to inquire at the Lyric Theatre about the possibility of her daughter playing the piano on Saturdays and Sundays for silent films.

There, while she was attending Marquette University, Hildegarde's love affair with the world of entertainment began.

The nearby Palace Theatre featured an act called "Jerry and Her Baby Grands." Nervously, Hildegarde went backstage and asked Jerry if she

Hildegarde wearing her famous long gloves.

could join the act. Hildegarde was hired for a junior act that played split weeks at small theaters throughout the country. Fortifying herself with daily prayers before making auditions, Hildegarde soon earned other bookings.

An audition for Martinus Poulsen, who owned the Cafe de Paris, London, England, resulted in an offer to appear abroad. Although Hildegarde's mother had supported her career in every way, this time she hesitated.

"I do not see how you can go to England now. Your father has cancer." Sadly, Hildegarde refused Poulsen's offer.

"Forever I shall be grateful that my father lived long enough to see me successful. The year before he died, I played the Riverside Theatre in Milwaukee in Gus Edwards' Revue. I reserved a stage box for my family so my father, who by this time was very ill, would not be disturbed by late arrivals. When I came on stage as the little German immigrant, wearing a beret, carrying a small carpetbag, using a broad accent, my father turned to my mother and smiled. Smiles had been rare and he would soon have no reason to smile at all."

After her father died, Martinus Poulsen called and repeated his offer for her to perform in England.

"Never before or since have I been more frightened than I was on opening night. As I sang my opening song, my voice trembled. I trembled too. The audience continued to talk and laugh. I was a flop! I left the stage to applause that came from one table only. 'Hildegarde,' the voices from that table called. 'Give us your German Band Song.' Those blessed voices belonged to Gilbert Miller, Cole Porter and H.G. Wells. They had heard me perform in America. I asked for a man's hankie to use as a bandanna. The audience quieted. My nervousness left me. The song and my kind compatriots saved me from disaster."

The experience opened Hildegarde's eyes to the need for more confidence, poise and style. Deciding to gamble on herself in a gigantic way, she waded deeply into debt for carefully fitted gowns. She hired tutors to instruct her in grooming, grace and protocol. Devouring books on nutrition and physical exercise, she trained her body as well as her voice.

Little did she realize that the long gloves that covered her now graceful arm movements and the dainty lace handkerchiefs would later be enshrined in the Smithsonian Institute Museum of History and Technology in Washington, DC or that the long-stemmed flowers she gave to members of her audience would become recognized by the floral

written by ANNE BIEBEL

world as a Hildegarde rose.

With her friend, partner and business manager, Anna Sosenko, Hildegarde left London for Paris. The popularity of her one-woman shows made her well known in Europe. But she returned to the United States unrenowned and unheralded.

Starting anew with fresh songs, chic gowns, practice, prayers and more practice, Hildegarde prepared for her opening at the Versailles in New York. They loved her.

"When I was invited to appear at the elegant Persian Room at the Plaza, everyone warned against it. 'She'll die at the Plaza,' friends whispered to Anna. I heard them. Both Anna and I were well aware of the dangers, chief among them being the size of the room. But, we decided to take a chance. Had I closed the door on this engagement, I wonder where I would be today."

Her six month contract with the Persian Room was renewed every year for eight years.

She was the star of her own NBC Network radio program "The Raleigh Room" on the ratings list of the top ten programs for four consecutive years. She also starred in "Beat the Bank" and "99 Men and a Girl." Among Hildegarde's million selling recordings are "Darling, Je Vous Aime Beaucoup" (her theme song), "I'll Be Seeing You," "The Last Time I Saw Paris," "All Of A Sudden My Heart Sings" and "Lili Marlene." She also introduced "April in Paris" and "Wunderbar."

The pigtailed, blonde child who had wailed at her mother, "Hildegarde! Hildegarde! Oh, this awful name you gave me. How could you do such a thing?" had become Hildegarde the Incomparable. The name she once deplored became an asset.

(See Selected Honors, Accomplishments, Publications, page 309)

lillian mackesy

On January 9, 1931, Lillian Sontagg-Plotkin wrote a letter of application to the *Appleton Post Crescent.* She stated, "If you have an opening in your organization I am willing to come to your city entirely upon my own responsibility. In the event that I should prove unsatisfactory, I shall

Through her years of commitment she did more than any other single individual in deciphering and describing the history of Outagamie County.

163

expect no consideration . . . I am willing to work for $22.50 a week and am eager to make a connection at once." Ten days later, on January 19, 1931, Lillian Sontagg-Plotkin began her 45 year association with the *Appleton Post Crescent.*

Her duties were varied. She was responsible for the daily column "Looking Back 100 Years." She wrote the weekly column "Historically Speaking" and edited the pictures for the weekly photograph series "Remember When?"

Lillian was also very interested in most aspects of theater production, helping with props, acting or publicity. During a production for Little Theater at Whiting Memorial Chapel, Lillian met James Mackesy. They were married in Green Bay on Christmas Eve in 1931 and later had three children.

She is most noted, however, as the energetic and bright woman who has done more than any other individual in exploring and sharing the history of Outagamie County.

Lillian became involved with history through her work for the *Post Crescent.* One of her first projects involved gathering material on former Appleton resident Harry Houdini. Controversy over where Houdini may have resided while in Appleton prior to the turn of the century precipitated her unearthing a vast amount of information. Out of this rose new questions, leading to more information and, eventually, to more questions. It came to a point where Lillian had acquired so much information on early Appleton she became recognized as Appleton's foremost local historian.

She was directly involved with five major projects that served to illuminate the heritage of Outagamie County for its citizens, including the research and writing of five lengthy articles for the "Appleton Diamond Jubilee" edition of the *Post Crescent,* co-editing a book entitled *Land of the Fox* with Ken Sager, writing and directing the County Centennial Pageant and coordinating the 1957 Centennial Edition of the *Post Crescent.* Lillian was also responsible for preparing the four-part supplementary edition to the newspaper in 1976. Lillian's part of preparing this edition was performed in ten virtually sleepless days and nights. For her effort Lillian received a second place award from the Wisconsin Associated Press.

Aside from her journalistic efforts, Lillian was inexhaustible in her attempts to provide Appleton and Outagamie County with a history museum. Finally in 1977, Lillian saw part of her dream realized with the purchase of an old church by the Outagamie County Historical Society, Inc., to be used as a History Workshop.

Lillian Mackesy died on September 30th, 1978. She bequeathed her collection of documents, papers and photographs to the Outagamie County Historical Society. This generous donation has enabled the continuation of investigations into local history.

(See Selected Honors, Accomplishments, Publications, page 311)

◀ *Lillian Mackesy* (courtesy, Outagamie County Historical Society)

mabel mannix mc elligott

A full and useful life often includes many little side excursions, but it is a rare person who can so direct all such byways that they converge on the main road of a successful career.

Mabel Mannix McElligott is such a rarity. Now Director of Continuing Education and Community Service at Mount Mary College, Milwaukee, she draws upon her past work with young people and in community service, her interest in several branches of the fine arts, her teaching, her belief in women's abilities, her executive know-how and strong leadership and upon many other resources and experiences from her past.

Before accepting this position, Mrs. McElligott had established a name for herself as dean of women and in other administrative capacities at Marquette University. When she was asked to become dean of women in 1935, she was probably the youngest woman to hold such a job. She also taught speech, mostly so she would get to know the students better, she said. For several years she also coordinated in-service training of graduate students who worked as residence hall counselors, in student services and in the office.

She was largely instrumental in developing housing for women at the university and founded the Association of Marquette University Women for that purpose. Several university halls were established, among them O'Donnell Hall, for which the first federal college housing loan in the country was issued.

A graduate of Marquette with bachelor of music and master of arts degrees, she also studied administration at the University of Chicago. While teaching in Milwaukee Public Schools, she thinks that she may have established another "first" in her use of music and speech as therapy for handicapped children.

Even her work in drama, in radio and with the old Wisconsin Players, has been grist for her career mill. Such experiences, she believes, have helped her understand how people think.

But her great personal warmth, felt by nearly everyone who comes in contact with her, can't be attributed to past career experiences. That must have come from the cradle.

And her Irish mother had a hand in it. It is from her that the young Mabel Mannix learned to "lose yourself in others and to be receptive" to whatever happens along. As a child she was never really curbed, she said, and as a consequence, she was never afraid to face up to challenges.

Then, too, her husband, Attorney Francis McElligott and their three children have been fully supportive of everything she wanted to try.

The listing of Mrs. McElligott's various activities and honors takes up a couple of inches of very small type in "Who's Who in America." She has been active in many branches of community affairs and is a leading spokeswoman for women's activities and associations. She is nationally known as a platform speaker.

Mabel McElligott is happy in her work, as she has been in all the other aspects of her long, successful career. She enjoys combining past experiences and drawing from them insights into new challenges.

(See Selected Honors, Accomplishments, Publications, page 311)

Right: Mabel Mannix McElligott, and left, using her talents at the podium.

written by CHERYL MAXWELL

marie sperka

Marie Spruyt Sperka states that her love for wildflowers comes from her Dutch ancestry. Her parents emigrated from Holland to Kenosha, Wisconsin, where she was born. Marie started growing wildflowers as a child. "I followed my Dad around the garden; he always had a beautiful garden." In her first garden she cultivated spring beauty, red lobelia, and many other varieties from the banks and woods near Little River, north of Coleman, Wisconsin.

Upon high school graduation, she left her beautiful surroundings for a year of business college. After their marriage May 17, 1937, Marie and Frank Sperka operated the Hillside Hotel, a guest house and retreat center, for the Carmelite Fathers at Holy Hill. A son was born during their last year there.

In 1945, the family moved back to Marinette County and established their present home. She

Her book is the most comprehensive guide on growing over 200 species of wildflowers.

Marie and Frank Sperka with friend of the family.

and her husband cut down trees and dug out stumps in preparation for building their home. Frank Sperka's talent as a carpenter added much to the beauty of their home.

Their 40 acres of woodland enabled Marie Sperka to pursue her dream of growing wildflowers. She established Woodland Acres Nursery 14 miles west of Crivitz on County Highway W, from which she sold quality stock wildflowers, ferns and hardy perennials throughout the country. For over 30 years, from early spring until late fall, she was in her garden by 6:00 a.m. working until evening.

Marie made another of her dreams a reality by publishing a book *Growing Wildflowers—A Gardener's Guide* (Harper and Row, 1973), the most comprehensive guide available on the subject. It gives detailed instructions on soil preparation, planting, and propagation. Lists of plants that grow well in various soils and locations are included, and an index of common and botanical names.

Marie Sperka feels that more people need to know wildflowers. She meets and talks with groups, shows her slides, answers questions, and emphasizes the dedication that preserving wildflowers requires. For example, the ladyslipper, if not grown correctly, may become the "passenger pigeon" in the horticultural field. These precious flowers cannot be grown from seed successfully.

While enjoying and caring for her flowers, Marie fell in love with the bleeding heart. She studied Mendel's Law of Propagation and taught herself botany. After many hours of work over the course of 16 years, she developed *Dicentra Luxuriant PP3324,* an everblooming bleeding heart with fluorescent red flowers. It is insect-free and withstands temperatures of 35° below zero.

She built up a stock, but could not sell a single

Marie in her Woodland Acres Nursery, Crivitz, Wisconsin.

plant of the new variety until she secured a patent, which required three lawyers and several years of waiting. After the patent was granted in 1973, Marie sold exclusive rights to Walters Gardens of Zeeland, Michigan. She receives a royalty for each plant sold, without having to water, weed, or cultivate.

Past 70, Marie Sperka is still at work, specializing in rare wildflowers. She devotes much time to developing an improved white bleeding heart that will have the good qualities of *Dicentra Luxuriant.*

When young people ask her how to get started, Marie tells them, "It is not easy, but with faith in yourself you can accomplish much. You must like your chosen goal, because you are going to work at it and be dedicated to your work if you are to succeed."

Marie's own dedication enables future generations to have and enjoy the wildflowers. The motto she most admires is, "The greatest work begins with the first steps."

(See Selected Honors, Accomplishments, Publications, page 313)

written by MARILYN THOMPSON

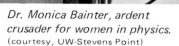

Dr. Monica Bainter, ardent
crusader for women in physics.
(courtesy, UW-Stevens Point)

monica bainter

An inquisitive nature may have sparked the lifetime career of Monica E. Bainter.

At the age of four she stuck her tongue on a pump handle and received a lecture on conduction, convection, and radiation from her father. By the time she was six, trailing him around the family farm, she knew as much about physics as most college students. "While my dad repaired machinery, I'd hand him wrenches and ask, 'why?'" she recalls.

Her childhood experiences were the beginning of a long career in physics that flourishes even though Monica Bainter has officially retired after 50 years of teaching.

Born in Lanesboro, Minnesota in 1910, she grew up in Rochester, Minnesota, where she was valedictorian of her high school class. She worked her way through the College of St. Teresa, Winona, Minnesota, as a switchboard operator and as a piano accompanist for vocalists. She majored in mathematics, physics and music. Later, she earned a master of arts degree from the University of Minnesota and a doctorate from the University of Wisconsin.

Her first jobs were in Chatfield and Spring Valley, Minnesota, where she taught mathematics and physics at the secondary level. From 1938 to 1943, at New Richmond, she was Wisconsin's only woman senior high school principal.

In 1947, Dr. Bainter joined the faculty of the University of Wisconsin-Stevens Point. During her tenure as department chair, she was instrumental in developing a curriculum that prepared physics majors acceptable to graduate schools and industry.

One of her earliest projects was in the 1930's at the Mayo Clinic where she was trained in measuring the radiation from radium gas (radon) collected in glass vials and used for treatment of cancer. While teaching at the University of Wisconsin-Madison in 1943, she participated in the Manhattan Project which measured the emissivity of uranium at very high temperatures. For several summers she worked in radiation physics at the Argonne National Laboratory. She spent a summer at Rensselaer Polytechnic Institute studying and designing the cores of nuclear reactors and another summer at Cornell studying the biological effects of radiation.

Dr. Bainter's name is included in a media guide published by the Atomic Energy Forum. The guide, primarily for the nation's news reporters, lists about 100 specialists in business, industry and education available for interviews about energy developments and issues. She is the only person from Wisconsin and the only woman listed.

Her career has not been without its snags. Good humor was a quality needed in 1980 when Lee Sherman Dreyfus, Governor of Wisconsin, and her former boss as Chancellor of the University of Wisconsin-Stevens Point, nominated Monica Bainter to serve on the State Public Service Commission. Because of her staunch support of nuclear power and her public comments after the Three Mile Island nuclear power plant incident, she was chastised by the press and by opponents of nuclear power. Ralph Nader, consumer advocate, came to Wisconsin to lobby against confirmation.

Although she withdrew her name, Dr. Bainter did not retract her statements. She argued it would be impossible for the nation to achieve energy independence without using some atomic energy. "We must have a combination of all possible energy sources if we are to get out of the mess we're in," she maintains. "By continuing to depend so heavily on fossil fuels, the world runs the risk of depleting resources that are vital for such things as medicine and the production of food and clothing."

Although she retired from the University of Wisconsin-Stevens Point in May 1980, she declares, "I'm not really retired; I still make two speaking engagements a month." That leaves her time for hobbies and activities such as knitting, bowling, golf, playing bridge, cooking, travel and "fixing" things such as television sets. "I constructed a color TV set from a kit," she remarked.

"I have enjoyed life," Dr. Bainter says. "Even though originally I wanted to be an actuary, I'm glad I wound up teaching. I liked my last year as much as my first. I enjoyed seeing the world open up to my students."

With her enthusiasm and continued interest in learning and sharing her knowledge with others, Dr. Monica Bainter will continue opening up the world to a lot of people in the years ahead.

(See Selected Honors, Accomplishments, Publications, page 305)

She is a beloved, internationally acclaimed writer of children's books about horses.

marguerite henry

The glow of childhood has never left Marguerite Henry. She is one of the best read children's authors in the world. Since the publication of her first book, *Auno and Tauno* in 1940, more than 13 million copies of her books have been sold. They have been translated into 13 languages; she is the recipient of literary awards too numerous to list and films have been adapted from some of her most popular books.

Marguerite has written more than 40 books, enthralling children with her carefully researched stories of horses, ponies, burros, birds, dogs, cats, and foxes. She writes of real people, real animals, and real incidents.

Born in Milwaukee, she is the youngest of four daughters and one son born to Louis Breithaupt and Anna Kaurup Breithaupt. Of her early years she says, "I grew up with one foot in printer's ink. My father had a printing company in Milwaukee, and I had the fun and rich experience of helping to proofread after school and on Saturdays."

At age 11, Marguerite won a $12 prize in a story contest for children, sponsored by *Woman's Home Companion.* There and then, she decided that writing would be the pleasantest way to earn a living.

At Riverside High School in Milwaukee, she wrote love stories that she sent to *The Atlantic Monthly* and *Harpers.* The rejection slips frequently were amended with notes of encouragement.

While she was attending Wisconsin State Teacher's College, now the University of Wisconsin-Milwaukee, she met and married Sidney Crockery Henry. He has always been her mentor and critic, encouraging her research and writing.

A "weft of fact and a warp of fiction" is her own description of her work. This blend takes her to many out-of-the-way, sparsely-inhabited areas. Her classic *Misty of Chincoteague* and its three sequels (about the annual swim of wild ponies from uninhabited Assateague Island to Chincoteague Island in the Atlantic tidewaters of Virginia) are responsible for attracting thousands of visitors from near and far to view the spectacular swim of the ponies each year.

Several of Marguerite's books have aroused interest in the welfare and preservation of wild animals. An outstanding example is *Mustang, Wild Spirit of the West,* which created a clamor to save the diminishing herds of wild horses from the toughest mustangers of the West. The book is a biography of Wild Horse Annie, a pint-sized secretary who almost single-handedly waged war against the cruel methods of the bounty hunters. *Brighty of the Grand Canyon* has also been instrumental in saving the lives of the wild burros who inhabit the Grand Canyon.

Children who read her books are given authentic, historical backgrounds of people and events of current interest. Her books have a universal appeal because she writes of people, animals, and conditions that children can understand.

◄ *Marguerite Henry* (courtesy, Tony Francis Photography)

Morning hours she spends in her study, with a supply of sharply pointed pencils. A file nearby is filled with story ideas just waiting their turn. In response to the question from a young fan, "When you write a book, do you type it down as you think of it?" she replied, "Most authors, I believe, write their first draft on the typewriter. I feel happier with a pencil in my hand. It is almost like caressing the words."

She takes time each afternoon to hike a mile

She is the horse lovers' 'Dear Abby,' receiving a constant stream of letters which she answers.

with her husband to feed Bugaboo, an elderly mare who awaits her apple slices with a nicker and a whuffle of anticipation. It is difficult to tell whether Bugaboo or the Henrys enjoy the interlude more.

Before moving to Rancho Santa Fe, California, in the early 1970's, the Henrys lived in the countryside of Wayne, Illinois. There at various times their pasture included Misty, the Chincoteague pony; Friday, a Morgan horse; a western burro (the model for Brighty); three fox cubs for *Cinnabar,* assorted families of cats and kittens for *Benjamin West and His Cat Grimalkin*; and a lively dachshund named Alex, who is featured in *Album of Dogs.*

Marguerite and Sid Henry have no children of their own, but through her books, all the children of the world belong to this couple. The children write to her, asking her advice on personal problems and sharing with her their thoughts, hopes and dreams. Bowls filled with photographs sent by boys and girls are found scattered through the Henry home. She tries to answer all their letters with warmth and empathy.

Writing for children these many years has kept her outlook on life and the world fresh and buoyant. Marguerite Henry is as ageless as her stories.

(See Selected Honors, Accomplishments, Publications, page 309)

She is the first woman architect registered in Wisconsin and has been designing passive solar homes since 1947.

lillian leenhouts

In the summer of 1933, Lillian Scott (Leenhouts) and a friend packed a cardboard suitbox with overnight things and a lunch and took the train to Chicago to see the Century of Progress Exhibition. To be there first thing in the morning, they had to take a late night train and sit in the depot until it was light. But the experience outweighed the discomfort, for while they were there, they stopped in to see the round glass house designed by Architect George Fred Keck.

Keck's workmen, who constructed the glass house in the wintertime, reported that even on the coldest days, if the sun was shining, they could work in shirtsleeves. On fair days the house was heated entirely by the sun.

Lillian never forgot their words. She became intrigued with Keck's work. While she was studying architecture and even after she graduated from the University of Michigan, she watched his development, his wall panels of fixed glass with louvers top and bottom, his experiments with heat

Left:
Lillian Leenhouts;
Below: A model of the library for the Theosophical Society in Madras, India. (courtesy, Milwaukee Journal)

174

She orients every building for the least disturbance of soil, the best use of wind, sun, trees, earth temperatures and prevailing breeze.

in tile and later his metal pans under concrete floors, his projecting roof above the glass for sun control. She also watched the buildings of Frank Lloyd Wright, Aldon Dow, Corbousier and other architects who were early proponents of passive solar and natural environmental orientations.

Lillian Scott was born June 2, 1911. Her father was an alderman in the little village of South Milwaukee. He died when she was seven and her mother filled his position in a building and loan office after his death.

Lillian remembers childhood evenings in the house that her father had built from designs of a consulting architect. She remembers her grandmother reading to the family, urging them to question and to seek the meaning of life.

When Lillian was 14, her mother died, leaving her and her 10-year-old brother Ronald orphans. They were sent to the Omaha home of one of her mother's sisters.

The ensuing four years were arid for Lillian. She closed up, could not respond to school or games. It was one of the saddest periods she was ever to undergo, but it ended with a happy decision. She was to attend a private art college, the Layton School of Art in Milwaukee, where self-expression in many media was encouraged.

Her first opportunity to practice her long-desired craft came when she began working for architect Harry Bogner, who was also the president of the Milwaukee Art Institute. When World War II came along and the government froze the use of building materials except for defense work, she became a wandering draftsman. She designed smokeless powder plants and naval stations in such locations as Wilmington, Baraboo and Atlanta.

The last of such stop-gap war jobs was in Hagerstown, Maryland, where she did perspective drawings of new and experimental airplane details for Fairchild Aircraft Company. It was here that she met and married Willis Leenhouts.

After the war when construction of private buildings resumed, the firm of Willis and Lillian Leenhouts, AIA, was founded. Two early passive solar houses in Milwaukee designed in 1947 and 1948 can be seen today in the 1200 block of East Concordia Avenue.

Lillian and her husband designed the first non-public, nonprofit housing for the elderly in the state, and, of course, it utilized passive solar design. Her dream was to create apartments economical enough so that retired persons in lower/middle income brackets could live independently and to make such apartments comfortable, convenient and safe. She realized this dream in the Cambridge Apartments. She worked tirelessly with Charlotte R. Partridge to obtain government sponsorship for the project and to promote it among the "doubters."

As her affection for this city grew and her career with her husband expanded, she and Willis began weekly trips to the inner core on Saturday mornings where they advised homeowners and renters on new and repair construction. For many years, they functioned as a duo "design review board." Mrs. Leenhouts began art lessons for underprivileged children and enlisted up to 21 teachers to give free instruction in art, reading, cooking, gardening and music.

This work led to her founding the first Community Design Center in the city, later known as CDC's, centers where other architects could come and give unpaid time to persons who could not afford such professional help. In 1948-50 she chaired the Mayor's clean-up committee to beautify parking lots, leading in 1966 to her becoming a charter member of the Mayor's Beautification Committee. She was the first woman to serve on the Wisconsin Architectural Licensing Board. Her encouragement of young women beginning their studies in professions formerly deemed inappropriate has greatly increased their numbers in such studies at MSOE and the School of Architecture and Urban Planning of UW-Milwaukee.

The Leenhouts' home has been visited by hundreds of people on tours for the benefit of one cause or another. It was designed to carry out the principles of sun use; it not only conserves fuels and natural resources, but is also beautiful. The house is in the heart of Milwaukee, yet it is nestled into a bosky thicket of about 40 trees, among them white oaks, silver poplars, ash-leaf maples mountain ash and mulberry.

The unpretentious interior is simple yet with aristocratic touches. Experimental windows and the imaginative glassed corner make possible the management of a riot of growing plants.

Now in her 70th year, Lillian Leenhouts does not give a backward glance. Her newest hope is that the city's beautification committee might shift its service for the next decade from geraniums to passive solar promotion for all city buildings and a beautiful River Walk downtown. Her selfless work continues.

(See Selected Honors, Accomplishments, Publications, page 310)

Above: The 14-story Cambridge Apartments showing solar windows, and, right: View through the solar windows of the Leenhouts home in Milwaukee.
(Photos, courtesy Milwaukee Journal)

*Affectionately known as "Mrs. AFS Wisconsin," she has long been
interested in International Relations.*

dorothy von briesen

When Dorothy von Briesen was a teenager, someone told her, "Service is the rent you pay for the space you occupy." She has lived her life by this maxim, serving her family, community and country in multiple ways.

The mother of four who earned her law degree from UW-Madison in 1937, Dorothy has always been interested in international sharing.

She has done volunteer legal work through many channels. Currently she does reference service one day each week for the Milwaukee Bar Association. In the past she has worked as a staff lawyer for the Legal Aid Society and has been a volunteer attorney for the Counseling Center of Milwaukee, Inc. When she was in law school, she aspired to be a juvenile court judge, but she says raising four children of her own somehow dimmed her interest

in telling other parents how to raise their children properly.

So how does this relate to international sharing? When her own children were in school, two of the von Briesen daughters were American Field Service exchange students. Involvement on the local level moved to state activity when she became Wisconsin chairman of AFS. For 10 years she worked in this capacity, and affectionately known as "Mrs. AFS Wisconsin," she has been a continual recruiter for host families and sponsors for international visitors and students throughout the state. As an articulate ambassador of international good will, Dorothy has been a frequent and popular area speaker.

An international outlook is a shared family habit, and the von Briesen household has been "home" to countless students and foreign visitors for long or short-term, planned or impromptu visits. Dorothy and her husband Ralph are world travelers with a keen interest in the world's peoples and their cultures. Their friendships are worldwide. Their four children continue the von Briesen pattern of international interest and concern.

Dorothy has been board member and vice president of the International Institute of Milwaukee and most notably worked as general chairman of the Holiday Folk Fair sponsored by the Institute. As chairman, Dorothy asked the groups to stress culture rather than nationality in each country's presentation.

Dorothy's unique collection of nearly 75 Christmas creches from different countries has been displayed at the governor's mansion during the holiday season.

As head of a State Department team, she went

*Dorothy von Briesen; Far left
top: In Lesotho hat with State
Department visitor from the
Union of South Africa;*
(courtesy, Interior Institute)
*Middle: Arranging nativity
figures from her worldwide
collection; Below: With husband
and daughter at the Great Wall
of China, 1980; Near left: Meeting
of selection of Foreign Visitors
Committee, Guatemala City,
Dorothy on far right.*
(courtesy, US Embassy)

to South America in 1978 to evaluate the Sponsored Visitor Program of the National Council for International Visitors. Under this program candidates with leadership potential visit the United States for 30 days. Included in the roster have been 33 heads of state.

In just 29 days Dorothy and her team interviewed 250 Latin Americans who had been visitors to see how their visits had enhanced their lives. Through the team's efforts the State Department learned about things they had been too polite to mention to their hosts at the time. The team findings were instrumental in bringing about many positive changes in the program.

During all this, she has been actively involved in her community, promoting social awareness in the Milwaukee area as vice-president of United Way.

"Dorothy's life is exemplified by continued concern for and service to others which she effectively renders in the board room as well as on the most basic one-to-one level," says one friend.

Dorothy von Briesen has paid and continues to "pay her rent" very generously. She has made "the space she occupies" a better world for all with whom she has come in contact.

(See Selected Honors, Accomplishments, Publications, page 314)

sister thomasita fessler, osf

One of the best known artists in the Midwest, Sister Thomasita Fessler, OSF was born in Milwaukee, Wisconsin on February 23, 1912. She attended Sacred Heart Elementary School and St. Mary's Academy, both in Milwaukee.

In those days, art classes were not considered an important part of the curriculum, so Sister did not get an early start in developing her artistic talent. However, she spent much time at home making soap carvings and creating little artifacts which he proudly displayed about the home. The family background shows a long line of architects, builders, artists, carvers and church decorators.

After entering the religious congregation of the Sisters of St. Francis of Assissi in 1929, Sr. Thomasita earned her Bachelor of Education degree in 1935 at the former Milwaukee State Teachers College (now the University of Wisconsin-Milwaukee), and her bachelor and master of fine arts degrees in 1947 at the Chicago Art Institute.

Shortly thereafter she was appointed chair of the Cardinal Stritch College art department. She transformed the fifth floor attic of St. Mary's Academy into an attractive studio and gallery which she named Studio San Damiano. Here she developed and taught college, adult and children's art courses.

Her aim was to rekindle the spirit of early Christian art. Her students enjoyed working in the

Sister Mary Thomasita Fessler, OSF, head of the
Art Department, Cardinal Stritch College. ►

"For her, life involves the discovery and appreciation in nature of subtle textures, intricate patterns and fascinating shapes."

—FATHER MICHAEL E. KOMECHAK

traditions of an 11th century workshop, at oak tables, kilns, looms, easels, with thick malleable clay, burlap, paints, dozens of other media.

Sister Thomasita believes that the greatest thing that can be done for people is to develop their creative powers. She has had ample opportunity to do that in her 33 years of teaching art. Her students are kindled with the dignity and wonder of what they are doing and becoming, for personal growth and a new grasp of beauty are as much part of the studio's purpose as the polishing of manual skills. The aim of the department is to develop not merely draftsmen or craftsmen but to help students live creatively. This aim is based on the premise that art is not simply the manipulating of materials and a making of things, but rather the making of people. Hence, art instruction at Cardinal Stritch College leads students to rediscover Creation and to develop a supernatural insight.

When asked how her art reflects her beliefs, Sister answered: "In order for something to be a work of art it has to be basically an expression. A lot of people go through life blindly. All they do is identify what they see but they do not experience it. I think that an artist is made by having all five senses in full gear all the time so that responses begin to accumulate and from that fullness comes what the artist says."

Among the exciting things that Sister has done in her busy lifetime is the conducting of world tours.

In her travels, Sister has taken more than 100,000 slides which she uses to inspire her

students and give them a world view. She also uses the slides to refresh her memory before beginning to paint. She thinks of her photography as "a quick paint brush."

During a nine month period in 1974-75, while teaching full time, Sister created 88 oil paintings which captured the colorful beauty of places she had visited. These art pieces were exhibited at Studio San Damiano under the title "The World is My Canvas." The paintings, done in oil and collage, possess a great range of interpretation in a variety of styles and forms. The expressions, ranging from semi-realism to abstraction, interpret the atmospheric quality of various parts of the world. The show was a sellout.

Her second major art exhibit, which was displayed in 1976, was entitled "America Is My Home," More than 70 paintings and collages depicted winter scenery, summer sunsets, old neighborhood churches, Lake Michigan's shoreline, and a variety of other impressions. At this special showing, most of the art pieces were sold within two hours of the show's opening.

Her third major art show, exhibited in 1977, was titled "African Reflections." The inspiration for Sr. Thomasita's paintings and co-worker Irene Kilmurry's ceramic sculptures was gained during a trip to Africa, in which the artists picked up techniques, ideas and moods to be translated into works of art.

Sister Camille Kliebhan, president of Cardinal Stritch College, says of Sister Thomasita: "Sister is, indeed, a genius with respect to visual expression, an inspirational instructor, and a dynamic organizer of creative activities. But—best of all—she reaches people and teaches in such a way as to draw out the best and sometimes hidden talent in every man and woman who studies with her."

(See Selected Honors, Accomplishments, Publications, page 308)

Left to right: Sister Thomasita at work; Amid samples of her work; "Amalfi Drive View."

written by JEAN TYLER

hannah swart

On a cold, snowy morning in 1918 in Milwaukee, three Werwath children and their governess were seen nearing the German-English Academy (now the University School of Milwaukee). The smallest of all, five-year-old Johannah, was straggling behind. She tried hard to keep up with the others, running nearly all the way. Her little legs and heavy, warm clothing hampered her, but, after the distance of nearly a mile was covered, she knew she would be with Tante Anna Gaulke and her wonderful

kindergarten. Johannah, called Hannah, was ready to open a new box of challenges.

Tante Anna used Friedrich Froebel's methods in her classroom. Colored cloth balls and unusual shaped boxes were part of the equipment in gift boxes that each child received. Each box contained something for teaching one of ten steps of learning in Froebel's plan. There was no competition among the students because each was given a set and allowed to open a "gift box" when he or she had mastered the skills of the previous box. Hannah was always thrilled when she could open a new box.

Johannah Seelhorst Werwath was the fifth girl to carry that name in as many generations of a family from Westphalia, Germany.

Her parents were well-educated. Her mother, Johannah Von Seelhorst before marriage, had been the head of the Foreign Language Department in Algiers University. Oscar Werwath founded the Milwaukee School of Engineering in 1903, just after emigrating from Germany. They were married in 1908 in New York City, then came to Milwaukee to live and work. Their four children were Karl, Greta, Johannah, and Heinz.

When the children were small, their governess, Freya Oeyler, a French Canadian student of the National Teacher's Seminary, and Tante Annie Luetzow, Mrs. Werwath's "kindermachen," cared for the children and lived as a part of the Werwath household. The family ate together only on weekends and special occasions. German, English,

Hannah Werwath Swart

and French were spoken in the home. During the school year, the children were reared in a highly disciplined manner. But in the summertime, they enjoyed a grand and glorious three months of complete freedom at their summer home, "Kinder's Glücklichkeit," on an island at Little Cedar Lake.

In traditional European fashion, it was assumed that the Werwath children would devote their lives to the family enterprise, the Milwaukee School of Engineering. Consequently, on the day of her graduation from Milwaukee University School in 1931, Hannah says, "Father introduced me to my first day of work. He took me to the school and showed me the instructors' classbooks in which I was to enter the students' grades. I was to work

Far left: Heinz, Hannah, Greta, Karl at Little Cedar Lake; Left: Werwath Summer Home, 1914-1932.

Above: Oscar Werwath family, Hannah on far right.
Right: Hannah and George's wedding, October 7, 1937.

from 7:30 to 11:00 each day. This was a day of bitter conflict for I had had my heart set on being a doctor of medicine or doing some other work in the medical field." It marked the beginning of Hannah's 20 years as Registrar and Head of the Records Department at the Milwaukee School of Engineering.

She spent afternoons as a part-time student at Milwaukee Downer College from 1931-34 and took courses at the University of Wisconsin-Milwaukee and MSOE through 1946.

In 1930 a young Fort Atkinson man, George Swart, enrolled at MSOE. He and Karl Werwath became "best friends" and he and Hannah met. "The two boys looked so much alike, it was unbelievable and what one couldn't think of, the other did," says Hannah. Swart received his

associate degree in welding engineering in 1934 and became the head of the Welding Institute at MSOE. He was also in charge of central purchasing for the institution during the difficult days of World War II.

Friendship led to romance for George and Hannah. They were married October 7, 1937, and four children have since blessed their marriage.

The years from 1931-1951 were some of the busiest and most exciting of Hannah's life. Her

Swart Family, 1979. Back row: Murray, son Paul and Nancy, George, Sr., Carolyn and George, Jr.
Front row: Ben, daughter Hannie, Amy, Hannah, Keith, daughter Toni and Chris.

home life, her part-time college studies, and her work at MSOE were supplemented with her outside interest in Girl Scouting into which she poured her energies.

The year 1951 brought great changes to the family. They moved to Fort Atkinson to rear the children in the rural environment where the Swart family had pioneered and lived for four generations. Hannah exchanged her daily associations at MSOE and the familiar sights and modes of life in Milwaukee for a new community and an unfamiliar kind of life. "I shed many a private tear those first years."

The changes brought out in them a special interest they shared—George and Hannah have always been history buffs. Their 10th anniversary gifts to each other were life memberships in the State Historical Society of Wisconsin. George's avid interest in local history influenced Hannah's efforts in that direction.

She has since written numerous newspaper and magazine articles on local current events and historical topics. These records of area happenings have ended the dearth of written resources in local history.

She has published several works including a pamphlet entitled *Footsteps of Our Founding Fathers* (1964) with Mary Hoard, a biography of Margarethe Meyer Shurz (1967) and *Koshkonong Country, A History of Jefferson County* (1976), a ten-year research and writing project.

On July 1, 1967, Mrs. Swart became curator of Hoard Historical Museum. Today, annual attendance exceeds 20,000 visitors from all 50 states and many foreign countries. It is considered one of the outstanding local history museums in the nation, valued at over $250,000 and is available year round to all citizens. The exhibits and

educational programs span a multitude of interests for every age group.

Johanna Werwath Swart continues to open new boxes of challenges.

(See Selected Honors, Accomplishments, Publications, page 313)

catherine cleary

The room is restful, filled with the softness of blue and with a pervasive sense of calm and balance. But at the sunlit center is an aura of vitality and excitement surrounding Catherine Cleary, the woman who lives here. Now in her sixties, fair-haired and blue-eyed, a dusting of freckles on her open face and more than a hint of the out-of-doors in her bearing, it is easy to visualize her as being first on the trail.

And, in fact, she has been a woman pioneer in the banking and business world, blazing the way for others to follow. She was the first woman president and board chairman of a major trust company (the First Wisconsin Trust), the first woman director of consequence in the corporate field (Northwestern Mutual Life Insurance Company, American Telephone and Telegraph, Kraft, Kohler and General Motors). A trustee of several important educational institutions and foundations (Lawrence University, Notre Dame, the Mayo Foundation, the Johnson Foundation, the Faye McBeath Foundation), she is former adjunct Professor of Business Administration in the graduate school of business in the University of Wisconsin-Milwaukee.

Responsibilities, commitments and honors become this woman. Her face retains interest, openness, the irrepressible urge to search, the eagerness to learn. Her talk focuses on challenges, opportunities, growth and her memories turn on the help and encouragement received from others rather than on her own achievements.

She began early to make the important decisions about the course of her own life. When she was in third grade at the Campus School in Milwaukee, a number of her friends were transferring to the Lake School and she thought she should, too. Her father, president of Northwestern Mutual, was in the habit of discussing things of importance with this eldest of his three children, she recalls. "We used to talk over the questions he was facing at work, my interests and problems, and whatever was happening in the course of our days." So when Catherine brought up the question of changing schools, they talked it over seriously and in depth. When the decision was finally made—not to transfer—she was the one who made it.

Not only was she allowed to make up her own mind at a young age, she was encouraged to feel that whatever she set her mind to, she could accomplish. "They say that an oldest daughter is especially close to her father and, for me, that was true." During these beginning years her mind was continually stimulated and shaped by fortunate circumstances. She grew up in a stable neighborhood in a loving family. "We never felt anything but loved and protected as we went from house to house to play." The families were always glad to see them, interested in them. At the Campus School too, this was an era of openness to new ideas, new ways of learning. "Everything I know today about running a meeting, about parliamentary procedure, I learned at school then."

Cleary attended Scripps College for two years and graduated from the University of Chicago with a major in English. She taught for a time in private schools in the East. She called her father one day and broke the news: she wanted to go to law school. "I could hear the thud across the thousand miles," she smiles. He approved and she went,

The first woman director of many national corporations, she has encouraged young women to pursue law, banking and financial careers.

Catherine Cleary

graduating first in her class in 1943 from the University of Wisconsin.

She worked for Kohler Company for a year and for a small law firm in Chicago for three and one half years. Meanwhile, her father died unexpectedly. The rest of the family was scattered, so she returned to Milwaukee to be near her mother.

There she ran into her first discrimination. "No Milwaukee law firm wanted a woman lawyer." One law firm reluctantly offered her a job, provided she would have no contact with clients. An opportunity with another firm would not have used her legal training. George Luhman, a neighbor from childhood and close friend of the family, the President of the First Wisconsin Trust Company, advised her that the latter firm was a good one, but called her back to offer her a job at the Trust Company that would utilize her legal background. George Luhman's offer was the real beginning for her, she feels. The trust business was growing exponentially, there were management opportunities, and the job was interesting and challenging.

Busy as Catherine Cleary was developing as a banker, she always allowed time to experience other aspects of herself. Her father always urged her to maintain an identify separate from her work. She remembers needed weekends at her cottage in Oostburg. She would drive there tied in knots, but, by the time she had carried in the wood, done some repairs, watched the birds for awhile, all that tension was forgotten.

Cleary thinks that more women will make career commitments, but she has reservations about the number of women in the executive suite. She sees it as a problem of priorities, not lack of opportunity.

"To get to a position of major responsibility in any corporation or agency requires a willingness to put in the kind of time necessary to do the job. For a young women, either married or about to be, that's not a problem. But when children come, sometimes women want to stop for a few years or work part-time, a valid personal decision. I would have opted to do that had I married and had children. However, one cannot develop at the same pace as the person who continues to make steady, continuing investments of time and energy in a career. I know I gave my work a disproportionate amount of time, it was part of the investment I made, and it paid off in interesting, responsible administrative work. My judgment is that, for me, it was not too high a price."

Catherine Cleary's future looks as rewarding and challenging as her past. Her assignments take her all over the country. She retired early to have time for herself, and still has not found it. So she reluctantly left teaching. She plans to write a nontechnical book on estate planning. "I think I have a feeling for discipline, for keeping some pressure on myself," she observes. "As you grow older, the continuity of human experience becomes more meaningful. You remember all your parents and grandparents gave you. And now I see my nieces and nephews, my students. You see yourself as part of the long chain of humanity. You are grateful for all that was given to you and want to pass it on."

(See Selected Honors, Accomplishments, Publications, page 307)

written by MARILYN STUCKEY

madame liane kuony

Preparing a luncheon for representatives of *Bon-Appetit* magazine or greeting each of her customers personally, Madame Liane Kuony presides over the Postilion II and the Postilion Great House Restaurant with much charm and grace. The daughter of a French father and a Spanish-Dutch mother, Madame Kuony was born in Belgium and brought up in Himes, a city in eastern Languedoc. She has traveled extensively and has lived in Lausanne, Switzerland and in central and South America.

Looking at the grand Victorian house at 775 North Jefferson Street in Milwaukee, the feeling of quality seems to be expressed in every way, from the semi-circle stairs entrance to the large spacious windows. Madame Kuony grew up in such an atmosphere of quality and appreciation of food. Her mother was a superb cook and her father an expert in fine wines.

Her philosophy is "Be sincere in life and be sincere in cooking, no difference."

Cooking with the best quality fresh produce one can find explains her naturalistic approach to cooking. According to Madame Kuony, "We must get back to the good earth and stop tampering and interfering with natural resources. If you are willing to pay the price, you can find good quality natural products. Anything that smacks of being processed or manufactured is not natural." Although sources of such natural products are

Madame Liane Kuony (courtesy Image Studios, Inc., Appleton)

somewhat guarded by each cook, Madame did share her source of Purebred Charolois Beef: Mr. Bruce Purdy of Apple Hill Farm in Appleton, Wisconsin.

Just before World War II, she met and later married John Kuony. For a brief time they lived in Portland, Oregon, then moved to Fond du Lac, Wisconsin. It was there she began her business ventures. One unsuccessful enterprise was her exquisite French cuisine frozen dinners, shipped in lovely packages to Maison Glass, Charles and Co. and other fine food shops. Due to inexperience in cost accounting, she lost money on this venture.

After finding and purchasing a lovely Victorian country home, she established the first Postilion House Restaurant on the outskirts of Fond du Lac. She began serving only luncheons, then enlarged to serve tea and Sunday dinners. The tea was not a wise innovation as it created an unfortunate image, and men stayed away for a time.

Before its closing in the late 1970's people flew their planes into Fond du Lac or drove many miles to enjoy her French cuisine, served with the dignity and flair of the past.

For business and personal reasons Madame moved to Milwaukee establishing Postilion II School of Culinary Art and the Postilion Great House Restaurant in 1979 and 1980. Although she closed the restaurant at Fond du Lac, the cooking school is still operating.

"There is a wonderful feeling to be wanted and needed and to be appreciated for your work," said Madame Kuony. "Many of us have wonderful memories of our mother's cooking; it is recognition for a lifetime."

She goes on to advise, "There should be no waste in cooking and using food. Everything edible should be used and brought to its utmost distillation . . . Only when you learn the rules can you take liberties in your cooking."

The students of Madame's school are mostly professionals, including food writers, chefs, caterers, and small restaurateurs. Many of the graduates are placed in homes of famous well-to-do people. Madame believes that perfecting the skills learned in her school takes time and practice and she counsels her students to begin in private homes so mistakes can be made on a small scale.

In the 33 years of the restaurant business and the 20 years in teaching classic cooking, Madame Kuony has never advertised. "Quality speaks for itself," she says proudly.

Another talent Madame Kuony displays is her interior design. She has decorated numerous

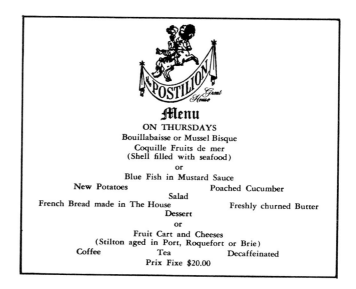

Menu

ON THURSDAYS

Bouillabaisse or Mussel Bisque

Coquille Fruits de mer
(Shell filled with seafood)

or

Blue Fish in Mustard Sauce

New Potatoes   Poached Cucumber

Salad

French Bread made in The House   Freshly churned Butter

Dessert

or

Fruit Cart and Cheeses
(Stilton aged in Port, Roquefort or Brie)

Coffee   Tea   Decaffeinated

Prix Fixe $20.00

homes and kitchens in Wisconsin and is known for her unfailing eye for color with home accessories. Many of these accessories are available in her culinary shop, which shares space with the Postilion Great House Restaurant.

Almost as famous as her cooking are her many hats worn even while supervising in the kitchen. They have become her trademark.

Madame Liane Kuony has spent nearly one-third of a century sharing her knowledge of cooking and her philosophy of living with the people of Wisconsin. We might say "Hats on" to a great lady of our state. She has enriched both the lives and cuisine of pupils, guests and friends with her elegance and skill.

(See Selected Honors, Accomplishments, Publications, page 310)

Some like it mild; some like it hot!
Courses redolent with pungent aromas of curry
and pineapple, lamb and chicken,
condiments from every part of the globe.

Far left: Typical Postilion Menu
Near left: Madame Kuony, wearing
one of her many hats.

written by MARILYNN RICHTER

clare kiepke

Silence and tension surround the event. The race begins. One woman contestant stands out, eager, applying herself fully to the task. She soars ahead, her face doused with whipping cream. She has done it, she has won the pie-eating contest. The winner is Clare Kiepke!

On the surface Clare Johnson Kiepke seems a chummy sort with whom you love to chat, to share your children's latest escapades or to discuss the latest best-seller. But Clare Kiepke is more than fun, games and good conversation.

For many years, Clare's life centered on her family and church work. She was so active in her church that the head of another congregation

Top left:
Clare Kiepke and her hearty laugh after a pie eating contest at a barbeque for the Outagamie County Health Center residents;
Far left: Three of the girls from Sunrise House just as they are going off to work. Note their van with its "Custo Cleaners." They're proud of it—Mary Cardin, Mary Schmitt and Jean Ruppel;
Left: Mary Lou McClenahan, executive director of both Casa Clare I and II with Clare;
Right: Clare and friend.
(courtesy, Appleton Post Crescent)

Reliable, insightful, with an unfailing sense of humor, Clare has been a catalyst for change, particularly for retarded and emotionally disturbed women.

193

questioned her pastor's judgment "allowing a woman to be so important in the church." Reverend Paul Brinkman describes Clare as a highly motivated person who extends herself to others. He relates, "She isn't a saint, however miraculous her accomplishments. Besides, she calls me 'boy.'" From her church involvement Clare developed a nucleus of contacts and resource people whom she would later call upon in other activities.

In 1967 Clare heard that an occupational therapy aide was needed at the Outagamie Mental Hospital. Motivated by a strong desire to help her two sons through college, she applied for and got the job. Shortly afterwards Clare became the hospital's first volunteer coordinator. Clare literally "opened the doors of the hospital to the community," according to the hospital's award committee. She initiated a program involving Appleton High School psychology students and enlisted the Girl Scouts and many others as hospital volunteers.

Always one to hit the road when necessary, Clare began the practice of taking adult patients to the Christ Child Camp which up to that point, had been used only for retarded children. Year after year she drove patients to Christ Child by car and camped with them.

Casa Clare I and II halfway houses were created for socially maladjusted women. Their purpose is to enrich and restore all who enter, to rehabilitate, not just provide a sanctuary. Casa Clare I was opened in 1972 with Case Clare II following in 1976. Opening Sunrise House, a Fairweather Lodge for chronically mentally ill women, also occurred in 1976. When the idea was first broached to Clare, even she was doubtful. The possibility of making self sufficient women out of patients who had been hospitalized for years with serious emotional problems sounded impossible. Not one to pass up a challenge, Clare made it work.

She tells of one woman in Sunrise House who was acutely deluded and dismayed everyone—but who now is "so completely sane, she scares me." Another success story is a resident of Sunrise who offered to cook and to manage household purchases. The resident became a dealer for such supplies to reduce costs. Later she began doing clothing alterations and now has a thriving business.

Clare's enthusiasm and hard work have benefited much of society. She has taught Sunday school for 36 years, has worked with Boy Scouts and Girl Scouts and has assisted migrants, drug offenders, gays, alcoholics and youth in trouble.

Clare started an "Adopt a Family" program and the Christian Clothes Closet, where items are made available at no cost to those in need.

Clare Olive Johnson was born in New London, Wisconsin, on December 19, 1918. She had an older brother from whom she became separated when their mother died in 1929. She was "farmed around" among relatives and eventually was reared in Merrill by a married cousin who had no children of her own. Although Clare's mother had been a teacher, her foster parents didn't believe in higher education for women.

So, following Clare's high school graduation at 16, she went to work: first at Montgomery Ward, then at a knitting mill where she met her future husband, Martin Kiepke. They married in 1940 and have three children. Eager for self improvement she attended night school and took over Martin's position in a paper mill when he went off to war.

In childhood Clare had dreamed of becoming a missionary in China. Much of her dream came true, if not in China, certainly in her missionary work nearer home. Now retired, she still helps others.

Clare and Martin reside in the north woods near Lakewood, Wisconsin. She drives to Appleton each month for meetings to help solve problems at the houses. She is also a working member of the national board of the Coalition for Community Living, and travels to other states to help in disseminating the Fairweather Lodge program.

After years of supporting Clare's dedication, Martin now enjoys the outdoor life. And because he's sharing life with a woman with an outrageous sense of humor, his life is never dull.

(See Selected Honors, Accomplishments, Publications, page 310)

Civic leader, University faculty member, promoter
of women's rights, she is also proudly a wife, mother and grandmother.

ellen benson humleker

"Don't worry about those things about which you can do nothing. If you can do something about a problem— then do it."
                                                    —Gustave Benson

These words, spoken often during Ellen Benson Humleker's childhood were to be an important influence on her adult life.

She was born February 2, 1918, in Madison, Wisconsin, the oldest of the three children of Mabel and Gustave Benson. Daughter of a full time homemaker and a patternmaker, Ellen spent her childhood at the family home on Lake Monona where her determination to achieve was nurtured. Senior class president and valedictorian of her high school graduating class, she then attended and graduated from the University of Wisconsin-Madison.

On June 6, 1941, Ellen Benson was married to Andrew Humleker at Evangelical Lutheran Church of Our Savior in Madison. In 1946 they moved to Andrew's home town of Fond du Lac, where he went to work for Sterling Lumber Company and where she began her career of community involvement.

The next several years were to be busy ones for Ellen, raising her family of two boys and two girls. While they were attending school, she became involved in many school activities, including PTA. In 1957 she became a candidate for the Board of Education in Fond du Lac and won election. With

Ellen Humleker, City Council member, and as Board of Education president. (Seated, front center.)

support and assistance from her family, she served two more terms.

Her second term as Board president proved to be three very difficult and distressing years. The city's only junior high school was judged unsafe by the State Industrial Commission. This led to the "morning and afternoon platooning of senior and junior high students" at the city's only public senior high school.

The old building was eventually demolished. A large scale building program then developed. Additions to the high school and some elementary schools were necessary to accommodate the growing population.

Mrs. Humleker is described by present Superintendent of Schools, Jerome Strupp, as "a particularly strong and effective board member, serving as president during probably the most critical years in the Fond du Lac School District's history." Strupp states further "she was always ready to listen to ideas and suggestions, always gave them fair consideration, and then acted on them in a manner felt to be in the best interests of the students. While very resolute and toughminded when an issue was at stake, her manner was consistently pleasant."

Upon leaving the board in 1966, Mrs. Humleker cautioned that "buildings do not necessarily make a grade-A educational program." She called for advancements in vocational education, a study of closed circuit TV and development of a program to teach students how to study.

She returned to the University of Wisconsin-Madison in the summer of 1966. She received her masters degree in nutrition the following year and joined the faculty of the University of Wisconsin Oshkosh School of Nursing. She taught there for 13 years until her retirement.

Meanwhile in 1970 Ellen Humleker won election to the city council. Two years later she announced she would not seek a second term. Phone calls and messages soon began pouring in, asking her to reconsider her decision. Reconsider she did; she was re-elected and voted president for three years, making her the first woman to hold that office in Fond du Lac.

Her decision to retire from teaching came in 1980 at the age of 62. In June of that year, Associate Professor Emeritus Ellen B. Humleker drove away from the University of Wisconsin-Oshkosh for the last time. Retirement, however, did not bring a retirement from her unsquelchable energy and involvement in civic commitments.

(See Selected Honors, Accomplishments, Publications, page 310)

mabel ruby mc clanahan

She is vice president and business manager of the company, handling all business phases of the corporation.

Mabel with Jim Crane, president of Crane Engineering with some of the products they handle.
(courtesy, Appleton Post-Crescent)

Long before it became fashionable or customary for a woman to enter the field of business, Mabel McClanahan was carving her niche as an outstanding businesswoman.

She was born and raised on a farm in Langlade County, Wisconsin, and attended Wausau Senior High School. Her favorite subjects were shorthand, typing and bookkeeping. She graduated in 1934 at age 16, but state laws dictated that she could not yet work full-time, so she worked part-time and took additional business courses at the high school.

In 1937 she was married and in 1938 had a son, Garrett, who is now a pilot for American Airlines.

From 1942-1946 she worked at a civil service job for the War Production Board in Wausau. While there she met Herbert Crane. He had recently closed his company, Crane Engineering, in Appleton, Wisconsin for the war years and he, too, was working for the War Production Board. In 1946, when Crane re-opened his company, he invited Mabel to join his staff.

Mabel moved to Appleton and joined Crane Engineering Sales, Inc. as a secretary-bookkeeper. The firm had six employees at that time and Mabel was the only woman. Representing several manufacturers, the company serves as a distributor of liquids' handling and pollution control equipment. It sells to industries and municipalities throughout the state of Wisconsin and the Upper Peninsula of Michigan.

Sales were less than one-half million dollars when she started. As the years progressed, Mabel became corporate secretary and office manager and for the past six years was vice-president and business manager, handling all business phases of the corporation. The firm now employs 23 people and has sales of $10 million.

As a woman in business, Mabel does occasionally run into a male counterpart who questions her role. More than once customers have asked to talk to the boss only to find out that Mabel is the boss.

Mabel has always been interested in legislation. She is active in the Republican Party on the county, state and national levels. She favors the Equal Rights Amendment and has worked for its ratification.

With a strong interest in small business and its relationship to government, she serves on the small business committee of the Fox Valley Chamber of Commerce and the Lt. Governor's Advisory Council on Small Business. In January, 1981, Mabel was a Wisconsin delegate to the White House Conference on Small Business, leading to her appointment to the steering committee for a Wisconsin Governor's Conference on Small Business. Mabel serves her community as President of the school board and as a bank director.

Mabel is an active member of the Business and Professional Women's Club. While serving as national president, Mabel spent every weekend from Thursday through Sunday visiting BPW chapters across the country. The only weekend she missed was Christmas. She has conducted numerous workshops on leadership training and involvement in community programs in Wisconsin and the Midwest.

To relax, Mabel devotes herself to gardening, a hobby fostered when she was a child on the farm. She particularly likes flower gardening and she

leaves the vegetable gardening to the rest of her family.

She never tires of learning. After moving to Appleton, she took evening credit courses at the University of Wisconsin-Fox Valley Center. Recently she began taking tennis lessons.

Many honors have been bestowed upon Mabel; she is a role model for young women of today. She is dedicated to her family, her career, her community.

(See Selected Honors, Accomplishments, Publications, page 311)

Far left: Reception at the White House for leaders of organizations involved in "Keep America Beautiful" in early 1968. Mabel is being greeted by President Johnson.
(courtesy, White House)

Left: Tea given by Mrs. Nixon to recognize women business leaders during their legislative conference in Washington. Mrs. Eisenhower, Mrs. Nixon, Pat Huttar and Mabel McClanahan.
(courtesy, White House)

Top: Board of Directors, Valley Northern Bank, Mabel only woman member.
(courtesy, Valley Northern Bank)

Above: Meeting with Mrs. Johnson in October, 1967. Mabel, then president of the National Federation of Business and Professional Women's Club, Inc., was invited to the White House for a private meeting with Mrs. Johnson to discuss the Federation's program of Crime Prevention for women's organizations.

section III: today . . .

written by VINCENT ABARAVICH

Margaret Abaravich (courtesy, Pleasant View School)

margaret mary abaravich

This is the story of a remarkable woman who overcame total deafness. She is a living example of what the hearing impaired can accomplish, and an uncompromising advocate for the rights and acceptance of the handicapped.

Margaret McCormack was born February 15, 1919, to a pioneer Irish-American family which settled in Milwaukee in the 1800's. Through her father James Leo McCormack, Margaret inherited a zest for life, his reliability and understanding nature, along with his quick wit and Irish sense of humor.

Her early childhood was spent in the area of North 13th and West Clybourn Streets known as "Tory Hill." Today it is criss-crossed by expressways bordering Marquette University. Until the early 1930's, an imposing building known as "O'Donnell's Flats" graced that area. This building was erected by Margaret's grandfather at the turn of the century. It contained eight apartments, each occupied by a member of the O'Donnell family, spouses and children.

In one of these apartments, her parents James and Margaret raised their family amid aunts, uncles and cousins. It offered a wonderful atmosphere in which to grow up, secure in the knowledge that a trusted relative was always close at hand. Thus Margaret lived her early childhood.

At age seven, Margaret entered Gesu parochial school. Her stay was interrupted at the third grade level when she became totally deaf after being stricken with spinal meningitis. Although she returned to Gesu after her illness, Margaret found the continuance of her education difficult and she lagged behind.

She lost her hearing from spinal meningitis when she was nine, accepted her handicap and overcame it.

This began a long and arduous struggle for the young girl who was determined not to be made different by her handicap. Margaret entered the Paul Binner School for the Deaf, a strictly oral school where manual signs were taboo. Stress was put on lip reading and speech.

Through high school, Margaret was mainstreamed with hearing children, without interpreters or manual communication. These were difficult years, but she persevered and graduated from Lincoln High School in 1938 in the top ten per cent of her class. After graduation she discovered that the only college for the deaf at the time, Gallaudet College in Washington, DC, required proficiency in manual communication, which had been prohibited in the oral track education for the deaf in which she had been trained. Her dreams of a college education suffered a setback.

Undaunted she enrolled in Milwaukee Vocational School, forerunner of the present Milwaukee Area Technical College, where her efforts to study journalism or library science were ignored. Margaret was assigned courses in shoe-making and millinery, neither of which interested her. Finally she did get into higher math and science, and found them extremely difficult. With no interpreter assistance, higher education became impossible.

Disappointed over the misconceptions about the capabilities of the deaf, Margaret was forced to abandon her dreams. Instead she hit the pavement in quest of employment. Again she met obstacles as she was both deaf and unskilled. Eventually she found part-time employment setting tables at a college dormitory and stuffing envelopes at a letter service.

When the army drafted men to fight in World

Above: Margaret and her husband Vincent, and Margaret relaxing with one of their grandsons on a recent visit.

War II, she sought employment in a war plant. Her first application at Cutler-Hammer Company was turned down, presumably because of her handicap. She persisted, reapplying daily until they gave her a chance. Her eventual job was as electrical tester, an easy task. She made friends quickly and soon was considered "one of the gang." In her spare time she did volunteer work for the American Red

Cross. She is proud of the Army-Navy "E" for excellence awarded for her work at the plant.

After marriage in 1944 to a deaf engineer, Vincent Abaravich, she continued to work for Cutler-Hammer until the birth of their first child. Subsequently two more children were born, all with normal hearing.

Margaret insisted that the family live independently. Innovations were required: a doorbell operated by electric light was installed; then came a "baby crier," an electronic device that picked up sounds and transformed them into light. In time, the home became a place of blinking lights, which served their purpose well. The children developed wonderfully.

Her unfinished battle with her dreams soon resurfaced, however, and Margaret returned to the Milwaukee Area Technical College. There she met a teacher who helped mentally retarded children as a volunteer. Margaret became fascinated with this work. Entertaining children of widely varied abilities is one of her special gifts. Desiring to utilize this talent, Margaret began working with the trainable mentally retarded at Pleasant View School. In 1973 she was hired as a teacher's aide. Meanwhile she attended sign classes in the evening and became proficient in this form of communication.

Gaining an understanding of manual communication opened new horizons for Margaret. She enrolled at the University of Wisconsin-Milwaukee and attended regular classes with the assistance of a registered interpreter. In the fall of 1980, at age 61, Margaret was awarded a bachelor's degree in education, realizing that long-delayed dream.

Inflamed with a desire to see corrections and changes in the interest of present and future generations, she has since become an active advocate for the deaf. Margaret spoke out at a Milwaukee School Board meeting on the oral versus the total communication methods of teaching the deaf in the Milwaukee Public Schools. Shortly afterward a two-track method was adopted in Milwaukee schools and currently is in operation.

She testified at Wisconsin Public Service Commission hearings to help the Commission become aware of its responsibility to provide certified deaf customers with telephonic devices that enable persons to communicate reciprocally over regular telephone lines.

Margaret also has participated in public hearings that resulted in the establishment of a much needed Bureau of the Hearing Impaired (BHI), a branch of state government that oversees the needs of hearing impaired citizens. She worked for passage of Public Law 504 seeking rights of the handicapped and for installation of emergency telecommunications devices in the Milwaukee County Sheriff office to comply with this law.

Margaret is a truly remarkable woman. If the hearing impaired have a problem, she works to solve it. Television captioning for the hearing impaired is relatively new; Margaret is actively fighting to improve this service.

The little girl from "Tory Hill" is a pioneer as zesty and steadfast as her Irish ancestors. And the quick wit and lilting humor endure.

(See Selected Honors, Accomplishments, Publications, page 305)

written by LINDA S. NOER

florence parry heide

" . . . Invisible - balloons on invisible strings, waiting to be pulled down . . . "

Florence Parry Heide, who defines the art of creative writing that way, has pulled a lot of those "invisible strings" since the first of her 60-plus books was published in 1967. And those "invisible balloons" contain not hot air, but inspiration for juvenile novels, picture books, songs, adventure stories and mysteries, as well as elementary school textbook primers and stories.

The total output of this writer since her first book is very visible. Among her best-known books

Above: Photo of Florence with her mother and brother taken a couple of months before her father died.
Right: Treehorn's Treasure *by Florence Parry Heide (illustrated by Edward Gorey), published, October 1981.*

Florence on a visit to a Madison school.
"The boy on the left has become one of my pen pals—
I have lots of those!"

is *The Shrinking of Treehorn,* which was translated into German, Swedish, Spanish, French, and published throughout the United Kingdom. The book won the Jugendbuchpreis in 1977 for the best children's book in Germany.

"If you want to pretend you're shrinking, that's all right," said Treehorn's mother, "as long as you don't do it at the table."

The book is a fanciful tale whose appeal and insight into the imaginings of children provides a delightful glimpse into Florence Parry Heide.

Treehorn wasn't pretending. He really was shrinking, and that didn't make life easy for him as he became smaller by the moment. "That's a stupid thing to do," said his friend. "You're always doing stupid things, but that's the *stupidest*." Treehorn's teacher said, "We don't shrink in this class," and sent him to the principal. Poor Treehorn spent an unhappy day and night until

he discovered a magical game that helped him solve his problem.

Mrs. Heide has written a sequel, *Treehorn's Treasure,* published in October 1981, which, like the first, is illustrated by Edward Gorey.

Florence Heide hopes that her books help to instill in children the "joy and excitement of reading." She encourages commitment and empathy ("how it might feel to be in someone else's shoes, someone else's skin") and teaches the young reader to question. She likes to encourage children to keep a notebook of ideas and feelings and to write something—anything, even a fragment—every day to get into the habit of putting their thoughts into words.

With her daughter Roxanne, Mrs. Heide writes two series of juvenile mysteries which will soon be available in paperback. The mother and daughter collaborators are presently writing their twentieth book.

Born in Pittsburgh, Florence Parry Heide came from a family that was "surrounded by words." Her mother was a drama critic and daily columnist for the *Pittsburgh Press* for many years. Mrs. Heide recalls that her mother made writing seem effortless and exciting.

Florence attended Wilson College and graduated from the University of California at Los Angeles. She worked in New York after graduation, always hoping to marry and "live happily ever after." This wish came true when she married attorney Donald Heide, raised five children and later began her writing career.

Mrs. Heide, now a grandmother, is still so intrigued and excited by young people that she travels extensively to speak in schools, at writers' workshops and to groups of all kinds. She is accessible and enthusiastic, a warm and gracious

As a writer of more than 60 books for children, she is widely recognized for her commitment to youth.

woman. Her commitment to quality children's literature is matched by her concern and pursuit of excellence for community educational programs.

Like Treehorn, she has found that the power to control the direction of her life lies in confidence, perseverance and a contagious optimism.

(See Selected Honors, Accomplishments, Publications, page 309)

Florence Parry Heide and a sampling of her work.

written by CONSTANCE THREINEN

kathryn clarenbach

In 1920 the right of women to vote was written into the United States Constitution, and in Sparta, Wisconsin, a third child, a first daughter, was born to the family of a country parson.

Eventually she became chair of the Governor's Commission on the Status of Women for most of its 15 year existence, founder and leader of the National Organization for Women, a founder of the National Women's Political Caucus, and executive-director of the National Women's

A thoughtful, articulate partisan for women's rights, she headed the Governor's Commission on the Status of Women for more than 13 years.

209

Conference on International Women's Year. Kathryn Frederick Clarenbach's influence has been felt far from her native town. But she recalls her youth with fondness, and traces many of her successes and convictions to the encouragement of her parents and the experiences of a large and loving household. Kay describes them this way:

"I grew up in Sparta, Wisconsin, in a family of three brothers and no sisters. I don't recall ever wishing for a sister. Our corner house with huge yard was large and attractive; it was also filled with music, lots of laughs, activity and people. There was love, respect, and abundant encouragement."

Top left: Frederick family, 1941. (Back) Gordon, mother, David, (front) Robert, father, Kathryn.
Far left: Kathryn Frederick, Senior Honors Convocation.
Near left: Speaking in Hawaii, 1970, first woman-in-residence at the University of Hawaii.
Above: Women's Equality Day, 1975, on the Capitol steps, Madison.

Her mother presented a role model, although Kay did not realize this at the time.

"I never thought of my mother as being especially independent, modern, or liberated. But within the context of her life and times I realize now that she was all three. I knew she was intelligent, dignified, gentle, and warm. I just didn't think in terms of liberation. But I remember she had her hair bobbed in the early 1920's without my father's knowledge and to his dismay.

"She was elected to the school board. She refused to take part in Ladies Aid and Mission societies in my dad's eight country churches, though she always attended one service a week with him . . . She made me the first pair of beach pajamas in Sparta, to the raised eyebrows of neighbors, and assured me when my friends were taught they shouldn't shampoo or bathe, much less ride bike or play tennis during menstruation, that I could and should be as active in all respects as I felt like . . .

"My mother had been a country school teacher . . . She was a natural teacher, and all four of us had a built-in tutor. Our three sets of encyclopedias and an unabridged dictionary were in constant use. No matter how hard she worked, my mother read every afternoon and had an arrangement with the library to phone her and give her 'first dibs' on every new book it acquired. Every morning she got up an hour early in order to write letters and write in her diary. She loved researching and writing her papers for the Sparta Literary Club and often ghosted my dad's annual paper as well."

Kay's father was all that a daughter could want as a mentor and supporter. His professional qualifications were unusual for any time especially for his era. He had BA and MA degrees from the University of Wisconsin in Hebrew and Hellenistic Greek, and a law degree from Georgetown University.

In Sparta his primary paid position was State Parole and Probation Officer but he was also preacher, lawyer, state humane officer, divorce counsel, court commissioner and newspaper stringer. Prior to his marriage he served in the Wisconsin Legislature where he was referred to as the Fighting Parson. With such a range of responsibilities and interests he was able to provide his family with experiences unknown to most small town children. Table talk was of public affairs, personal crises, the role of government, and the responsibilities of individuals.

Kay remembers that her father frequently drew her attention to the achievements of women. Most significantly, he included her in his expectation to see each of his offspring through a master's degree before sending them on their own. He was suspicious of Kay's chosen field, political science.

But it was a natural for Kay. She completed her MA in political science at Madison and, with the demand high for women workers during World War II, she spent 1942 to 1944 in Washington, DC with the War Production Board as an administrative analyst.

At the war's end she returned to Madison and earned a PhD. She met Henry Clarenbach, also a graduate student, who was not frightened off by her mother's advice to give Kay a long tether. Their marriage followed a pattern now common but unusual for 1946. Kay went off almost immediately to teach at Purdue, and Hank to Columbia to work on a PhD with frequent visits back and forth.

By the time they returned to Madison they were rearing a family of three. Hank opened a real estate business arranging a flexible schedule so Kay could have opportunities outside the home and he could participate in parenting.

Right: Upon returning home, husband Henry carrying David, Kay, Sara carrying Janet; Kathryn, 1981.

The return of the Clarenbachs to Madison occurred at a propitious time for the women's movement. Kay joined the UW faculty as a counselor to initiate a continuing education program for women. She encouraged many to begin new lives. As an administrator she worked with deans, faculty members, and secretaries to accommodate the new clientele.

The creation of the Governor's Commission on the Status of Women in 1964 set a new direction in Kay Clarenbach's life. She was appointed by Governor John Reynolds as its chair, a position she held for the full 15 years of the commission's existence with the exception of one term. Under her leadership issues were articulated, public awareness was stimulated, and support kindled for changes in Wisconsin's law and practices, that place the state in the lead in progress for women.

With her organizing ability, calm manner and broad perspective on social and political matters she became a national figure instrumental in the formation of NOW and the National Women's Political Caucus. Kay spent 18 months in Washington, DC as executive director of the National Commission for International Women's Year and, in that capacity, was responsible for the overall planning and policy implementation of the National Women's Conference held in Houston in November 1977.

Besides the positions that she concurrently holds—faculty member of the UW-Extension and chair of the Women's Resources unit, regular

commentator on Radio WHA's "Morning People" program, member of the National Continuing Education Committee and of the Alverno College President's Advisory Council—she is frequently a guest lecturer for campus classes and for professional and lay groups in Wisconsin and around the country.

(See Selected Honors, Accomplishments, Publications, page 306)

If her views seem radical to some, they provide for many others an unfettered analysis of reality and a reasonable program for political action.

Sister Remy Revor, and blockprint and batik fabric exhibited with "Objects: USA." (photo by John Ahlhauser)

sister remy revor

"Awakening in students an awareness of beauty in the world around them" Sister Remy Revor considers her most important accomplishment.

Said one student at the University of Tennessee, Knoxville, "I've never had an art teacher open my eyes the way she has."

"She's a cool lady with a whole lot of wit," said another. "She makes you do more than you have to; she makes you more demanding of yourself."

Sister Remy is professor of art at Mount Mary College, Milwaukee, Wisconsin. The school began as St. Mary's College in Prairie du Chien in 1872 and was moved to Milwaukee in 1928.

Sister Remy is an artist, a designer, lecturer and an educator of international repute. She was a Fulbright Research Scholar in Finland in 1969 and 1970. Under a Louis Comfort Tiffany Foundation Grant, she spent four months of 1963 in Sweden studying Swedish methods of textile printing.

The art professor was born in Chippewa Falls, Wisconsin of parents of French extraction. After graduating from high school she entered the School Sisters of Notre Dame in Milwaukee, a teaching community numbering over 4,000 in the United States and Canada and 5,000 throughout the world, in Europe, Central America, South America, Japan, West Africa, Micronesia and Puerto Rico.

Originally a science major, Sister Remy transferred to art after her first year of college. She received a bachelor of arts degree from Mount Mary College and a bachelor of fine arts degree from the School of the Art Institute of Chicago where she also earned her MFA.

Of her choice of medium Sister Remy wrote, "My electing textile design as my medium was

Sister Remy, enjoying her work.

She is professor of art at Mount Mary College and a textile designer of international repute.

largely a happenstance. I happened to be assigned to Margaret Artingstall's class when I was fulfilling the requirements for my first degree at the Art Institute. All the work of the class was done in 'flat pattern,' and included the designing of record albums, wall papers and stained glass windows as well as textiles. It was in textiles, however, that I felt most at home. A carpet pattern entered in a national competition while I was still an undergraduate won third place and gave me a sense of assurance.

"When I returned to Mount Mary I entered textiles in the art exhibit at the Wisconsin State Fair and the Wisconsin Designer craftsmen annual exhibit. From the start these fabrics were awarded prizes. Now that I no longer feel it necessary to compete I still feel the need to create. And so my textiles are frequently shown in invitational exhibits. They can be seen hanging in various places at Mount Mary. I also send textiles to the annual Channel 10 auction."

Sister Remy has given lectures, seminars and workshops in textile design on many campuses including the Universities of Kansas, Wisconsin, Louisville, North Carolina State and Northern Illinois, Cleveland Museum of Arts, Rochester (NY) Institute of Technology and Lawrence University.

She has conducted study tours in West Africa, Finland and Sweden. In 1978 she organized a workshop at Mount Mary College by the Marstrand Designers of Sweden, the group she had worked with during her 1963 stay in that country. From 1969 to 1981 she taught summer classes at Arrowmont School of Arts and Crafts, Gatlinburg, Tennessee. In 1980 she spent a semester at Notre Dame Women's College, Kyoto, Japan. The news media has used her talents on TV programs and the Voice of America.

"Although the greater part of my time is spent in teaching, I find time to print my own textiles, mostly for the sheer joy I find in doing so. I would like to think that this feeling is evident in my work. Half my graduate work at the Art Institute of Chicago was done in painting, the other half in pattern design. Both disciplines involve the application of paint to fiber, but while a painting is usually an entity, pattern design involves the repetition of motifs. I do not feel that on this account it is a lesser art and I take pride in making my fabrics as beautiful as possible," Sister wrote.

"Ideas for textiles evolve naturally from the world around me, and I convert these sketches I do of shadows, textures of bark, shells, wood grain, to units of design which will adapt to textiles. I do not exclude anything and find equal

delight in stones, bugs, reflections in glass, buttons and baskets. Since working with the Marstrand Designers in Sweden and for a year in Finland where I became acquainted with the Finnish Designers my work has become bolder, larger in scale and richer in color.

"While the bulk of my work is done with the silk screen process, I also work with dyeing techniques, batik as well as block printing."

Her enjoyment of her life commitment is reflected in her relaxed, self-possessed expression of satisfaction that is conveyed to all who meet her. She shows that inner vitality so essential to an artist. She inspires her students and awakens in them an appreciation of the beauty in the world around them.

(See Selected Honors, Accomplishments, Publications, page 313)

Far left: Sister Remy accepting Alumnae Madonna Metal from Sister Ellen Lorenz, president of Mount Mary College.
Near left and above: In classroom studio with Mount Mary students.

written by ANNE G. NILES

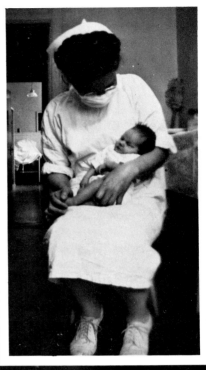

signe skott cooper

*Let us never consider ourselves finished
nurses. . .We must be learning all our lives.*

Although this statement is attributed to
Florence Nightingale, it might well have been said
by Signe Skott Cooper. Professor Cooper has been

in the forefront of continuing education since 1955 when she founded the first university continuing education program for nurses in the United States. Under her direction, the department has been recognized for innovative approaches to programming and has been a pacemaker for the nation.

How did she do it?

"Well, I happened to be in the right place at the right time for a starter," Mrs. Cooper suggested. But it takes more than luck to continue the professional climb, and that's what sets Signe Cooper apart. Words like self-directed, creative, determined, dedicated, sincere and non-compromising come to mind. It is a unique combination of such traits that propelled her to leadership in the field of continuing education in nursing. Louise Smith, professor emeritus from the school of nursing, University of Wisconsin-Madison, calls her a "spark plug."

Signe Dorothea Skott, the second of four children, was born in Clinton County, Iowa, on January 29, 1921, to Clara and Hans Skott. She grew up on her parents' Jackson County, Iowa, farm, attending a country school through seventh grade.

"Going to a one-room school was great," Mrs. Cooper recalls. "I could listen in and be

Signe Skott Cooper, conducting Educational Network Telephone class. (photo by Gary Schulz, courtesy, University of Wisconsin-Extension) *Insert: Signe on the obstetric unit at Wisconsin General Hospital, Madison, 1947.*

challenged by all the interesting things others were doing. I think it was a mind-stretching experience."

During Depression days on the farm, her mother became a stringer for five newspapers, an intermittent occupation that bridged six decades of newspaper writing. Watching her pound the typewriter must have had a strong influence on Signe, for she has become one of nursing's most prolific writers, has been a member of several editorial boards, and has taught and encouraged other nurses to write for professional publications.

"We have always been a close-knit family," Professor Cooper states, "And my grandparents, aunts, and uncles lived nearby during my childhood. They all gave direction to my life. But my father, in particular, influenced me as a continuing learner. He was a curious person and never went any place without first learning about it and then talking to people to find out what was going on there."

Signe Skott knew at five years of age that she wanted to be a nurse. "Occasionally, I gave thought to becoming a veterinarian," she says. But the profession of nursing pulled the strongest, and she planned to enroll in the Methodist Hospital School of Nursing in Madison. Entering nursing students were required to be at least 18 years of age, and being just 17, Signe decided to attend the University of Wisconsin for one year.

These were the hardship days of the Depression, and the tuition of $27.50 was not easy to come by for anyone with several children to educate. By this time, the family was living in Middleton, and Signe and her younger sister, Kathryn, would put a dollar's worth of gasoline in the Model "A" Ford each week to commute to the University. Because the course of studies interested her, she remained until 1943, completing the University's graduate nurse program.

Following graduation she joined the US army and was stationed in the China-India-Burma theater. "It was an experience I'm glad to have had, but would hate to live through again." After serving 27 months and after a brief marriage, she returned to the Madison campus for more studies and to work at the University's Wisconsin General Hospital.

These were the Baby Boom years, which, along with a shortage of nurses, meant working 18 hour days during busy periods. However, Mrs. Cooper was able to attend classes and graduated in 1948 with a baccalaureate degree. Although teaching had not been a career goal, she joined the faculty of the School of Nursing and after a summer session at Teachers College, Columbia University, began a teaching career that would continue throughout her professional life.

Seven years later she became the first chairman of the Department of Nursing in University Extension. The department, which recently celebrated its 25th anniversary, has grown from one professional staff member to a dozen. It has developed from a department with no initial guidelines to an internationally recognized leader in the field of continuing education for nursing. Nearly 100,000 students have enrolled in Extension Nursing courses.

Of early Extension days, Theodore J. Shannon, onetime dean of Extension, recalls, "Whenever there was a snowstorm, hail, or sleet, we used to joke that chances were that Signe was on the highway somewhere to teach a class or chair a meeting. A mark of her dedication," he emphasizes "is the fact that she took a leave of absence from the University for employment in a small community hospital in order to reorient herself

and better understand the perspective of the practitioner."

Professor Cooper's interest in history has led her to become Wisconsin's foremost nursing historian, and she has worked closely with the State Historical Society in the acquisition, preservation, and presentation of nursing memorabilia.

Of her personal beliefs Mrs. Cooper says, "I believe in a do-it-yourself philosophy. Each person was put on earth to do something, and I'm concerned because too many people were 'letting

She has dedicated herself to solutions of health care problems in Wisconsin
through personal and professional involvement in research, advisory and teaching efforts

219

George do it'. People ought to do what they can to make this world a better place. But people also need to find out their own words of wisdom. My words won't help anybody else. They really have to find what is meaningful and what makes sense to them."

Helen Tobin, director of centralized staff development at the University Hospitals of Cleveland, friend and frequent traveling companion says, "Although continuing education is Signe's major thrust, she is certainly far from narrow in her knowledge of nursing and the delivery of health care. In spite of the fact that she has gained national and international recognition for her contribution to the development of continuing education in nursing, she remains a very conscientious person, willing to share her expertise through many publications, leadership in committees and groups and individual conferences. She is never too busy to share with those who seek her help."

(See Selected Honors, Accomplishments, Publications, page 307)

Left to right: Signe Skott Cooper on the air; receiving the Linda Richards Award from Rita E. Miller at the National League Convention; teaching an Extension Nursing class at the Wisconsin Center, Madison.
(photos by Gary Schulz, courtesy, University of Wisconsin-Extension)

written by BETTE BROWN & MARY ELLEN STONE

isabel brown

A few years ago, Round-up Jenny, a Polled (hornless) Hereford cow was very sick. A number of veterinarians attempted and failed to relieve her ailments. They gave her a 10 percent chance to live and said they could do no more.

But Isabel Brown did not give up. She encouraged and nursed Jenny for weeks, until, finally, the cow began to respond. Today, three healthy calves later, Jenny shows no signs of her near-fatal disease.

This is an example of the work of Isabel McKerrow Brown of Hartland, Wisconsin. Her

ability to understand animals is reflected in their trust of her. Whether checking for disease or helping with a calving, Isabel can read a cow like a book.

Expertise with animals is just one of her many talents. She is farmer, accountant and nursery-woman, working with her husband Warren in their W.W. Brown farm operation. On weekday mornings, she goes to her office at Merton School and, as financial consultant, administers a one million dollar budget.

Isabel Brown has been a member of the Arrowhead High School Board for 15 years, the Wisconsin Livestock Breeders Association Board for five years, Wisconsin Polled Hereford Association Board, two years, and the Waukesha County Fair Board, 12 years.

Mrs. Brown's pace would tax a marathon runner. In the nursery, she waits on customers, pots and digs trees, and supervises the work crew. Then there is her cowgirl side. She maintains the herd's health, gives shots and pills, pulls calves, trims hooves and gives annual vaccinations. She can recite each animal's ancestry, generations back, with specific details about dispositions and performance data.

Many a round-up finds the agile gray-haired lady in the middle of the action. One cowboy, hired to work a few weeks before the Browns' annual sale, commented, "We'd be working cattle and, time after time, Mrs. Brown would end up doing most of the haltering, with us watching from the sidelines. It was almost embarrassing."

Crop work is a big part of the Brown operation. With Warren busy with the nursery in the spring, Isabel runs the corn crew. In 1980, she, her daughter, son-in-law and a part-time hired man planted over 500 acres of corn. Isabel can and does run all of the machinery, including the corn planter, and attends seminars to keep current on fertilizers, application rates and other recent developments.

Isabel Brown is past president and 30-plus year member of the Hartland's Woman's Club, founding president and member of the Wisconsin Cowbelles, member of the Wisconsin Pollettes. She plays bridge and was a member of the Schoolhouse Players, a theatrical group, for 12 years. She has served as Richmond 4-H Club general leader for 20 years and Sunday school teacher for almost as long.

Born and reared on a 500-acre sheep and dairy farm, Isabel was the oldest of five children. When she was a little girl, her father, Gavin McKerrow, made a deal with her mother and grandmother. If Isabel would practice piano for an hour after school, she could then help tend the livestock.

So she practiced diligently and bolted out of the house to enjoy her favorite pastime.

Isabel spent a lot of time with her father who was the founder and president of Golden Guernsey Dairy Cooperative. She learned much about running a business. Photographs of her father and grandfather are displayed in the Steenbock Library at the University of Wisconsin-Madison, and in the Saddle and Sirloin Club in Louisville, Kentucky.

Left: Isabel Brown at work; (lower far left) At seven years old; (near left) 1969 Champion Bull Award.

In her free time on weekday mornings, Isabel goes to her office at Merton School, and, as financial consultant, invests and appropriates a $1 million budget.

Carolyn McKerrow, Isabel's mother, always a lady and eternally positive, played no small role in her daughter's development.

Working side by side, Warren and Isabel Brown have a special and supportive relationship that has developed during their 40 years of marriage. If Isabel attends an out-of-town meeting, Warren covers for her at the home front. And when she brings home a purchase, a bull or a heifer, he "ohs" and "ahs" to make her feel it was a good buy. Usually, it is.

Coming from a nationally renowned livestock family, Isabel could have rested on the laurels of her forefathers, using their sheep and dairy bloodlines. Instead, she and her husband began from scratch in the beef business, buying their first Polled Herefords in 1953. They are pioneer breeders of Polled Herefords in Wisconsin.

The Browns' herd has won many awards, including premier exhibitor and breeder at Midwestern state fairs. Their cattle have been sold nationwide and in Hawaii and Costa Rica.

Until the fall of 1980, the Brown farm had around 150-200 head of cattle. With the children out of the nest and the difficulties of raising cattle amid urban sprawl, the Browns reduced the herd to about 50.

In spite of all her extra-curricular activities, Isabel Brown has never neglected her domestic skills. She is an excellent cook, bakes bread, and loves to entertain. She makes handknit sweaters. One of them, donated to a Polled Hereford benefit auction, brought $125.

Her homemaking skills were partly self-taught, and partly the result of her college education. She attended Carroll College in Waukesha and the University of Wisconsin-Madison, majoring in home economics. At Madison, she won the Miss Milk Maid contest. She also won an award as the top Ayrshire judge in the nation. She is a certified livestock judge, traveling to fairs throughout the Midwest.

Love of animals and the out-of-doors are common denominators among the three children, Carolyn, Randy and Bette. Their careers reflect their mother's interests—education, horticulture and economics.

Isabel Brown's list of accomplishments is impressive, but her most endearing qualities are difficult to document—the sparkle in her eye, the quiet smile, the warmth, the patience when teaching a newborn calf to nurse.

Isabel Brown is a ray of sunshine to all who cross her path.

(See Selected Honors, Accomplishments, Publications, page 306)

She has been national president of the League of Women Voters and assistant secretary, US Department of Energy.

ruth clusen

Ruth Clusen began as a teacher and a volunteer and today is a national consultant in environmental affairs. She introduced the televised presidential debates of 1976 and later became Assistant Secretary of Environment in the US Department of Energy.

Ruth Chickering Clusen was born June 11, 1922, in Bruce, Wisconsin, the daughter of Elmer and Ruth Breed Chickering. Her father was a teacher so the family lived in several cities in Wisconsin and spent seven years in Kentucky before moving to Eau Claire where Chickering

Ruth Clusen, as president of the League of Women Voters, facilitating the Presidential Debates of 1976.

taught at the campus school and his daughter graduated from Eau Claire High School.

In the household that included one brother, there was always interest in public affairs and the political scene. Ruth tells that the whole family enjoyed reading, an interest still avidly pursued.

Ruth graduated from the University of Wisconsin-Eau Claire in 1945. The same year she married Donald E. Clusen and the couple moved to Montana where both had teaching jobs.

In a few years they moved back to Wisconsin to Green Bay where Ruth taught English and speech at East High and at Franklin Junior High. "I really enjoyed teaching as I like working with young people," she said.

The Clusens have two daughters, Kathryn of Milwaukee and Elizabeth, Green Bay. There are two grandchildren.

"My husband has always been supportive of my activity. Yet I do not feel this was something my family let me do. I wanted to teach so I did. My greatest challenge came in trying to mesh in an acceptable way an active life outside the home with the responsibilities of a young family at home in a climate where this was not the norm."

In addition to activity in the League of Women Voters, Ruth was a volunteer in the PTA, at her church and in the hospital auxiliary. By 1958 when she was becoming more active in the League she gave up teaching.

In the 1960's Ruth Clusen became interested in environmental issues, developing expertise and political contacts.

She was elected to six years on the national League of Women Voter's board as her portfolio in "Environmental Quality" grew. She drew the attention of the White House. Under five administrations Ruth Clusen was sent all over the world representing the State Department.

Mrs. Clusen has had a distinguished career in public service. She has been a leader in promoting an integrated approach to environmental improvement through planning, coordinating, administration, monitoring and financing. She has encouraged public education and attention to such natural resource issues as energy production and conservation, land and water use, management and air quality improvement. She has promoted public involvement in water quality planning and solid waste management.

A long-time advocate of a global approach to environmental problem solving, Ruth Clusen served as a US delegate to several international environmental conferences. Over the past 14 years she has been named an emissary for the government on 13 missions to foreign countries.

Of her own commitment to these causes, Mrs. Clusen explains, "It basically comes down to energy, directing that energy towards personal achievement and remaining persistent in attaining selected goals."

(See Selected Honors, Accomplishments, Publications, page 307)

Right: Swearing in as Assistant Secretary, Department of Energy. Ruth with daughter Kathryn LeClair, granddaughter Christine and Secretary James Schlesinger.

"Nothing has come easily to us in trying to achieve our equal place in society — not education, or employment, or the franchise. But we surely have learned a lot in the process. . ."

—RUTH CLUSEN

She turned the office of village president into a full-time plus job.

angeline thompson

It all began April Fool's Day, 1975, when Angeline Thompson won the election for president of the village of Haugen by one vote as a write-in candidate. Little did she know what challenges awaited her during her term in office. Haugen is a small community of 250 about 65 miles northeast of Eau Claire and Angie has been a resident for over 30 years. Prior to election day, she enjoyed a quiet, private life as a homemaker and mother.

Angie Thompson was born in 1922 in Barron County. She graduated from Rice Lake High School. She married Vernon Thompson and they have three children.

At the age of 53, Angie lunged into a new career. Since that April day both the personal life style of Angie Thompson and the character of Haugen village have undergone numerous changes.

In just five years this community experienced more improvements than most towns do in 50 years.

Angie turned the office of village president, for which she received only a small commission, into a full-time job, not to mention her overtime hours. Besides serving as president, she chaired the centennial celebration in 1976, served as president of the Senior Citizens Center in 1977, helped organize the Haugen Community Club and supported youth activities.

No matter how insurmountable the project, Angie is ready to tackle it. In 1976 she jumped right into a complex public works project—switching from septic tanks and individual wells to a community water and sewer system. To understand all the legal requirements Angie attended DNR courses with the other specialists in the field. She qualified for licenses to become the required water operator, waste water operator, local public works inspector, lateral inspector, plumbing code inspector and waste water analyst.

With the assistance of consultants she applied for the million dollar grant to finance the project. For two years she acted as administrator, record keeper (turning her home into an office), serving as all the commissioners rolled up into one and contributing her own physical labor. It was not an uncommon sight to find the president down in a manhole wearing a hard hat or climbing the water

Left: Angie and her own 8-point buck ("All mine!") (photo by her husband Vern)
Right: Sixteen years old, 1938 (photo by sister Eunice Sheldon)
Far right: "One of my better catches." (photo by son Howard.)
Below: Sketch by Bill Hrudka representing Angie as village president;

tower to make sure everything was operating well. She also took water samples of the wells.

There was a time during this project when Angie worked a seven-day week from dawn to dusk in order to beat the arrival of the freezing temperatures in the northern part of Wisconsin. There were days a person could not see across the street because the dirt and dust were so thick in the village. On other days workers wallowed in mud up to their knees.

There were telephone calls to the president at all hours of the night. She personally cleaned the 60 manholes of debris before the system could be turned on. She literally knows her little village from the ground up. She said, "I'm just thankful our village wasn't any larger. God helped me get through this six-year period to come out on top."

Angie spearheaded an impressive list of community achievements: new bank and post office buildings; installation of a community water and sewer system; renewal of all village streets; upgrading of the local recreational ball park; organization of a Senior Citizens Center that now includes 88 members; the establishment of a low cost housing unit for the elderly.

Two new subdivisions have been developed. A laundromat and cheese house are welcome additions to the village. Established homeowners and businesses showed pride in their community by refurbishing their properties.

Angie brought life to Haugen and has set a healthy trend for future development. The village of Haugen and surrounding rural areas are proud to have had Angie Thompson as their leader. Her strength and courage guided her community during the trying period of rapid growth. The village board would not let her resign after her first three year term. Haugen needed Angie Thompson!

At times Angie looks back with nostalgia to her private quiet life as a homemaker. In May 1981 her term as president expired and she is now a "counseling housewife" helping others with water and waste water problems.

The whole community of Haugen benefited from a woman who gave so much of her energy and talent to the community's development and progress.

(See Selected Honors, Accomplishments, Publications, page 313)

Four generational photo: daughter Sandy, mother Florence Sheldon holding first granddaughter Julie, and Angie. (photo by Vern Thompson)

written by MYRNA M. TONEY

barbara thompson

Remembrances of her family working as a team planting, harvesting and marketing tobacco, the farm's cash crop, come easily to Barbara Storck Thompson. "It was backbreaking work for all of

Above: Barbara Thompson, age 5, first grade
(photo by Reierson's Studio)
Below: Barbara at the National 4-H Club Congress representing the state of Wisconsin as outstanding 4-H member.

us, and a lot of it under the hot sun, but it secured the ownership of our farm."

Recalling the early days, Barbara cherishes her hardy roots. Life for the Storck family, as for many other Wisconsin farmers during the depression years, was filled with long days of hard work. The Storcks operated a dairy and tobacco farm on the northeast edge of McFarland, Wisconsin.

John and Marie Storck strongly believe in the German work ethic and instilled it in sons, Norman and Curtis, and daughter, Barbara. "It really took the work and cooperation of the whole family to come out ahead. The rewards were there, too, in the satisfaction of knowing you had contributed to the overall successes."

From the parental helm came encouragement to participate in church and 4-H activities and to take pride in one's work. Friends growing up with Barbara remember her concern for others and her boundless enthusiasm in school and community activities. "I believe that my participation in 4-H

projects laid a strong foundation for the development of leadership and communication skills. At 16 Barbara was selected as Wisconsin's representative to the National 4-H Congress in Chicago, Illinois.

Encouraged by teachers and professors, Barbara chose a career in education. Her professional career included the roles of classroom teacher, reading specialist, school psychometrist, school administrator and educational consultant, leading to her election in 1973 as state superintendent of public instruction, the first and only woman to serve in this capacity in Wisconsin.

As state superintendent, Barbara used her family's team approach to involve citizenry and

parents, through advisory councils, in working toward educational goals. She believes involvement in the shaping of Wisconsin education must be sought from individuals at the grass roots level.

Early in Barbara Thompson's administration as state superintendent, she addressed the problem of sex discrimination and sex and minority role stereotyping in Wisconsin schools.

Throughout her terms in office, Barbara worked for quality education and improvement of delivery systems so that all students might have access to education regardless of where they live. She led the fight on many fronts: improved vocational education opportunities, retaining the arts as basic to education, strengthening the basics and providing appropriate educational services to students with special needs. She advocates that the best interests of the child should prevail at all times. "I consider the opportunity to serve students and their parents a very great privilege," she states.

In 1944, when Barbara was 19, she and Glenn Thompson were married. They have two sons, David and James. Having personally experienced positive benefits from 4-H involvement, Barbara and Glenn gave firsthand support to 4-H Club work by serving as leaders. Barbara maintains that the support and encouragement provided by her husband and sons has made it possible for her to pursue various options and to demonstrate that women can fulfill more than one role successfully. In 1969 Barbara and Glenn Thompson received PhD degrees in Educational Administration at the University of Wisconsin-Madison.

The Thompsons developed their own family farm at Mount Horeb. Happy are the times when they can get together with their family for visiting and reminiscing. They enjoy visits to the Storck family farm to visit Barbara's father, who at 90 continues to work on the land. What Barbara once said about her early life applies to her career as well, "Sure it was hard work, but we reached a goal that meant a lot to us, and we were able to do it by working together."

(See Selected Honors, Accomplishments, Publications, page 313)

Left to right: Barbara with UW President John Weaver and UW Regent Bert McNamara; UW Chancellor Jean Evans with Barbara, receiving the state and national 4-H Alumni Award, 1976; Barbara with Milwaukee Superintendent Lee McMurrin (courtesy, UW - Extension, Madison).

Above left: Mary Lou Munts—baby picture, 1925;
Below left: With brother; Above: Outside the Capitol
in Madison, Wisconsin.

State Representative Munts was ranked one of the most effective legislators in the Madison Assembly.

mary lou munts

Asked what it is like to be a woman legislator, Mary Lou Munts says, "When we were only seven out of 132, obviously, we couldn't afford to be mediocre. We are now up to 20 and I feel that our diversity and accomplishments are recognized. I have always felt a special obligation to take on at least one major project each session of importance to women. Marital property reform is my blockbuster challenge this session (1981)."

As representative of the 76th Wisconsin Assembly district since 1972, Munts' legislative record includes significant public policy successes in mental health and developmental disability laws, solid and hazardous waste management, energy, natural resources, mining reclamation, utility plant siting, divorce reform, equal rights and ethics legislation. She thrives on tough issues.

Her record of legislative accomplishments is the result of solid behind the scenes effort. "One of her special fortes," as noted in a *Milwaukee Sentinel* article, "is bringing competing and conflicting interests together informally to work out problems with proposals long before they hit the floor, or even a committee hearing."

An eldest child, Mary Lou Munts grew up in the Chicago area, where her father was Director of the Research Laboratory for Standard Oil of Indiana. "I had a loving relationship with my father," Munts relates. "I don't think there's much question that the reason I have intellectual self-confidence is because of all the encouragement he gave me. My mother had the harder job of taming a superactive child." In looking back, Mary Lou now perceives how much she was also influenced by her mother's intellectual quickness and her demanding

Mary Lou Munts with Senator Thomas Flynn and Representative James Rutkowski at a hearing on AB370. All are co-authors of the Marital Property Reform legislation.

standards.

"My younger brother Tom and I shared an idyllic life in the summer on Lake Michigan in the Indiana Dunes, the kind of childhood that makes you reluctant to grow up. My parents had both

been high achievers in school and were a hard act to follow. My brother is the creative one and is now a novelist. I turned more toward the world of people and action.''

Munts' civil rights activism, political interests and leadership qualities emerged early. While a student in economics at Swarthmore, she was in the vanguard of the movement that saw the first Black student admitted to the small Quaker college in Pennsylvania. At a student leadership training institute on Campobello Island, she was inspired by Eleanor Roosevelt. These were heady years.

Swarthmore was followed by the University of Chicago where she received a master's degree in economics. ''It never occurred to me to proceed to a PhD, Munts explains. ''I never had any professional expectations. Most women of my age at that time did not look ahead and ask, ''What will I be doing (professionally) ten years from now?''

After her marriage to Raymond Munts in 1947, she worked as a research assistant and college

"I learned as much from my volunteer work as from any job. Being on a multitude of boards and committees enabled me to organize and to be effective in the legislative committee process."

MARY LOU MUNTS

235

teacher until she quit to have the first of their four children.

"I'm glad that I didn't have the pressure of a career when my children were young. I loved that period and made the most of it." But she was not a recluse from public and community life. She served as a board member of the League of Women Voters and worked for candidates in partisan and non-partisan elections.

Then followed ten stimulating, provocative years in the Washington, DC area. Stirred by civil rights activism, Munts was a leader in efforts to desegregate public accommodations and promote fair housing in the suburbs. When her youngest child was five, she took a job as a part-time economist for a Washington consulting firm.

In 1967 her husband accepted a position on the faculty of the University of Wisconsin-Madison School of Social Work. "I had deep community roots and was still feeling my way about whether to pursue a career as an economist, so the move was a very difficult one for me," Munts explained.

Shortly after moving to Madison, the family suffered a devastating blow, the drowning death of their son, Roger. "Looking back, I realize now that I was seriously depressed after this happened," she confides. "It was a ghastly time, but gradually I began to find my way back. The loss of our son has made us even closer as a family, more open and sharing with each other."

Looking for new avenues for her energies, she entered the University of Wisconsin Law School, at age 46, while continuing her community and political activities. She received her JD Degree in 1976.

In her first year of law school, she ran for alderman on the Madison Common Council, but lost. However she discovered her potential as a candidate, and when a state Assembly seat opened up in 1972, she ran and was elected. She has served as representative of the 76th Assembly district ever since.

Munts has chaired the Assembly's environmental committee for four terms and also that of the National Conference of State Legislators. Her current agenda includes leading efforts to preserve quality services for the handicapped and the disadvantaged in the face of budgetary cutbacks.

Through all of this, "it's important to remember how wonderfully human Mom is," her daughter Polly adds. "She loves staying up 'til all hours talking or reading a good mystery. She bought her first pair of running shoes at age 52. She'd be just as content weeding her asparagus patch as leading debate on the floor of the Assembly."

(See Selected Honors, Accomplishments, Publications, page 311)

Left above: Mary Louise Rogers, 1941;
Left to right: With Eleanor Roosevelt when she spoke
at Swarthmore College; Relaxing on the river
with husband Ray and son Andy; Munts family, 1980.

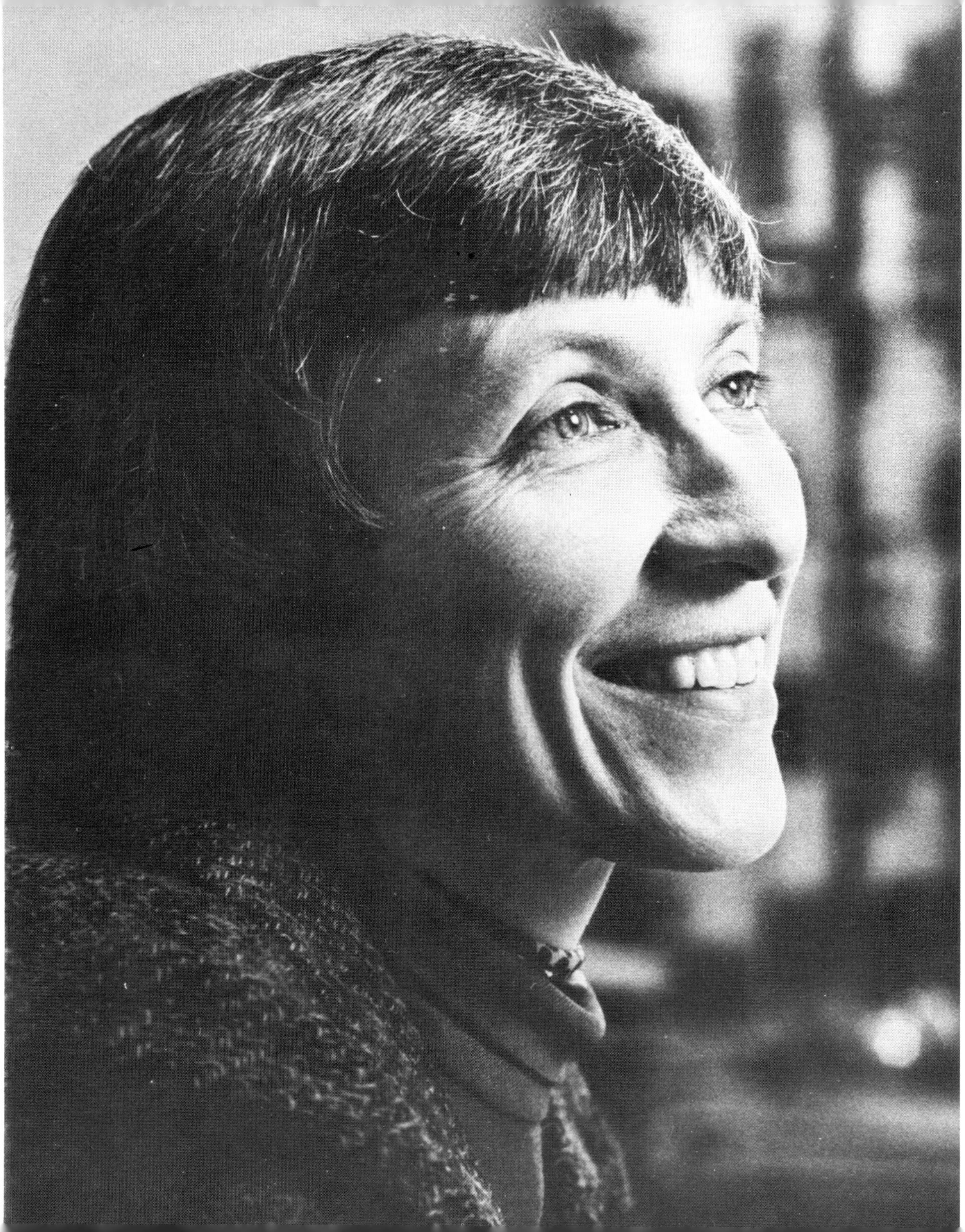

written by MAY MURPHY THIBAUDEAU

sister joel read

"In 1967, I was in Washington, DC, to lobby for the International Studies Act. At the same time, the first organizational meeting of NOW (National Organization for Women) was underway. I was aware of that meeting through the Milwaukee press, so I went. On the spot, I was asked to work on the first Board of Directors and did so for two years."

Thus, almost by chance, Sister Joel Read assumed a leadership role in the women's movement which she is convinced is "a permanent part of history. The question is not whether you will have to change, but whether you can shape change to continue the values in which you believe."

In 1968, when Sister Joel became president of Alverno College, she was in a position to do just that, to implement change in the education of women to help them cope with changes in their lives. Alverno is a professional and liberal arts college for women, owned by the School Sisters of St. Francis, and directed by a lay Board of Trustees.

Her leadership has brought Alverno to the forefront among women's colleges with innovative programs that have attracted national attention. The curriculum enables students to master the knowledge base in their selected areas of study while developing high level abilities in

Far left: Sister Joel Read, president of Alverno College; Above: Taken the day before she entered the Community of the School of Sisters of St. Francis, January 31, 1942. Left: Sister Joel.

238

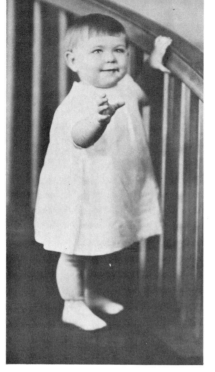

*"The women's
movement is a
means for a better
life for all. . .
together women
and men can create
a more humane
world."*
—SR. JOEL READ

*Above:
Janice Read, one
year and one day old
Right:
Mother and Janice,
1926.*

communication, problem solving, and other areas important for functioning in the contemporary world. A sophisticated assessment program assists students to become lifelong learners by developing their own self-evaluation skills.

Off-campus experiential learning helps students to test theory in practice and to continue learning in unstructured situations. New time frames, such as the popular Weekend College, provide flexible scheduling for women with jobs and family responsibilities. Support services, such as babysitting and career counseling, are available. A research center sponsors programs and works to document and clarify changes in women's lives. It maintains collections of books, magazines, and articles, and is one of the few such centers in the Midwest.

Sister Joel Read is the descendant of Irish immigrants who settled in Chicago. Into this community, Joseph Read, one generation out of Ireland, was welcomed when he came in 1910 from Canton, Ohio, to work as an accountant in the steel works of south Chicago. He married Ellen Sweeney, daughter of retired downstate landowners.

Prior to her mother's death in her early teen years, Sister Joel says,

"My mother and my father educated my sister and me to believe that we could do anything we wanted to do, we could be anything we wanted to be, provided we got the education for it and made the effort. I had little sense that women were excluded from any profession.

"But in my high school Latin class, when we were translating Caesar's Gallic Wars, *I was struck by the word* impedimenta. *It stood not only for 'baggage,' but also translated into 'old men, women and children,' or anything that impeded the males.*

"About that time, I was thinking about college and considered majoring in theology. When I asked our parish priest where I could go to study theology, I was greeted with uproarious laughter. Women didn't study or major in theology in those days. That, plus many other experiences, began to show me there was a difference between what my parents assumed to be possible for women, and what others thought. All were early pointers to feminism."

Shortly after graduating from Loretto Academy, Sister Joel entered the convent of the School Sisters of St. Francis, Layton Boulevard, Milwaukee. She had been impressed by the Sisters as they worked in her home parish. She believed that within the framework of a diversified order, there would be room to develop her talents and to lead a celibate life in a social, caring setting. The combination of a home background of early responsibility because of her mother's illness and death and the perspective gained through wide reading and travel made the serious commitment logical.

She earned her BS in Education at Alverno and her masters in history at Fordham University. Then she returned to Alverno as instructor in history, later to become chairperson of the History Department and eventually president of the college.

"One cannot study history without coming to some insights into the efforts that were made in this country in the 19th century to upgrade the role of women. Women's colleges in this country find their origin in the early 19th century. The colleges of the later 19th century—the famous Seven Sisters—were organized to show that women could be educated on the same basis as men. Finally, with the westward movement came the development by Catholics of women's colleges throughout the midwest, like Alverno, which began in 1887."

President of Alverno College, Sr. Joel Read, in action.

As a historian, Sister Joel considers NOW a major effort to continue the work on behalf of women that goes back to pre-Civil War days. "The movement was dormant for a time, but was renewed by NOW in the 1960's." Sister Joel has served on NOW'S Board of Directors, on the United States Commission for the Observance of International Woman's Year and on the Governor's Commission on the Status of Women.

"In these critically difficult times for women, colleges like Alverno have a crucial role. Women's work is extraordinarily important to society. The better women carry out their traditional functions, the better off society is. But women's work must be connected with the larger world of decision-making and women must be enabled to participate in the work world as they choose."

(See Selected Honors, Accomplishments, Publications, page 312)

written by BARB ZELLMER

audrey jane dernbach

Audrey Jane Dernbach is a remarkable woman who doesn't think she's remarkable. She is the recipient of numerous awards for her achievements in public education for the early detection of amblyopia (lazy eye).

Lazy eye is a defect in which the muscles in one eye are not as strong as those in the other. In the preschool years when a child's vision is still developing, the child with a lazy eye gets a blurred image from one eye and unconsciously turns off or disregards the weaker eye, increasingly

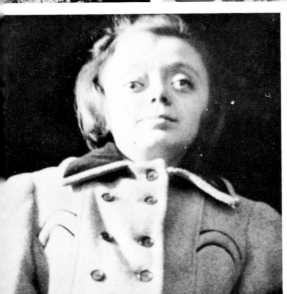

Her interest and determination resulted in the development of a program to detect Amblyopia (Lazy Eye) in children at an early age.

depending on the stronger one. As a result, the lazy eye progressively weakens, its vision decreases, and blindness in this eye usually ensues.

According to Dernbach, "Ignorance of so serious a problem as amblyopia has kept this sneak thief in operation too long. I was graduated from the Columbia School of Nursing in Milwaukee in 1947. Either I slept through that class or it was not mentioned. I found that nurses graduating as late as 1972 had never heard of amblyopia. But who can look into the child's brain and see that he or she is seeing a blurred picture? Every parent thinks and knows that his child is perfect."

Dernbach and her husband Robert discovered their oldest son was not perfect. When his lazy eye was diagnosed, it was treated by patching. Dernbach explains: "Patching is a very difficult time for the afflicted person. With a patch on the good eye and the lazy eye not working, the child is temporarily blind, Gradually, the lazy eye starts to work. The child will try every trick to remove the patch, so often the mother's patience is tried to the limit. When our child's eye was patched, he

Left (clockwise beginning at upper left):
Audrey at 11 in Nekoosa with long curls she wore until she was 17 and 5'7" tall. ("I learned all about being teased.");
High school graduate, 1944 in Wisconsin Rapids, curls cut;
Teaching Health Class at Altoona. "I have always had a parttime nursing or teaching job to help with Lazy Eye expenses."
Audrey reading "Charlie" to James Root and Laura Jones;
Delores Schmidt, Audrey's blind friend who suffered a lot and was the most beautiful person she has known.
Right (above): Sons and husband, John who is "Charlie," husband Robert, Paul and Bob Jason;
(Below) "Charlie" of booklet fame.

He covered Charlie's good eye with
A little patch of black
To force his "lazy eye" to work
And bring its vision back.

It seemed in just a little while
That Charlie's eye was straight.
He wore the patch for several months
And patiently did wait.

Some kids wore glasses with their patch,
And never once did cry.
Some kids had operations to
Correct their "lazy eye".

But Charlie was a lucky boy.
His parents sure were right
To get him to the eye doctor
In time to save his sight.

would cry so much that the patch often had to be changed seven times a day. It was an insane time. After six months of patching, our son had to wear the patch for a few weeks every year, until he was eleven.'' John's vision improved to 20/35 in his right eye, from 20/200 when his problem was discovered.

Because her son had been spared blindness in the lazy eye by early detection, Dernbach became concerned about the children whose plight would not be discovered in time. She asked John Bacharach, Director of the Eau Claire City-County Health Department what his department was doing to find children with lazy eye in time for correction. His negative response prompted her to urge him to do something.

After months of discussion and preparation, Bacharach, Dernbach and Anabel Airis, a registered nurse volunteer, started a central screening program for preschoolers in 1960, continuing through 1965. Only ten percent of the three and four-year-olds in the community were brought in for screening. Bacharach decided that parents, when given a simple enough method, could screen their children in the privacy of their homes.

The Eau Claire Home Screening Eye Kit for preschool children was developed in 1966. The kit consisted of an introductory letter from Bacharach, an instruction sheet, a card with a large Snellen E and a small Snellen E, plus a stamped, self-addressed post card with a number corresponding to the child's name at the Health Department to be returned with the test results.

Dernbach says, ''I was very skeptical of the kit. I was its severest critic. But the records show that it is a success. Eye patches are a common sight in this community. Parents, children, old and young citizens, all working together have developed an almost sure method of finding every lazy eye.''

On the basis of the kit and previous community

Far left:
The many-talented, hard-working Lois Walker Cameron —"Lou"—who rhymed the "Charlie" book, set up Lazy Eye, Ltd.
Near left:
Audrey working in the upstairs office of Lazy Eye, Ltd.

effort, Bacharach received an $8,000 Neurological and Sensory Disease Project Grant from the Public Health Service for a two-year study to determine the frequency of all eye problems in preschool children and to find out whether parents could accurately screen their children. Dernbach became the volunteer project nurse.

The first year, Dernbach rechecked every child whose parents used the kit and returned the post card. Parents did a good job, but not all responded. The second year, she checked every third child to whom the kit had been sent. She learned that the kit was put aside when parents did not understand or when the child did not cooperate. More eye problems were found.

Changes were made. The kit was sent to all four-year-olds. If the post card was not returned within two or three weeks. Dernbach telephoned the parents. If parents needed help, Dernbach checked their children.

Results of the two-year study were sent to *Public Health Reports,* and printed in the May, 1970 issue. Requests for reprints and additional information poured in from all over the world. Seventy-two foreign countries and almost every major medical school in the United States responded.

At the end of the original two-year study, Dernbach compiled a list of problems needing further explanation. She put them into a simple story aimed at the busy parent reading to a child. She felt that a child's book about lazy eye would be a simple way to provide information about this blinding condition and the need for detection through home screening. The illustrator, Bill Maki, created "Charlie," named and patterned after Dernbach's son, John Charles, now an attorney in Pennsylvania. Dernbach's friend, Lou Cameron, an Eau Claire registered nurse, rhymed the text.

In 1972, Dernbach and Cameron formed Lazy Eyes, Ltd. of Eau Claire County, a nonprofit organization, funded by unsolicited contributions and memorials, to promote the eye kit and the book, *Charlie's Lazy Eye.* They distributed information, handled mail requests for kits and books outside Eau Claire County, and eased the financial burden of the Health Department. They helped other communities start programs in their areas by making materials available at minimal cost.

By 1972, with the home screening program running smoothly, Dernbach and Cameron turned their attention to Lazy Eye, Ltd., and became full-time volunteers, using every opportunity to publicize the program.

While growing up in Nekoosa, Wisconsin, Dernbach had a teenage friend who was blind. She credits her friend as being her inspiration. "I hated the blindness. I'd think, 'God, I can open my eyes and she can't.' " Dolores could not attend school but Dernbach claims Dolores knew more than she did. She had an "innate, uncanny, sense of right and wrong. She was pure, not painted with prejudice." Dolores had been in constant pain since the age of five when a brain tumor was removed. She died at 20 of cancer. Says Dernbach, "I owe her memory."

(See Selected Honors, Accomplishments, Publications, page 308)

written by *IRIS GRUNDAHL*

gene boyer

A total commitment to women's liberation is evident in all of Gene Boyer's activities. She is a co-founder of the National Organization for Women and she is chairman of the Wisconsin Women's Network, which she helped found in 1979 when Governor Lee Dreyfus abolished the Governor's Commission on the Status of Women. This network provides a communications link to coordinate activities of organizations and individuals concerned with women's issues.

A Milwaukee native, Boyer credits her parents, Nat and Rene Cohen, for many of her present beliefs. Although the female members on both sides of her family were strong, independent role models, her father was largely responsible for her non-sexist upbringing, and he encouraged her to think of a career at a time when this was unusual for girls. At an early age, Gene realized there was something amiss in society, and it was difficult for her to understand why the attitudes with which she was familiar at home were not apparent in the real world.

Boyer's father owned men's haberdashery stores in Milwaukee. At the age of 10, she began working for him at 10 cents an hour, literally starting at the bottom, taking inventory in the basement.

When Boyer entered the University of

Above: Gene Boyer; Left: Gene (seated right) among four women influential in building the women's movement in this country, Catherine Conroy, Kathryn Clarenbach and Mary Jean Collins.

Wisconsin-Madison she hoped to pursue a career in architecture or law, but when informed that women weren't welcome in these fields, she changed to journalism and art. It was her first taste of sex discrimination.

After college, she married Burt Boyer, a professional baseball player in the New York Yankees' farm system. They have one daughter. The Boyers eventually moved to Beaver Dam where they own a furniture store.

For many years, Gene focused on the business world. She was the first woman to serve on the Board of the Wisconsin Retail Furniture Association, is a member of the National Association of Women Business Owners and other retail associations, and has held offices in professional organizations.

In 1962 she took on what she calls her first "activist thing". She founded a women's division of the Beaver Dam Chamber of Commerce. "There was no other way of making visible the presence of business women in the community," she states.

As a result Gene Boyer was invited to Madison for a conference on the changing roles of women. The keynote address by Kathryn Clarenbach was a revelation to Gene, as it so accurately paraphrased her feelings about women's rights. She had always felt very alone in her convictions. Most early feminists were beginning to discover each other, and in the 1960's the movement began to come together.

In 1966 Boyer attended a US Women's Bureau National Conference on the Status of Women held in Washington, DC. Inactivity of the government-appointed Equal Employment Opportunity Commission in the area of women's rights incensed a nucleus of concerned women. Gene was one of

On August 26, 1970, the first Woman's Equality Day, Gene staged a one-woman demonstration on the sidewalk in front of their furniture store in Beaver Dam, distributing NOW literature and discussing feminist philosophy with passersby.
"It must have started a mini-revolution, because today we have many women active and visible in city government and the power structure of our community," says Gene.

those who then formed the National Organization for Women.

Until this time, Gene's achievement in business was her primary concern. In the winter of 1967, she underwent critical major surgery. For a time she felt she might not recover, and she developed an enormous sense of urgency in her work. She reversed her priorities—she became a part-time business woman and a full-time feminist. She was driven, working for the movement many days and nights for 16 to 18 hours.

Her husband has always been supportive. She has often been away from home for many days at a time, attending and chairing meetings and making innumerable speeches. She plans to remain active in the 1980's, promoting current issues, such as pay equity and marital property reform.

Like most activists, she has experienced ridicule and hostility. One day a lady on the street beside her at a stop light said in a concerned voice, "I surely hope that no one sees me talking to you and tells my husband, as he will be very upset with me."

Fifteen years ago she gave a speech on the women's movement to a men's service club in Beaver Dam. The members sat with glazed eyes and seemed disinterested. Not long ago the same organization asked her to speak again. She decided to present the same speech, polished and updated. One of the men who attended both meetings came up to her and questioned "Why haven't you ever told us all this before?"

She sums up her feelings about the changes in which she has been involved, "The world is catching up. The kinds of things I realized needed to be done 20 years ago are starting to get done. I hope I live long enough to see more of these things come to fruition. I'm not a throwback; I'm a throwahead, I was born into a world that was alien and uncomfortable. It's just now starting to get comfortable."

To a more comfortable world for all women, Gene Boyer has been a major contributor.

(See Selected Honors, Accomplishments, Publications, page 306)

Her business career began at 10 years of age in Milwaukee where she took inventory in her father's menswear store at 10¢ an hour.

She is the author of such public publications as "Are Women Equal Under the Law?" and and articles on the ERA, Women and CEPA and Women and Power.

written by KATHLEEN WINKLER

Mary Linsmeier with her preschoolers.

mary linsmeier

"I guess I'm addicted to teaching! There were teachers in my mother's generation, in her family before her, there are teachers in my generation, and now they are starting in the generation after me—my life is filled with teaching."

That's how Mary Linsmeier, founder and co-

She is founder and co-director of 31 preschools throughout Wisconsin.

director of 31 preschools throughout the state of Wisconsin, describes her interest in the world of education.

"By age 13 I was teaching piano to children and adults in the neighborhood, and in a few months I had 35 students. Now, I know I wasn't a very good teacher at that time in my life, but it trained me to be interested in education. It gave me a frame of reference that is different from the typical teacher —I tried to figure out how to teach each of those students individually, instead of giving the same lesson to all of them. Some of my adult students would ask me, 'Why did you teach this or that a certain way?' Because I had no formal training in education, I didn't have an answer for them, but it made me think a lot. It raised a lot of questions in my mind as to why people teach the way they do."

Education was so much a part of Mary that it was inevitable she would go to college and get a degree that would enable her to teach. With a bachelor's degree in Spanish from Marquette University, she began teaching Spanish in a Rochester, Minnesota high school.

How to get through to high school kids, a group that is very hard to reach, became a challenge. "I kept thinking," she remembers, "why are kids so turned off to learning? Why is there so often a constant battle between the teacher and the kids? After all, children should like to learn. We all *like* to learn but not necessarily in the classroom. It seemed to be because they couldn't see the value of what was going on there.

"So I moved to Milwaukee and took a job teaching third grade in a Catholic school. I thought it would help to get them earlier, before they were so turned off, but I found they were already turned off! That year seemed to be the turning

Mary Linsmeier

point at which they were no longer receptive to learning, but were trying to figure out how to get out of doing what they were assigned to do."

The next year Mary married Frank Linsmeier. "I kept thinking, what am I going to do for my own children? How am I going to develop attitudes in them that will make them see learning as a worthwhile lifetime project?"

By the time she had a couple of preschoolers of her own, out of a family that would eventually number eight, Mary began to hold preschool classes in her basement several mornings a week for her own children and those in the neighborhood.

"I was doing it just for fun," she says, "but then the *Milwaukee Journal* called and asked if I'd be interviewed about what I was doing for my family.

I said 'no', but that same night the *Journal* ran a story about a woman with a large family who said that all she had time to do was to keep their shoes tied, and she couldn't wait for them to go to first grade so the teachers could start teaching them. I was so incensed, I called the *Journal* back and said, 'In defense of mothers with large families, I will do the interview.'

"And that's where it started. As soon as the article appeared, the phone started ringing. And it never stopped for three months. In those days of the early sixties there were plenty of nursery schools around, but they were typical preschools where you put a bunch of kids together, watch them play and make sure they don't hurt each other, and that's about it. But I was very non-traditional in my thinking about educating preschoolers. That's what people were interested in. I finally had to hire a 'phone sitter' to answer the telephone so I could take care of my family and teach my classes! I started running meetings on Sunday afternoons for people interested in preschool education. People came from as far away as Chicago, and many of them were teachers.

"Meanwhile, the class in my basement kept growing, and eventually I got my masters degree in educational psychology from the University of Wisconsin-Milwaukee. By the next fall we'd outgrown the basement completely and opened our first school in Wauwatosa. Later that year we had a request to open a southside location, and so many people came to the informational meeting that I had to stand on a table to talk to the people who packed the room. The second, third and fourth schools opened rapidly. From that beginning we grew steadily until in 1980-81 we have 31 schools, 150 teachers and over 1,000 children. After the eighth school opened my husband Frank quit his job and became our full-time business manager. I'm sure that is a big part of the reason for our schools' success, the quality of his business management. That also leaves me free to do my part of the job—supervision of schools, teacher training and developing ongoing curriculum—a job that will never be done!"

What makes a Mary Linsmeier school different from a typical preschool? She says, "The Linsmeier method is a specially developed, individualized educational program. We stress developing the individual's self-concept. And we feel that you can't build a self-concept without also building skills. So we build skills both in areas of the child's interests and in basic areas like math and reading and practical skills that include care of himself and the environment.

"I also believe that you can expect a child to comply with the rules of society from little on. We have basic rules in our classrooms and the child is expected to obey them. I don't think that inhibits children; I think that gives them security. Discipline makes a child feel free."

What about the future? Mary says, "Someone once approached me and said, 'Come with me and we'll open schools all around the United States and you'll be a millionaire.' But I knew I couldn't live with myself wondering what was going on in this school and in that school. I'd like to expand, but I don't ever want us to grow so fast that I can't be sure we have competent people offering quality education. I don't want to be in the business of 'Kentucky fried kids.' I don't want to ever get so big that the quality we offer gets lost. There are more important things than being a millionaire!"

(See Selected Honors, Accomplishments, Publications, page 311)

lorna balian

Lorna Balian is an award-winning author and illustrator of 11 children's books to date. Her stories lead wonderfully imaginative characters—like the Humbug Witch, a tiny sprite with an enormous papier-mache head, like the "aminal" and the giant baby girl, not to mention the Easter Bunny and Santa Claus—through all sorts of adventures.

The Sweet Touch came out of a gumball machine. Lorna's daughter came into the kitchen one day with her eyebrows shaved off. When asked what she had done, she said, "I put a penny in a gumball machine and got a ring, and I rubbed it and a magic genie named Ralph appeared. And he's the one who shaved off my eyebrows." Lorna created a gumball machine genie who granted only single wishes.

Lorna Juanita Kohl was born on December 14, 1929, in Milwaukee, Wisconsin. Her father, Henry W. Kohl, was of German descent and her mother,

Writer/illustrator Lorna Balian is inspired by things her six children have said and done, by memories from her own childhood.

Molly Pope Kohl, had Swedish and Danish ancestors.

Her mother died when she was only three and her sister Mary was two years old. Great Aunt Marea Oleson Pope Jackson, whom she called Nana, helped raise Lorna and Mary. "She was just a fantastic person, a super, loving, caring woman. She kept telling us how wonderful we were. And one of the nicest things about her—she was at an age when she really couldn't keep up with us—was that we were free to run most of the time, a very undisciplined childhood."

The family home was near the old Washington Park Zoo, Milwaukee, a favorite place. Her father, who worked for the telephone company, had grown up on a homestead farm near Readfield, Wisconsin. When his parents died, he was the only son of nine who could afford to buy his brothers' shares of the homstead. One of his brothers operated the farm for him and on weekends and during the summer, Kohl would pack up his two daughters and Nana and head for the farm.

With 365 acres of farmland to roam and explore, Lorna "just showed up for meals and band-aids." She loved to wander through the woods and search the cliff and swamp for treasures. There were plenty of farm animals to enjoy—chickens, pigs, even peacocks.

The broom would not move an inch.

Left to right:
"Country Stream" needlecraft design;
Lorna pauses at her drawing table; "Humbug Witch;"
"Wildflower Party Skirt;" and the Balian home,
a converted schoolhouse, Hartford.

On rainy days, she did a lot of reading. She liked to draw and spent many hours sketching anything that captured her fancy. The *Milwaukee Journal's* Green Sheet helped her learn to read before she started school.

Her teen years were not happy ones. When she was 11 years old her father remarried. Raised on "wicked stepmother stories" Lorna and Mary did not accept their new mother. "She really is a marvelous person and we are very close today," Lorna says now. A year after the marriage Great Aunt Marea died.

Above: John and Lorna on a coffee break at home; Right: Lorna, working on drawings for her next book.

In spite of such emotional drains, during her senior year, Lorna drew cartoons of the students and athletes for the yearbook. She also designed costumes for the high school plays.

Kohl urged his daughter to become a nurse. Only after much persuasion did he agree that she could attend the Layton Art School for one year, starting the fall of 1948. The next summer Lorna enjoyed her job as an artist for the American Lace Paper Company in Milwaukee so much she continued working and did not return to school.

In March, 1950, Lorna Kohl married fellow art student, John J. Balian. The couple moved to Hartford, where they purchased an abandoned one-room red brick schoolhouse and remodeled it.

The next several years were their "feast or famine" period as freelance artists. When their third child was born, John took a job to provide a steady income. The Balians now have six children; the last child left the nest in 1980.

As they were growing the library became a favorite place. After reading thousands of books to her children, Lorna began to feel she could write better stories. The librarian suggested she try revising and illustrating the old story, "Six Blind Men and the Elephant." She did and it was published as "The Elephant?"

"I have an instinct to write simply. But I do have some big words. I think children should encounter words they don't know or they'll never learn. But you can't have so many it discourages." To create the marvelous details and colorful pages in her books Lorna spends 2,000 or more hours illustrating each book.

Several years ago two of her stitchery designs received awards in *Family Circle* magazine's stitchery contest. Her work caught the eye of one of the judges who worked for Bucilla and he asked her to design stitchery kits for his company. Each year since Lorna has designed two or three embroidery or crewel kits.

Lorna travels to four or five states each year giving talks to children and adult groups, discussing her experiences in writing and illustrating children's books. She often appears on local television shows. She has the ability to make the adult remember how it was to be a child and children to laugh out loud.

In Lorna, young and old readers feel they have a really special friend.

(See Selected Honors, Accomplishments, Publications, page 305)

"Surprise comes naturally to Lorna and she projects ideas in a warm and unaffected manner."
—JOHN BALIAN

written by PATRICIA SMITH WILMETH & ALICE SEDGWICK

roberta boorse

One magical evening in 1944, a 13-year-old girl watched spellbound as Danilova, Markova, Youskevitch and the dance company of the Ballet Russe de Monte Carlo moved across the stage of the old Pabst Theater in Milwaukee. Young Roberta Rehberg had been taking dancing lessons since she was four and had begun formal ballet training at the Bonnie Larson School of Dance just the year before. This however was the first professional ballet performance she had ever seen. The memory of that evening still lights her eyes.

Roberta Rehberg Boorse went on to become dancer and teacher of dance, founder of the

She founded and organized The Milwaukee Ballet Company whose unanimous critical acclaim has created a tremendous surge of interest and enthusiasm for ballet.

Roberta Marie Rehberg Boorse
and The Milwaukee Ballet Company.

Milwaukee Ballet Company, its managing director, fund raiser and board president. At the height of the Milwaukee Ballet's success, philosophical differences between Roberta, Jean Paul Comelin, her hand-picked artistic director, and the new board president became irreconcilable. Comelin's and Roberta's association with the Milwaukee Ballet came to an end.

"I was committed to doing what I felt destined to do."

Roberta grew up in the shadow of the Depression. She was in high school as World War II broke out, was waged and won. Her late teens were spent as America began an era of growth, prosperity and opportunity.

Born to a mother who had always wanted to study dance, Roberta Boorse fulfilled her mother's dream. Her after-school life was devoted to dance—performing in civic concerts and recitals, high school musicals, variety shows and plays. When she was 16, she was engaged as a summer dancer by Barnes and Carothers, a national touring company that produced grandstand shows for state and county fairs throughout the country. She danced with them for three years.

Eager to begin serious professional training, following graduation from West Division High School, she enrolled in the Stone-Camryn School of Ballet in Chicago. To pay for her training and to survive, she began a series of jobs that would later prove useful to her in her years of managing her own school of dance and the Milwaukee Ballet Company.

She studied daily and performed whenever possible. Meanwhile, she worked in a hospital, in a factory, as a waitress, as a receptionist, as a secretary. She had to change jobs in order to fit them in with her class and performance schedules.

And then a professional fund-raising job with United Productions opened up. She had to withdraw from ballet school and from dancing to accept the position. She did, and devoted a year to this company, during which she moved from city to city, staged and directed benefit shows, organized ticket drives and solicited program advertising and contributions to raise funds for non-profit organizations. By the end of the year she had saved enough to return to school.

However, there was a new obstacle. When she returned to working and studying ballet, the pace she set to get back into shape proved too strenuous. In poor health and physically exhausted, she returned home to Milwaukee, to regain her strength. While recovering, she began to teach dance for the city and suburban recreation departments and as a volunteer at a school for the deaf.

"Milwaukee's dance scene was as barren as a desert," she recalls. "Major ballet companies bypassed Milwaukee on tour, and there was little opportunity to study or see professional ballet."

When Roberta Rehberg was 20, she opened her own school, The Roberta Rehberg Academy of Dance Art in West Allis. Devoting herself to teaching and promoting the art of dance in the community, she put the enthusiasm and energy, the discipline into the academy that she had committed to her earlier dance training and work as a dancer. The academy enrollment grew to 250 students. In addition to the annual recitals, she presented over 200 lecture demonstrations and special dance concerts in schools, hospitals, nursing homes, libraries and public parks. A part of the community was being educated, readied.

In 1955, Roberta Rehberg married gregarious, outgoing Donald Boorse, president of Equipment

"Everything I did eventually served to help me in my professional career and with the ballet company."
— ROBERTA BOORSE

257

Lease Corporation, licensed pilot and instructor and champion midget auto racer. They have four children. When she talks about family, Roberta has an easy sunny laugh; her dark eyes flash with pride. From the first, Roberta's husband backed her career and the pursuit of her dream.

By the mid '60's, the various worlds of ballet began to come together in Milwaukee. Roberta Boorse's Academy of Dance Art was a success. Students' achievements were being widely recognized. The University of Wisconsin-Milwaukee School of Fine Arts started its dance department. Lupe Serrano, prima ballerina of The American Ballet Theatre, was living in Milwaukee with her husband, Kenneth Schermerhorn. The Performing Arts Center was being built and the major performing groups of the city had joined together to form the United Performing Arts Fund. Adolph A. Suppan, Dean of the School of Fine Art, was interested in ballet. Jury Gotshalks, former leading dancer of the National Ballet of Canada and Myron Nadel, chairman of the UWM Department of Dance, had the necessary background, artistic talent and skills that a professional ballet company required.

This timely set of circumstances stirred Roberta Boorse into action. Judging that the time was right for dance to take its place among the other major performing arts represented in the community, she used her Academy of Dance Art's annual recital as the symbolic turning point. "I pledged to turn over the proceeds of the recital to the United Performing Arts Fund to be held in escrow for the purpose of establishing a resident ballet company."

The $800 the recital raised was turned over to the UPAF. Boorse approached Dean Suppan, Gotshalks and Nadel with the idea of forming a ballet company within the University. The Milwaukee Ballet was incorporated in association with the UWM School of Fine Arts in January, 1970.

There were no funds for an office or administrative staff. Except for the artistic director and dancers, everyone was a volunteer. Mrs. Boorse became president and manager.

In 1974, the UPAF included the Milwaukee Ballet as its eighth member. Mrs. Boorse hired Jean Paul Comelin as artistic director. The company's growth consumed more and more of her time. That year she closed her school. "I couldn't do both, and I was obliged to devote full time to the Milwaukee Ballet." She served as the board's president for five and a half years and managed the company for eight years.

These years 1975-1980 were the golden era. The company had a 30-week season performing "Swan Lake," "Coppelia," the annual Christmas "Nutcracker," new ballets like "Florestan." The company toured the United States with triumph following triumph. The original $800 had grown to a budget of $1.1 million. And behind the success were long hours of hard work. "It was a labor of love. . .there were always obstacles; one solution to a problem seemed often to open the way to another problem." In 1980 this era ended.

Can an end be a beginning? Her dream has been realized—the Milwaukee Ballet is established, accepted, renowned. And what about Roberta Boorse? Tall, willowy, dark with a dancer's easy grace of movement, she says, "Dance will always be a part of my life."

(See Selected Honors, Accomplishments, Publications, page 306)

written by ELAINE EDWARDS

carol hough merrick

Wearing black tights and sometimes sitting in a position she uses as a teacher of yoga and meditation, Carol Merrick talked about the life experiences that meant most to her—completing the miracle of birth six times and enjoying a wonderful relationship with her husband of 31 years.

"I do feel a fierce sense of pride in my children but I honestly don't think I have lived vicariously, through them," she says. "Now, with one at home, I can truly enjoy having given the best to my children and being free."

Earlier in her life, Carol was influenced by her father, who believed in her and with whom she was very close, and her mother, who had a lively sense of humor. As a teenager, Carol read the biographies of Elizabeth Cady Stanton and Eleanor Roosevelt and was awestruck. The stories of their lives inspired her to stand up for her beliefs. The name Eleanor Roosevelt still evokes strong feelings.

"I heard her speak at Indiana University when I was 16," Mrs. Merrick recalls. "My father was an ardent Republican, so I went in with an opposite bias. She came to talk about the United Nations and about the poor and health problems. She really cared. I went out and read a book about her and those issues, and I became a Democrat."

Carol "dropped in" to college for two semesters and then "dropped out" for 23 years. She married Dr. John Merrick, a veterinarian, reared her children and helped her husband as a laboratory technician, surgical nurse, and receptionist, all skills learned on the job.

As a young married woman with energy left over after taking care of children, home, and animal

Carol Merrick (photo by Tom Anger);
Right: In sari at Ashram in Val Morin, Canada;
Far right: Speaking at Wisconsin Women's Network meeting.

She launched her own battle to help the displaced homemaker and the battered woman and to create a local woman's network.

259

clinic duties, she pursued interests that directed her toward her current line of work. Yoga was one of them.

"I really got to know myself as an adult at Ashram, a monastery in Val Morin, Canada. I was 1100 miles away from home and children, then aged nine to nineteen," she says. She decided to go back to school, get a degree, and help other women.

"What I gained was self-knowledge and self-acceptance. I wanted to give support to other women, so they, too, could survive. I knew the name of the game was credentials, credit, and knowledge." So she earned a bachelor's degree and later a master's in guidance and counseling-vocational sequence. Along the way she also picked up a master's in coaching certification and now teaches a physical education course in yoga at UW-Parkside.

Mrs. Merrick speaks of "dharma" (truth) as most important to her philosophy. In helping people sort out their values in counseling, she has come to appreciate openness and honesty more. She takes the perspective that there is "no me, no you, just

written by ANNE ERNST

oneness . . . things aren't good or bad, they just are." She works toward being non-judgmental.

"I feel responsible for finding my own way to enlightenment," she says. "I take responsibility for myself and others. I don't want to set conditions for loving them. I hope to achieve unconditional, positive regard for others."

Carol describes herself as a "very tough" vocational counselor. She believes in the ability of people to change because she has changed. "I've done what I had to do," she says, "and now I can say to people, 'you've got to believe in yourself'."

Mrs. Merrick has worked with battered women whose self-esteem was low, but who, with direction and a good support group, have made changes in their lives. She founded the Kenosha Women's Network, and was the co-founder of Women's Horizons, a shelter for battered women. She trained as a facilitator and ran the first displaced homemaker support group in Kenosha.

Self-admittedly competitive, Carol believes she is mellowing. "I love to win. I was always that way. I was always first in school foot races until they kicked me out—they were only for boys. I won all my piano contests. The teacher and other students assumed I would win. I was first in ping pong in high school and John and I were first in the Midwest in mixed doubles. I swam anchor on the Indiana University team. I won a letter playing varsity tennis at age 40 at Parkside. But I never felt upset if I lost if I felt I had done my best. Competition made me work harder."

(See Selected Honors, Accomplishments, Publications, page 313)

audrey sickinger

Audrey O'Connell Sickinger was born July 19, 1934 in Manitowoc County, the older of two daughters. Growing up on the family farm near Grimms, she did her share of chores and tractor driving. Her father was her inspiration and encouraged her interest in farming. After graduating from Valders High School, Audrey

attended Milwaukee Business Institute. She married Jerome Sickinger three months after graduation.

She combined her herd of 11 registered Holsteins with her husband's and the young couple began to farm, renting until they were able to purchase their own 200-acre farm. After many long, hardworking hours, it has grown to 2,750 acres and 135 dairy cows.

Active in many farm and community organizations, the Sickingers began to realize that no matter how hard Audrey worked, she was not receiving credit for her talents under existing laws.

In 1974, Audrey purchased 200 acres as a sole proprietor and began farming on her own. She has overcome the many problems encountered by a woman operating a business and especially a farm business where the word "farmer" has designated a male. Under her management the operation grew

to 750 acres and 135 head of cattle.

Audrey enjoys farming, and has instilled this love in her seven children, who are either working on the family farm or in ag-related jobs. She is extremely active in community organizations. She is involved in lobbying for legislation affecting agriculture. She encourages family activities and was an active delegate to the Governor's Conference on Families in 1980.

Past president and vice president of the Christian

In 1980, she attended a consultation with Rural American Women at the invitation of the White House, and participated in the farm women's seminar on "Government Decision-making."

Left to right: Audrey Sickinger
(photo by Welnetz Studio)
Audrey addressing group after having been awarded the title of Farm Wife of the Year (1980) by the Colby Chamber of Commerce.
(photo by Florence Rachwal)

Mothers Society of St. Michael's parish, Whitelaw, Audrey believes faith is important in the life of the family. "If it's not the center of your life, it's hard going. You have nothing to base your relationships on. And a farmer uses all the tools of technology to produce food but realizes a great respect for his Creator because he is so closely involved with growing and living things."

Audrey is convinced that young persons wishing to start farming can still do it with a lot of hard work and determination. "If you realize that the average age of a farmer today is 53, the opportunity to farm is there."

Her concern for agriculture led her to promoting attitude changes toward farming. "We're trying to take away the image of the 'dumb farmer'. We are trying to impress upon people that food is important and that the farmer is an elite 3% of the population. The American farmer must be a professional person—he has to be knowledgeable in marketing strategies. Even with modern technology, farming is hard work. It takes a special dedication as well as experience to be a successful farmer."

Audrey is an able spokeswoman for agriculture. She is currently serving in her second term as president of Wisconsin Women for Agriculture and is secretary of American Agri-Women, a national coalition of farm women's organizations. She was present when it was formed and has always been an active member. She has testified in Madison and in Washington, DC, and spoken before many civic and business groups. She is convinced that "at no other time has American agriculture reached so far and touched the lives of so many people as it does today."

(See Selected Honors, Accomplishments, Publications, page 313)

written by MARION BATES

shirley abrahamson

A conference session of the seven Wisconsin Supreme Court justices has just concluded. One is ushered into a quiet, pleasant office by a serenely gracious woman with a captivating smile and expressive eyes. On a corner of her desk is a collection of small seashells, momentoes of hours shared with her husband and son.

The conversation is of law and jurisprudence. A gentle voice warms to the subject. Justice Abrahamson's love for law is of long duration. At age six, her goal and course were set. She would be a lawyer. There was no particular event or incident that prompted this choice, nor was it her earliest ambition. Her first aspiration was to be President of the United States. This was a youngster to be reckoned with.

Justice Abrahamson's parents were strongly supportive of their daughter's aims. She grew up with the precept that "I could be anything I wished to become." Her parents, who had emigrated to the United States from eastern Europe, owned a neighborhood grocery store on the west side of Manhattan. The desirability of a formal education and the responsibility to support oneself and children were instilled.

Shirley Abrahamson proved a fine scholar. She was educated in one of New York City's high schools for the gifted and talented and subsequently was graduated near the top of her class from New York University.

Shortly after graduation, she married a zoology student, who pursued graduate study at the University of Indiana, where she enrolled in law school and finished at the top of her class. This was the year 1956. Her husband accepted a

She is the first woman justice to be appointed to the Wisconsin Supreme Court.

Justice Shirley S. Abrahamson

position at the University of Wisconsin-Madison. A relieved Dean of the Indiana Law School informed her that he was glad that she was leaving the State of Indiana, as she probably would not be able to obtain a job with a law firm in Indiana. Of course, he assured her, there were good law librarian positions available.

The years that followed took the Abrahamsons to Madison, then to Rutgers University, Newark, New Jersey, and Columbia University, New York City, before returning to Madison in 1960. Her husband accepted a faculty position in genetics and zoology in 1961.

In 1962 Justice Abrahamson received a Doctor of Juridical Science degree from the University of Wisconsin Law School, after which she joined the Madison law firm then known as LaFollette, Sinykin, Doyle and Anderson, later to become LaFollette, Sinykin, Anderson and Abrahamson. After hours were spent with the Wisconsin Civil Liberties Union, helping draft an open housing ordinance for Madison, and working with the League of Women Voters and law students.

In 1966 Justice Abrahamson was appointed to the faculty of the University of Wisconsin Law School. Practice was combined with teaching tax law. The diversity of her professional contributions at the national, state, and local levels reflects the range of her abilities, which span tax, constitutional and insurance law, legal drafting, court structure and judicial organization and administration, criminal law, appellate practice, legal aid, legal education, legal educational opportunities for minority persons, education in the humanities, and the status of women.

While drafting the open housing ordinance, Shirley Abrahamson became acquainted with former Governor Patrick Lucey, then a Madison realtor who strongly supported the ordinance. He was impressed, and when in the summer of 1976 a vacancy occurred on the State Supreme Court, he offered her the position—the first woman to be named to the Court.

Elected to a full ten-year term in April, 1979, Justice Abrahamson receives high praise from her colleagues for her legal abilities. It is not surprising that her name was among the women suggested to President Reagan as qualified to be named to the United States Supreme Court to replace Justice Potter Stewart.

Justice Abrahamson foresees a future in which "there will be more women jurists since there are more women educated and trained in the law and prejudices and stereotypical attitudes are on the wane."

Her philosophy embraces a belief in the dignity of the individual and in the obligation of each individual to the community. "Our system of government rests on the concept that all persons are born equally free and independent and have certain inherent rights. But if the individual sins against the community, he or she should be punished. And the community must deal firmly and fairly with the individual according to the laws it has established."

The law is both Justice Abrahamson's profession and avocation. "Reading law and cases is my hobby," she assures one. There may be some midnight oil, but she loves it. This finely gifted woman, at ease with leadership, is an inspiration to all who strive to achieve their full potential.

(See Selected Honors, Accomplishments, Publications, page 305)

written by LOIS TATE KLIEFOTH

ada deer

One night as Ada Deer was walking home from the office in Washington, DC, two men suddenly jostled her. One ripped her purse off her shoulder and ran off. Ada immediately ran after them "screaming and yelling" as she tells it. A couple told her that the men had boarded a bus. Ada flagged down a squad car, climbed in and they followed the bus. The police stopped it and when a man jumped off, they followed him into an abandoned building and captured him with the help of a German shepherd. Ada's purse was found on the floor of the bus with the money missing but with credit cards and identification intact. When a Madison friend read the account in the paper, she commented, "Of course, that is what Ada would do. She's a fighter."

Ada Deer is a Menominee Indian. She is a social worker with a BA from UW-Madison and an MSW from Columbia in New York. At both universities,

Ada Deer in action working in the Office of Native American Programs.

Ada Deer

she was the first Menominee Indian to get a degree there. She is an advocate, a humanitarian—most of all, she is an activist. She makes things happen.

Ada Deer was born August 7, 1935, on the Menominee Indian Reservation in Wisconsin, the product of two cultures. Her father is a Menominee Indian and her mother, a white woman who had come to the reservation to work as a nurse. Ada is the oldest of five children and lived most of her first 18 years on the reservation in a cabin without electricity or running water. She says her mother inspired her to become involved in social causes.

She gained nationwide recognition for her role in the restoration of the Menominee Indians to reservation status. During this effort, the public, the press and some of the Menominees were not sympathetic, but she came through the chaotic period with her sense of humor and idealism intact.

Northeastern Wisconsin has always been home to the Menominee Indians. The 1850's brought a period during which several treaties were negotiated with the federal government. In return for ceding 9½ million acres of land, the Menominees agreed to accept the reservation as their homeland.

Then in 1954, the Termination Act was passed "to get the government out of Indian business." This meant the termination of federal supervision over tribal affairs. Thrust into an uncertain status, the Menominees voted to become a separate county, a cultural, economic and political disaster for the tribe. Without reservation status, their land base was endangered, members lost vital health and educational services. The county was soon in deep financial trouble. In effect the tribe was being destroyed.

As the years passed, the Menominee frustration and opposition to termination increased. Finally

Noted for her role in the restoration of the Menominee Indians to reservation status, she is an activist who works within the system.

267

in 1970, a grassroots organization called DRUMS (Determination of Rights and Unity for Menominee Shareholders) was founded.

As its spokesperson, Ada Deer spent the next two years in Washington, DC lobbying for return to reservation status for the Menominees. During this time she became friends with Comanche Indian activist LaDonna Harris, whose husband Fred is a former senator from Oklahoma. Senator and Mrs. Harris helped her make contacts in Washington and taught her how to operate as a lobbyist. Bills to restore the reservation were introduced in both Houses of Congress. With the hardworking support of the majority of the Menominee people, Ada Deer lobbied and the Menominee Restoration Act was signed into law by President Nixon on December 22, 1973. It repealed the termination policy and restored federal recognition and protection to the tribe.

Representative Lloyd Meeds, a Democrat from Washington State, told the *Washington Post,* "I don't know anyone who could have brought that bill so far so fast. Restoration was a dead issue before she began working on it."

But this was not the end. Then came the task of making the transition to reservation status. This became the work of the nine-member governing board called the Menominee Restoration Committee. Ada Deer was elected chairperson.

Frustrations were plentiful. Unrealistic expectations were held by some members of the tribe who called themselves the Menominee Warriors. Their frustrations finally culminated in the takeover of the abandoned Alexian Brothers' novitiate near Gresham. The warriors held the novitiate for a month demanding that the building be given to the Menominees for a hospital.

The episode was particularly painful for Ada who believes in working within the system. In the end, all the outsiders who had gathered around the Warriors went home leaving the Menominees to clean up the mess.

Finally late in 1976, the tribal rolls were validated with 5,292 persons to establish an electorate to vote on the constitution and bylaws. Soon after they were adopted, Ada Deer resigned. "We did more than we said we would do. It was time for independence and new leadership," she says. "Individuals must come and go, but the tribe continues. . ."

She moved to Madison and accepted a position on the University of Wisconsin faculty. She brought with her an undaunted enthusiasm for involvement. "Basically my continuing effort is being an advocate for Native American issues. . . and for women's issues, and a lot of other issues."

She has since studied under a fellowship at Harvard's Institute of Politics and worked as legislative liaison for the Native American Rights Fund in Washington, DC. She is also the first American Indian to run for statewide office in Wisconsin as Secretary of State. At the University she is currently instructor in the School of Social Work and manager of the Office of Native American Programs.

She loves her fast-paced life. She is one of those likeable persons whose enthusiastic optimism is contagious.

Ada has proved that one person *can* make a difference.

(See Selected Honors, Accomplishments, Publications, page 308)

She is president of Barnhill-Hayes, Inc., a management consulting firm
specializing in human resources management.

helen barnhill

"It is unusual for someone to get married at age 15, have seven children, continue going to school and college, to have a variety of jobs, and eventually wind up where I am today."

Today Helen I. Barnhill is the president of Barnhill-Hayes, Inc., a management consulting firm specializing in human resource management. Services available to clients include analysis and design of personnel systems and procedures, management skills training and development, and affirmative action/equal employment opportunity training and program development. The firm also provides career development counseling for interested individuals.

Helen Iphigenia Ponds was born in Ponce de Leon, Florida, the oldest child in a family of two girls and two boys. She came from a hard-working family. Her mother, a school teacher, lived away from home during the week. Her father got the children ready for school—preparing breakfast, combing and braiding the long hair—before he, too, left for work.

Her grandfather owned a general store in the area. Her grandmother "was a friend, and friends have always been important to me." Though she had only a fourth grade education she taught Helen to read at the age of four.

"One of my grandmother's sisters was my teacher in the one room school I attended. My educational background may be different from many southern black children, in that I had to do it right because it was my great aunt who was the teacher. I read *Heidi* from cover to cover when I was five years old. When I was a second grader I tutored eighth grade kids in reading."

She learned to cook when she was very young. Her father taught her to shoot a gun and work with animals on the farm. When she was about eight her grandfather taught her how to use an ax. He told her not to use her foot to hold the piece of wood. But since he always did, she thought she could too, and almost cut off her toe.

The family moved to Milwaukee when she was 10. Helen's first job was "at the dry cleaner. I was 14 and my dad did not want me to have a job. I bugged him so that he finally said, 'O.K., if you can go out, and tell the truth about your age, and find a job then you can have it'. He knew, and I didn't, that the laws would prevent me from working. But I knew there was some reason that my dad would say that to me. So I promptly went out, lied about my age, and got the job."

The mother of four girls and three boys, Helen has been divorced since the youngest child was about a year old. She is motivated by challenge. Rarely will she try to outdo someone else who may be doing the same thing. She is more likely to team up with that person and say, "If we're going to do the same thing let's really do it."

"In the company I want us to be the best

Left: Conference in office of Barnhill-Hayes, Inc., Helen, president, and Dr. Cynthia C. Stevens, vice-president;
Upper left: Mother Faustanna with brother James, sister Glendal and Helen; and father Willie Ponds holding baby Helen with Agnes Campbell, a major influence in Helen's childhood.

consulting firm in the area. I'm highly competitive, but not against individuals. I think competition is proper as long as it does not hurt someone. I don't have to put down someone else to get where I want to get."

Helen's counsel is frequently sought by women trying to get into the corporate structure, women seeking career changes, women returning to the work force, young women who are just graduating from college. "I tell them they are going to take all the fun out of life by planning it to the last detail. They must know themselves first. We women have been used to standing back and waiting until somebody else told us we were good at something before we stepped out to do it. You have to get a hold on who you are, what your skills are, and what your capabilities are.

"While many women object to being told that they have to emulate male models, I think it is important for us to understand what it was that helped men to be successful. Before we reject something we ought to understand what it is we are about to reject, and make sure that it doesn't have any value for us."

Helen talks often about responsibility to Blacks, to women, to other minorities. "When we know that we have a legitimate right to certain things that have made up the so-called good life, we also have to know that partaking of them demands a parallel responsibility. I tell them that the only thing that affirmative action can do is open the door. You will sink or swim on your own."

The freedom of being her own boss, the challenges of business, church and community commitments, and fulfilling these roles to her standards of performance are not the "fait accompli" of a detailed plan for her life.

"I still don't know what I'm going to do when I grow up. That's kind of my approach on life. A part of me says if it feels good, do it. That means that I'm willing to take on unusual challenges. I'm particularly willing to take them on if somebody thinks I can't do it."

(See Selected Honors, Accomplishments, Publications, page 305)

Clockwise (beginning from upper left): Helen's favorite current photo; Receiving honorary doctorate at Lakeland College — president Ralph Meiers, Helen, Catherine Cleary, Congressman William Steiger (courtesy, Kuehnel Farms); *Helen at work; Speaking at release of nationwide study on employer attitudes toward affirmative action.*

*"I've stared burnout
in the face, and
the only way to lick
it is to keep moving
and thinking of
creative ways to solve
your frustrations."*
—HELEN BARNHILL

margaret hawkins

"Natural talent is great, but you must believe that whatever you are doing is the most important thing in the world," Margaret B. Hawkins says. "Grow in the present, establish short-term goals to satisfy yourself—and you will develop ability and your reputation will grow."

The choral conductor for the Milwaukee Symphony Orchestra was born in Binghamton, New York, on January 28, 1937. Her family moved to Racine, Wisconsin, where her father, a publisher, worked for Western Printing Company. Margaret was in junior high school at that time.

She earned her BS in Music Education from the University of Wisconsin - Milwaukee and her master's in choral conducting from Indiana University. She studied under Margaret Hillis, conductor of Chicago Symphony Orchestra and later with Kenneth Schermerhorn, former conductor of Milwaukee Symphony Orchestra.

She began her career as choral director at Pewaukee High School where she stayed for 12 years, developing an award-winning chamber chorus. She believed in her students: "High school kids can do anything." They toured extensively and gained a national reputation. Milton Weber, then conductor of the Waukesha Symphony, saw them perform and afterward hired Margaret Hawkins to conduct the "Music for Youth Chorus."

As her personal reputation as a conductor

Margaret Hawkins

As Choral Conductor of the Milwaukee Symphony Orchestra, her formula for success is, "Take one step at a time, always doing your best."

273

increased, so did her willingness to invest unrepressible hours and efforts into her work.

Today she is choral conductor of the Milwaukee Symphony Orchestra. Under her direction, the group made its New York debut with the orchestra at Carnegie Hall in May, 1980. The *New York Times* lauded its "crisp discipline." Byron Belt of *Newhouse Newspapers* wrote, "When it (the orchestra) was joined by Margaret Hawkins' spectacular chorus the results not only raised the roof sonically, but sent the music soaring to one beautiful effort after another."

This chorus of 230 voices—the Wisconsin Conservatory Symphony Chorus which she regards as her chief accomplishment—reflects only part of her energies. She also works with about 100 of its members who do double duty as the Conservatory Singers. A very few, the "cream of the crop," those with solo caliber voices, enter the ranks of the Conservatory Chamber Singers which she also conducts.

"Music is fun, but music is also hard work. To rehearse a group involves tension and relaxation. One must exercise discipline with humor," says Margaret Hawkins. "When I conduct I have a great responsibility and I need to concentrate. After a concert I experience a violent winding down process, wondering if I did all I possibly could do. Then the nervousness and fear set in."

Four nights a week, from September to June, Margaret rehearses. On Wednesday nights she leads the chamber orchestra. Five days a week she teaches at the Conservatory and at the Milwaukee School of the Arts. Five weekends out of the season, she listens to the Symphony Chorus perform massive choral works with the Milwaukee Symphony. This is when she's not traveling throughout the country and giving lectures or performances, or serving as co-chairman of the Choral Advisory Panel of the National Endowment for the Arts, or conducting the Milwaukee Symphony Orchestra herself.

It's a hectic schedule, but it has never occurred to her to cut back.

"Pleasure and work are entwined in one. . .Perseverence, intelligence, a sense of humor and willingness to sacrifice are more important than talent."

(See Selected Honors, Accomplishments, Publications, page 309)

One Christmas,
from Kenneth Schermerhorn,
she received a bouquet —
not of roses —
but of conductor batons,
each engraved with her name.
It was his tribute
of respect.

She has grassroots, national and international experience in efforts to improve opportunities for women in education and employment.

sarah harder

"A feminist is someone who knows how far women have to go before we achieve equality—and who is willing to do something about it."

That is the working definition of Sarah Harder, whose view of how far women have to go and how much needs to be done extends beyond Wisconsin to the nation and the world.

Many aspects of Sarah's childhood and early adult life laid the foundation for her involvement as a leader in promoting issues important to women and families. Born in 1937, the older of two girls, she lived in Chicago in a close-knit neighborhood where her parents and grandparents had grown up and where many relatives provided an extended family environment. Her mother operated a ballet school, and while Sarah and her sister were often unwilling participants as dancers, they were continually drawn into major productions and developed a sense of theatrical involvement and making things happen. Even as the family moved from the city to small towns, her mother always managed to organize extravagant shows, pulling "everyone into the event who could dance or sew or pound a nail."

When Sarah was nine, the family moved to the suburban countryside, giving her the opportunity to explore fields, to fish, and to enjoy the river. Starting in a new school meant carving her own niche for the first time. As Sarah says, "In a small school of 200 students where I was an outsider, I really had to re-form my ideas about what one needed to connect with people. I had automatic

Far left (top): Sarah Harder at 10, fishing and climbing the willow at the house on the river, and (below) at age one; Near left (top): At age eight, and (below), at four-and-a-half with sister Susan in snowsuits; Left: Sarah Harder today.

connections in our small world within the large world of Chicago. Now thrust on my own, I was frankly not very successful in making friends. I had always been a bit outspoken and outrageous. But while my family was tolerant, Algonquin grade school didn't beat a path to my door."

It was a period of learning the advantages of independence, reading voluminously, and coming to rely on her own resources. Another move to a small town reinforced the sense that Sarah was going in different directions than most of her peers. This became clear at 8th grade graduation. "The class was so small, each graduate stood up to announce plans for the future. Because of a passion developed in my years on the river, I stated I was going to be curator of butterflies at the Field Museum of Natural History in Chicago." There was a cascade of laughter from the crowd.

Her parents owned a hardware store where Sarah quickly learned the inventory, to cut glass, mix paint and find the right bolt. Her mother developed a gift and toy section in the store, and in helping with its organization, Sarah says, "We had to accommodate our own tastes to the tastes of the community. I became aware of the significance of responding to the prevailing ethic in a place if one was to be successful."

After graduating from high school, she headed for the University of Iowa, determined to conform. While her first two years of college were successful academically and socially, she lacked direction. It seemed the best way to avoid difficult decisions was to get married. So she dropped out of college her junior year, got married and became a homemaker in La Crosse.

With the support of her parents, she continued going to school, but, "I was an aberration on the La Crosse campus. It was a particularly strange thing to be a pregnant student at that time." After the birth of two sons and a third unsuccessful pregnancy, school become more and more important. She began to recognize that she and her husband lacked common goals and interests, and after tumultuous inner searching, she finally decided to obtain a divorce. Once her parents recovered from the shock, they provided financial support for her commitment to continue her education.

At 25, Sarah accepted a graduate assistantship at Bowling Green, Ohio, and began a master's program in English because she was told, "Women can't get anywhere in history." She attended classes and taught courses in composition and Shakespeare, discovering that she loved teaching. She shared her office with Harry Harder whom she married. "Ours was a marriage from the first that shared family responsibilities and reinforced professional roles," she says. They have a daughter and a son.

In 1968 Sarah and Harry were looking for teaching jobs as coprofessionals. They eventually landed positions at the University of Wisconsin—Eau Claire, and happily settled into a life where family and profession were strong complements.

Today Sarah is assistant to the chancellor at the University of Wisconsin-Eau Claire with responsibility for education and employment innovations promoting equal opportunity. She serves on AAUW's National Board of Directors as chairman of the Committee on Women.

As floor manager of the Wisconsin delegation to the 1977 National Women's Conference in Houston, Sarah became involved in feminist issues at state and national levels. She was appointed to the National Continuing Committee formed to carry forward the work of the conference and

attended the presentation of its plan of action at the White House on March, 1978. The Continuing Committee publicized and encouraged participation in the 1980 White House Conference on Families and the UN mid-decade Conference on Women in Copenhagen.

Sarah recognizes the urgency of issues faced by the majority of the world's women. "I remember the words of a friend," she says. " 'Women make wonderful statements on paper . . . They moulder to dust in file cabinets and on library shelves.' While our principles are on the side of the angels, we are said to have little that's practical to offer the earth.

"We need to see clearly the task of achieving equity for women. We must have the courage to take up a lifelong task, to begin in our own backyards and to reach out from there. Our challenge is to make whole a world that emphasizes divisions, distinctions, separations and barriers.

"This time, instead of putting words on paper, we must really change the world."

(See Selected Honors, Accomplishments, Publications, page 309)

Above right: Bentley and Jennifer Harder in a neighborhood 4th of July parade (photo by Jules Chan); *Right: Sarah in the May 1980 ERA March in Chicago.*

written by LOUISE C. SMITH

Barbara Nichols, MSN, RN, president of the American Nurses' Association.

barbara nichols

Barbara Nichols always wanted to be a nurse. She long admired a great aunt who was a public health nurse and she identified nursing as a profession that seemed non-discriminatory toward Blacks. Today she is national President of the American Nurses' Association, the organization that officially represents registered professional nurses in the United States. She is the first black person elected to that office. She is also the mother of three young children and she meshes her professional and personal lives with admirable ease.

Barbara was born July 19, 1938. She does not have many bad memories of overt race discrimination, but she can describe social situations where discrimination occurred, frequently with a sense of humor. Once she missed a role in the high school play because she would have had to kiss a white boy. It was difficult for her to understand that even though she qualified for that role, she was barred for this reason.

She received a diploma in Nursing from the Massachusetts Memorial Hospital School of Nursing in 1959 and applied for admittance to the Navy Nurse Corps. Her initial interest was stimulated by a classmate who had been a WAVE. Another attraction was 30 days paid vacation with opportunity for travel. At this time, Barbara's parents were stationed in Alaska where her father worked in the Coast Guard. She enrolled in the United States Navy Officer Command course, and met her future husband.

In 1960, she was commissioned an officer in the United States Navy Nurse Corps and cited by the Navy for exemplary care in an intensive care open heart surgery unit.

Barbara has good memories of her three years in the Navy. They helped her develop discipline. She became aware that she was one of only two nurses of the 100 in her unit who did not have a baccalaureate degree. She knew what her next step would be after her tour of duty.

In 1964 she enrolled at Case Western Reserve University and in December of that year she married Larry Nichols. They moved to Madison, Wisconsin in 1966, and she has been continuously associated with St. Mary's Hospital Medical Center ever since.

Since 1970 she has been Director of Inservice Education. From 1974-77 she also held a position as Assistant Clinical Professor of Nursing, University of Wisconsin-Madison, a joint appointment with St. Mary's. In 1978 she was the first black to be elected president of the American Nurses Association and was re-elected in 1980. She travels extensively, speaking to groups all over the country. Barbara has been cited in over 600 publications and also interviewed on many radio and television programs. She is the first nurse to be awarded an honorary degree from the University of Wisconsin-Milwaukee.

She espouses nursing vigorously, "I believe that professional self-determination belongs in nursing . . . Nurses will be viewed by the individual families, groups, and the communities they serve as the most accessible providers in the health services network."

How has Barbara Nichols managed the multiple activities of her professional life and maintained a successful family life with her husband and children? "You don't get this far without help." When she accepted the nomination for president of the American Nurses' Assoication, Larry proudly assumed primary care responsibility for the children with the help of parents who live nearby.

The children have adjusted their lives to her frequent absences. Sometimes they accompany her on trips. The whole family met in the summer of 1980 at Calgary, Canada, after Barbara gave a speech at a meeting of the Canadian Nurses' Association. She says that she does little cooking but tries to spend the time with her family in doing things together and "interacting with them to give them memorable experiences."

Barbara Nichols emanates inner strength and a steadfast commitment to achieving her goals. She has high standards, high aspirations and a deep and loving commitment to her family.

(See Selected Honors, Accomplishments, Publications, page 312)

"Members of the nursing profession today are educated and certified to perform health assessments, health-teaching, family counseling and a number of other health care services."
—BARBARA NICHOLS

written by *JEANNE LAMSAM*

She is the Governor's Advisor for Women and Family Initiatives.

marlene cummings

As a wiry little eight-year old, Marlene Cummings was entranced with the heavy summer rains in her home town of Indianapolis. She would rush out-of-doors in the downpour, throw herself to the ground, and press her ear to the damp earth to listen. The heavy erratic drumming of the rainfall filled her with fascination.

The elders of her family—her aunts and the solicitous grandmother who took her into her home after the death of Marlene's mother the previous year—observed the child's action with concern. They questioned whether Marlene imagined hearing her mother's voice in the rain, and, having experienced the trauma of her burial, was pressing her ear to the earth to hear her. They wondered if they had done enough to ease the child's bereavement.

In fact, although she grieved over her mother's death, Marlene had absorbed enough of the devout Baptist family's Christian beliefs to be solaced by the conviction that her mother lived, forever happy, in heaven with Jesus. She would not have dreamed of trying to communicate with her mother in the ground. On the contrary, it was a spirit of daring that brought her flying out of the house in the rain. Her motivation was a tale related by a teenage acquaintance. "When it rains and the sun is shining," the friend told her solemnly, "deep down in the earth, the devil beats his wife. He makes an awful racket. But up here, you can't hear it so well. You've got to be perfectly still and listen." Marlene, with her lively imagination and eight-year-old naivete, swallowed the myth whole. The family's misunderstanding of her attempts to hear the drama underfoot, recounted with peals of laughter, illustrates Marlene's early perception of the fallacy of one person's attempts to judge another.

Especially detested by Marlene Cummings are the one-word judgments of labels. "Labels limit a person. Anything you can label, you can define, and thereby, limit. There are certain labels I was born with and accept. I am a woman. I am Black.

Far left:
Marlene Cummings;

Near left:
Marlene in front of a class of children, explaining skin color differences.
"I like this picture because it reminds me of my earlier efforts to help children accept each other's differences better. Knowledge about differences is the key to eradicating biases."
    —MARLENE CUMMINGS

(Photo by Roger Turner,
Wisconsin State Journal)

A Baptist, who has converted to Catholicism, so I am a Baptist-Catholic. But I won't accept other labels. I won't tell my age, for example, because age has become a label. I reserve the right to be who I am, just as I respect the right of other persons to be who they are. Everyone is born with gifts, which are different in each person, and all people have the right to develop their gifts, to become who they are. No individual should be defined and limited by a label."

Marlene's imaginative war on the evil of labels has cut a wide swath and propelled her into key responsibilities on behalf of children, women and people in general. The inspiration for her life's work comes from two women—her grandmother, Anna Mary Thomas, who reared her with the admonition "Use your gifts to leave the world a better place than you found it" and Mary McLeod Bethune. She is the eminent educator and founder of a college for black women, who listened to her pastor read the Scriptural passage (John 3:16) "Whosoever believeth in Him shall not perish, but shall have life everlasting." Bethune heard it one Sunday as though for the first time, moved to her very soul by the realization that it was not only Jews or Gentiles, but *herself* being addressed. From that time, she flung away pessimism and refused to entertain feelings of inferiority. Marlene Cummings, as a girl, read the account of this experience with sympathy and quickening self-recognition.

Faithful to her ideals, Marlene completed her education as a registered psychiatric nurse, married, and became the mother of four sons. When circumstances permitted, she worked as a visiting nurse, sharing 50 per cent of her salary with a carefully chosen babysitter.

For 10 years, while maintaining her absorbing family life, Mrs. Cummings served as human relations coordinator for the Madison Metropolitan School District. In teaching about her own and others' precious individuality, she wrote a weekly column for the Sunday *Wisconsin State Journal*, "Dear Mrs. Cummings".

Today she is producer-writer-hostess of a live weekly television series, "Very Important People" that attempts to develop awareness and understanding of individual differences, self-respect and respect for others. Carried by WISC-TV, CBS-Madison, the program has brought Mrs. Cummings and her ideas into thousands of homes, and her personality has made its own impact.

On April 2, 1979, Governor Lee Dreyfus announced he would disband the Commission on the Status of Women. His aim was to establish a new era in which women would always be at the

table when policy matters were discussed. Two months later, he appointed Marlene Cummings as Governor's Advisor for Women and Family Initiatives, effective August 1, 1979. He said of her, "She carries that key responsibility of providing me with the best advice she can give me—anything related to women's issues—and also to serve for the entire administration, including the cabinet, as a kind of constant conscience on those issues."

Marlene Cummings' goal in her present job is the removal of barriers and procedures that are stumbling blocks to women simply because they are women. She seeks to have women provided with choices, to be able to use their gifts and have these gifts valued by society. She extends this goal, beyond women, to include all people. She stands for reforms in the economics of marriage and the elimination of taxes in the transfer of assets from one marriage partner to the other.

When asked what she considers her own greatest

"Never compete against another individual. This is a trap that sets one up for envy, failure and loss of self-esteem. Rather, look upon your mistakes and improve. Compete against your own past record."
—MARLENE CUMMINGS

opportunity, Marlene answers promptly, "Being born."

"And what do you believe in most, Marlene?" Her pealing laugh rings out, and the answer comes like thunder, "People!"

On the door of her office, under the sign bearing her name and title, appears the question, printed in crisp, black type, "In Whose Image?" Marlene Cummings has answered that question for herself. Her philosophy, life and work challenge the people she meets to answer it for themselves.

(See Selected Honors, Accomplishments, Publications, page 307)

Left to right:
At the Cerebral Palsy Telethon, January, 1981; (courtesy, Channel 27, Madison)
Marlene and boys, Casey, Steve, Patrick, taken in June, 1980, in New Orleans at Steve's graduation from Loyola University; and Jeffrey (Chip) just prior to his 1980 graduation from West High School, Madison.

jill geisler

The phone rang and Jill Geisler of Milwaukee's WITI-TV Channel 6 cradled the receiver. It was Skycamera Six, the station's helicopter. A body had been discovered in a field and the crew had arrived before the authorities reached the scene. They shot some rather dramatic close-ups—exclusive material. But should it be shown on the air? Would the viewers be offended? Jill opted for a shot taken from a greater distance.

This is typical of many decisions the dedicated news director of Channel 6 has to make daily, usually beginning at 8 a.m. and sometimes working as late as 10:30 p.m. If crisis news breaks, she camps at Channel 6 during the event, overseeing all the news broadcasts and bulletins.

Her duties as news director continually interrupt Jill's social relationships. Her relatives have resigned themselves to the fact that she will be late for Christmas dinner. She has learned that people understand television to be a demanding business. Her yearly participation in the Muscular Dystrophy Telethon, for example, and her ongoing work with the Association for Retarded Citizens keep her away from home but happily involved in a commitment to others. Through her work with these groups, she helps heighten public awareness of the needs of the developmentally disabled. She produced a program entitled, "I've Never Known Someone Like You," the story of three mentally retarded teenagers at summer camp. In 1980 the National Association for Retarded Citizens recognized that work with its Arc of Excellence Award.

"When you have power to reach so many people, you have tremendous responsibility to use it for good," said the news director. "A lot of false

Jill Geisler   (photo by Chris Schmidt)

importance is placed on a television personality; people think you are a little bit brighter, a little more attractive, because you are on television. But if you never transcend this image, you are not doing very much."

Throughout her career Jill has devoted much time to talking to women, women's groups and the general public about women's roles in society, the depiction of women in the media and women in management. She places a high priority on education and women's issues. Through her speaking engagements, Jill seeks to inform women about what television can do *for* them and what it has done *to* them. She stresses that the image of women on television has changed.

Jill was born in Milwaukee in 1950. Her father was an installer for the Wisconsin Telephone Company. Her mother, ill for many years while Jill was growing up, died at 42 just after Jill had finished college.

Her parents encouraged Jill all through school, but believed that if she wanted more education, she must bear the cost. She became the first college graduate in her family, earning her way. Jill has a younger brother, Jack, whom she later also helped through school.

As a child, Jill loved writing, reading aloud and being "a little ham." In fourth grade her teacher began teaching her Spanish and by sixth trade, she was teaching her classmates the language.

For Jill the most rewarding responsibility of her years at Pulaski High School was as editor of the School newspaper. She worked after school in a candy store in downtown Milwaukee where she became manager at age 16.

Her determination led her to excel through college, graduating from UW-Madison as "Outstanding Journalism graduate of 1972." Then,

at the age of 23, Director of Communications Carl Zimmerman of WITI-TV asked her to join the basic news staff. "Here Lil Kleiman, my friend and co-worker (now managing editor of the station) taught me the value of being aggressive without being overbearing in pursuit of a story," Jill commented.

Within a year she was promoted to an anchor position. In 1978, she was named news director. At that time there were fewer than 10 female television news directors in the country. In this position Jill has sought to supervise and deliver the news well, to look for constructive information with sensitivity and to influence the way people view their world and themselves.

As news director, Jill is responsible for setting the standards and policy for news coverage at Channel 6. As a woman in a highly conspicious position, she sees her strongest impact on the community today as that of a role model.

"Using the power of the media as a force for good and using my visible position in the media as a positive role model for other young women, have been the most satisfying elements of my work. And I love that work!"

(See Selected Honors, Accomplishments, Publications, page 309)

She is the driving force behind the Ko-Thi Dance Company who teaches, choreographs and manages .

ferne caulker-bronson

Ferne Caulker-Bronson was born at a mission hospital in the village of Rotifunk, Sierra Leone, West Africa. Her childhood was spent on the campus of Fourah Bay College, located on Mount Aureol, 800 feet above sea level, overlooking the Atlantic Ocean. Her father, Solomon Caulker, a University director, was also a tribal elder and drummer.

Her childhood was filled with play on the warm, sandy beaches, freely running and playing in open terrain away from harm's way. She mixed with people from far away places—England, Switzerland, Austrialia, Italy—as well as those from other African countries. She learned as a child to value the person, whether illiterate or highly educated, whether rich or poor. Her life cut across all these barriers, as well as those based on the color of skin.

The freedom and stimulation of the African environment made firm early impressions.

When she was four, Ferne traveled with her parents to a small village called Mambo, the ancestral home of the Caulker family. Not a single child in Mambo spoke English. Ferne spoke no Sherbro, the language of the village and the people. Within two days, Ferne had organized the children into marches and games that she knew. She answered all questions with the one Sherbro phrase she managed to learn, "Ah chen thay potho,"

Left: Ferne Caulker-Bronson;
Right: In "Musical Interlude," Alverno College
(photo by Chuck Miller, courtesy, Ko-Thi Dance Company)

meaning, ironically, "I don't speak English."

The years in an English boarding school in West Cornwall were her first encounter with a society that opened the door to questions about "self" and "being." But the English gentlemanly approach did not prepare Ferne for the assault that the United States society of the middle sixties would fling upon her. It was during this period that her ideas began to crystallize.

She attended Custer High School in Milwaukee, 1964-65. She received professional training in dance at the University of Wisconsin, both Madison and Milwaukee campuses. In 1969, she studied African dance and art at the University of Ghana, West Africa and in 1972, she earned her bachelor's degree at UW-Milwaukee.

Dedicating herself to sharing her African heritage with her Afro-American peers, she began teaching in Milwaukee, and later, at the University. Her students were enthusiastic and her classes popular. UW-M Professor Jack Waldheim describes her as an inspirational teacher. "For several semesters I have seen her class, clumsy raw material, enter this room and come out magically transformed at the semester's end."

The Ko-Thi Dance Company is a major vehicle through which this sharing takes form. Ko-Thi means "Go Black" in the Sherbro dialect. Ferne founded the company in 1969, without funds, facilities or equipment, but with an abundance of discipline, energy, drive and talent.

As a professional group, Ko-Thi is not primarily an entertainment group, but rather an educational and inspirational endeavor. It seeks to strengthen the understanding of African cultural roots. The company runs studio classes, performs throughout the Midwest, gives lectures and demonstrations through public and private schools, colleges and universities, and performs for organizations.

"We see ourselves not only as folklorists or keepers and documentators of a culture, but also as ambassadors," Bronson says.

Ko-Thi has never had an unfavorable review. *Milwaukee Sentinel* Jay Joslyn described the performance, "Enriching modern dance and jazz techniques with the grace and discipline of African tribal movements, the company mimed the horror of slavery, the release of religion, the strength of dedication." Louise Kenngott, *Milwaukee Journal* dance critic, stated, "They hit you with power, pulse, and flair. They dance like crazy, until you think they'd drop with the next step."

Chicago Reader reviewer Dorothy Samuelson was "most impressed by Bronson's *Hey! You!*, a modern piece that she choreographed for herself in which she seemed to personify the plight of the black, invisible to the larger society, who pleads for recognition of his or her own presence."

"Drum Talk", a recording released in 1981, featuring the Ko-Thi drummers and African songs, is designed for use in teaching and demonstrating African rhythms and dance.

It has been a long road from a baby's cry in a mud hut hospital to the stage of a recent performance in the Brooklyn Academy of Music's Dance Africa '81, one that attests to the courage, determination, and talent of Ferne Caulker-Bronson.

She has touched the lives of innumerable Black youth in a positive way. Through Ko-Thi, she has brought hope and accomplishment to many who would not have shared in the joys of the American dream.

(See Selected Honors, Accomplishments, Publications, page 306)

She is the first American to win three medals in speed skating in a single Winter Olympics.

sheila young ochowicz

As a young child, Sheila Young preferred the shelter of her mother's dress when entering a roomful of strangers. Her sister, who was taking ballet, tried to teach her the graceful movements, but abandoned the venture in exasperation with her clumsy pupil. The shy and clumsy child became a renowned athlete, winning three world speed skating titles, three Olympic gold medals and three world cyclist titles.

Sheila's father, Clair Young, a bicycle racer, skated to remain in shape during the winter. Her brothers and sisters became enthusiastic skaters and enjoyed racing. Sheila enjoyed skating, but could not be persuaded to race. As she became less intimidated by strangers, she talked and played games with the other skaters. After watching a friend's enjoyment during competition, she thought, "I could do that."

Ignoring her aversion to being observed, she entered the first race. Skating soon had Sheila hooked. She liked the sensation of speed, the thrill of racing and the graceful motion.

Sheila was 13 when her mother died, and skating became an important focus for the Young family. Recalling that sad period, she feels that the shared interest in skating helped to fill the void and was instrumental in keeping the family together.

As she continued to compete, the national championships were experiences in frustration and perseverance. She won second place seven years in

Sheila Young Ochowicz at Innsbruck, Austria.
(courtesy, Sports Illustrated)

a row. At 15, she was introduced to the metric style used in the Olympics and won second place in a junior class short distance race. This became her favorite event.

Her high school years were a study in perpetual motion. Weekends were reserved for skating events. Each winter, she took a month off from school for intensive training sessions in West Allis.

At the 1971 Olympic trials, she earned a position on the speed skating team which represented the United States in Sapporo, Japan. She placed fourth in the 500 meter race, missing third place and the bronze medal by .08 second.

She considered retiring from competition after the 1972 Olympics, but, after observing the happiness of Anna Henning as she was awarded a gold medal, Sheila decided to continue. Her goal was an Olympic gold medal.

To stay in shape during the summer, Sheila followed her father's example with bicycling. During the summer of 1972, she placed third in the world cycling sprints in Marseilles, France. She determined to do better, and the following year in Spain, placed first.

In the summer of 1974, she began to work with Peter Schating, who trained the Austrian Team. Coach Schating promised, "Train with me for a year, and you'll be Number One."

On the first day of training in the beautiful countryside of Innsbruck, Austria, Sheila felt sick as she was doing a hard tempo run downhill. She was hot, tired, sweaty; her legs hurt, she was nauseated. She demanded to know what he was doing to her. His unsympathetic reply was, "You either pay now or pay later."

Workouts were physically demanding, but they were made less tiresome by inventing games. She continued to work hard, perfecting her turns and crossovers with smooth and powerful strokes.

At the end of a day's practice, Sheila had just enough energy to crawl on the bed and write a letter or read a book. She took courses in German to increase her fluency. Occasionally there was time for clowning with friends, dressing up in skintight skating uniforms, wearing mittens on feet, mimicking skin divers. The antics helped break the monotony of training.

In 1973, in Oslo, Norway, Sheila fulfilled Schating's promise by taking first place in the world sprint championships. She not only broke the world record for the 500 meter race, but the record for total points as well.

She had continued success in cycling competition that summer, finishing first in the sprints of the world cycling championships in Spain. She became the only athlete to hold world titles in two sports.

Sheila admits to being superstitious in her preparation for a race. The hat she wore in a good race at the beginning of the season became her lucky hat for all races. The clothes became her lucky outfit. Laying her jacket down ahead of her competitor's was a good omen. She had a favorite method of lacing her skates.

A month before the 1976 Olympics, Sheila's skating was fluctuating from race to race. Her coach, training several other competitors, was dividing his attention. Finally, she called her fiance, speed skater-cyclist James Ochowicz. He quit his job and flew from the United States to Davos, Switzerland to lend his support. A week later she broke the world record in the 500 meters with a time of 40.91 seconds. Elated with the victory, she was still concerned because the Olympics were now only a week away.

The first race, the 1500 meters was not her best

event but she won the silver medal that day, in what she considers her best race ever.

The climax of Sheila's career came when she won the coveted gold medal in the 500 meters. As soon as she took off her skates, she began pushing through the crowd in search of her father. When they met in tearful embrace, he did not have to tell her how he felt. She could see it in his eyes.

Sheila went on to receive the bronze medal in the 1,000 meter race. She became the first American to win three medals in a single Winter Olympics.

In the summer of 1976, Sheila competed in the world cycling championship spring event in Italy. For the second time, she became the only athlete to hold world championships in two different sports.

Then she announced to a stunned sports world that she was retiring at age 25 to marry Jim Ochowicz. "Sports are fun and exciting, but there is another aspect of life that must be fulfilled."

She did not leave sports completely. She took tennis lessons, ran and cycled for pleasure. She served as a member of the United States International Skating Association Board of Directors and Executive Board member of the US Olympic Committee. She traveled with her husband and, after her daughter was born, the baby went along. Sheila worked for the Lake Placid Organizing committee for the 1980 Winter

Above: Sheila and her daughter;
Right: Olympic Winter Games, Lake Placid 1980. (courtesy, Sports Illustrated)

Olympics, and was a commentator for ABC television for speed skating events.

During the summer of 1980, as Sheila coached young skaters and worked out with them, seeds for a comeback were planted. Her goal was to return to national and world competition and finish among the top ten at the world sprint championships.

Training took on the logistics of army maneuvers as she worked around her husband's hours, limited rink hours, household chores and babysitting arrangements. She earned a place on the United States team at the world sprints in Grenoble, France, finishing seventh. Sheila talks about her comeback, while cuddling Katie on her lap. "After being laid off for five years, skating as well as I did is very satisfying. I can't tell you how proud I am of myself."

Sheila Young is looking at her options and considering long range goals. Whatever she decides, she will give it her best.

(See Selected Honors, Accomplishments, Publications, page 314)

susan shannon engeleiter

Susan Shannon Engeleiter was the youngest woman in the United States to be elected to a state legislature when she was elected in 1974. She was 22 years old when she won a seat in the Wisconsin State Assembly, and she is still setting records.

Great support came from her husband, Gerry Engeleiter, an attorney and former Congressional aide. Her parents, Art and Jo Shannon, and her younger brothers enthusiastically joined her campaigns for the State Assembly, the United States House of Representatives and the State Senate.

Susan was born in Milwaukee March 18, 1952, and grew up in a politically aware household. After she graduated from UW-Madison in 1974 with a teaching degree in English and Communications,

she ran for State Representative of the 99th Assembly District (the Elm Grove, Brookfield, Menomonee Falls area). She had lived in the district all her life, and was familiar with the issues because of her four-year part time job in the Senate during college. She won the election and became the youngest state legislator in the country.

Susan admits, "I found age to be a problem as a candidate. It was something of a handicap. But I ran in 1974, the middle of the Watergate period, when many people were disenchanted with the incumbents. I did a lot of door-to-door campaigning, to almost 1200 homes, and I think people felt that somebody who was younger, and a woman who was not an incumbent, might be worth a try."

In 1978, Susan became a candidate for the United States House of Representatives. She lost to James Sensenbrenner by approximately 480 votes out of 73,000, about one-half of one percent of the vote. Her workers were disappointed, but Susan was a gracious loser, and considered the campaign a positive experience.

In her next try for public office, she won the race for State Senator from Wisconsin's 33rd District, and became the first Republican woman to hold that office. Susan likes the greater diversity of communities that are contained in the larger Senate districts as compared to the smaller Assembly districts. She feels it is easier to debate issues when only 33 people are involved.

Susan Shannon Engeleiter;
Far left: Engrossed in session.

Historically, government has been dominated by men, although this is finally changing. Wisconsin's legislature now has 22 women, a record number. Susan believes, "As in any field where there have not been many women, women in government must work harder initially to prove themselves. Mediocre men in government are tolerated, but mediocre women are pointed out as examples of why there ought not be more women. I find that a very unfair standard." Susan has been around long enough, four years in the Assembly, and a year and a half as Governor Lee Dreyfus' legislative Liaison, that her male colleagues are comfortable with her. She feels that it is important to keep a sense of humor while working as a woman candidate or legislator. She recalls her first campaign when she was frequently mistaken while walking door to door for the Avon lady. During her early days as a state representative, lobbyists coming to see her sometimes mistook her for the secretary. Sue learned to see the humor in such situations.

It is important that women are not identified only with women's issues, Susan feels. She involves herself in a great variety of issues. She is author of the law that put the uniform donor card on Wisconsin drivers' licenses. A severe shortage of kidney donors has been nearly eliminated as a result. She has also worked to reform Wisconsin's sexual assault law and has spent much time on reapportioning Wisconsin's legislative seats.

Keeping up with her tough schedule requires boundless energy. In addition to legislative sessions and committee work, she is available regularly in town and village halls, usually on Saturday mornings. A typical week also includes meetings with local officials, visits to industries and talks to school and scout groups and civic organizations.

Despite her busy schedule, Susan found time to complete her law courses and was admitted to the Bar on June 16, 1981.

According to her former aide, Ruth Humphries, "Susan has the unique ability to sift through to the core of a problem right away. Her Senate colleagues call her approach judicial because she likes to look at the pros and cons of an issue, recognize where the basic problem lies, figure out the bottom line and how to solve it in the most reasonable way."

She sums up her goals for the future. "I hope to break the jinx of no woman ever being re-elected to the State Senate. I want to do a good job for the area I represent. The Senate is still very male-dominated, so the better job I can do, the easier it will be for other women in the future. One reason I like to speak to school groups is that I can be a role model for girls who might be interested in government careers, and help boys to understand that girls can be in nontraditional roles. To do the best job I can brings a sense of fulfillment, it makes me a happier person."

(See Selected Honors, Accomplishments, Publications, page 308)

written by JANN MC BRIDE

jill ann lieber

"A great symphony is a man-made Mississippi down which we irresistibly flow from the instant of our leave-taking to a long foreseen destination."
Aaron Copland

A symphony in sports best describes the approach Jill Ann Lieber orchestrates as columnist and sports writer for the *Milwaukee Sentinel*. Her special kind of music is what led her to New York to join the Research Staff of *Sports Illustrated*.

As a sports reporter, she aims for the heart, resulting in a story so real the reader becomes the witness.

Jill Ann Lieber

From early childhood, her mother describes Jill as "very enthusiastic about every aspect of life. She seemed to pursue any event with equal excitement. Not once did we ask or tell her to do her homework or practice her violin. In fact, on occasion, we'd ask her to stop practicing! She's always been very self-motivated."

Born in Neenah, Wisconsin on July 15, 1956, Jill became the valedictorian of her 1974 graduating class of 559 from Neenah High School. Her reminiscence is that "high school taught me not to be a member of any particular clique, but to be my own person."

Jill applied herself in high school with good study habits and a hard-work ethic. Music became a discipline for Jill. She studied violin and piano at the Lawrence Conservatory of Music and the University of Wisconsin.

Stanford University was Jill's choice to pursue a profession in violin. There she was among music

majors who were "playing better at a hobby than I was at a career. I couldn't stand just being average."

It is not surprising that one who revered the rhythm, form, emotion and movement of music would become interested in sports, the expression of bodily movement.

From eighth grade on, Jill and her father attended many area sports events. She remembers him kidding her about becoming the first woman sportscaster.

By the end of her college freshman year, Jill was on her way to fulfilling her father's prediction. She studied sports psychology and kinesiology.

Her goal was "to write for a major metropolitan newspaper, especially indepth features, eventually becoming a columnist or sports editor."

Jill earned a bachelor of arts degree in communication in March 1978. She held a double minor in music performance (violin) and physical education. Jill had participated in classical violin performance, solo and ensemble work as well as the Stanford Symphony and chamber orchestras. She wrote for the *Stanford Daily,* covering major sports events and became sports editor in 1976-77.

Prior to her post with the *Milwaukee Sentinel* Jill worked as intern for WBAY-TV, as sportscaster for KZSU radio, as a stringer for the *Palo Alto Times,* the *San Francisco Chronicle* and the *Milwaukee Journal.* In 1979 she was included in "Best Sports Stories" for her award-winning "Noah Jackson Wasn't Inhibited."

Left to right:
Jill in the locker room interviewing Milwaukee Brewer pitcher Pete Vukovich;
(photo by John Biever, courtesy, Milwaukee Sentinel)
In New York, working for Sports Illustrated;
On TV as Milwaukee Sentinel sportswriter.
(photo by John Biever, courtesy, Milwaukee Sentinel)

The most memorable highlight of Jill's career was covering the 1980 Winter Olympics. The assignment was a confidence-booster, the most rewarding event she has yet experienced. "It is still difficult to believe that I was actually there, competing among the very best writers from everywhere." She returned with impetus for a new column, "Dusting Off the Gold," where she presented comprehensive features about Olympic stars.

Jill's style is the ultimate complement to her career. She is the culmination of writer, musician and athlete. As a journalist Jill believes that a person has to create her own opportunities. "Being a pioneer is hard, but I do have a cause. I worry that I might never see my potential used to the fullest; but then I think of women who will follow me."

Jill has suffered her share of discrimination on either side of the locker room door. She thinks of herself as a skilled writer, not a woman in a man's world. "Luckily for me, I've received the support from writers of the 'new breed' who hold broad perspective in my area."

"I work very long on melodies. The important thing is not the beginning of the melody, but its continuation; its development into a fully completed art form."
—*Strauss*

(See Selected Honors, Accomplishments, Publications, page 310)

Beth Heiden

written by MARY HELEN BECKER

beth heiden

A cheerful voice on the telephone agreed to a meeting and refused an offer of transportation saying: "I'll come on my bike or I'll just run."

When the doorbell announced her arrival, Beth Heiden had indeed run two miles from her campus apartment. Wearing an old sweatsuit and a backpack, her face red from running into a chill wind, the small figure looked considerably younger than her 21 years. She seems familiar because of all the photographs in the news media, but she is a more complex and interesting young woman than the sports pages reveal. Friendly, natural, and radiating energy, she communicates her enthusiasm for her many activities. Her eyes light up as she describes her work for the Special Olympics and tells how the retarded youngsters improve their sports skills when they receive good instruction.

Elizabeth Lee Heiden, born September 27, 1959, in Madison, Wisconsin, is the daughter of Jack and Nancy Heiden and grew up in the pleasant community of Shorewood Hills near Madison. Beth and her brother Eric began ice skating as toddlers. Though they started out in the Madison Figure Skating Club Beth declares that they "always wanted to skate fast." She recalls skating in a race at Vilas Park sponsored by the Madison school board when she was six and Eric was seven. Members of the Madison Speed Skating Club who were there asked the Heidens to join.

After enrolling in the speed skating club Beth, at

seven, began skating competitively. By age nine she was Pony Girls National Indoor Champion. While speed skating turned out to be her favorite sport, Beth is an all-around athlete, excelling in diving, track, bicycling and tennis.

Dianne Holum who won bronze and silver medals in the 1968 Winter Olympics and silver and gold in the 1972 Games came to Madison in 1972 to attend the university and became coach of the Madison Speed Skating Club. The only woman who coaches world-class skaters today, Holum found the young Heidens promising and before long was investing her time and talent devising training programs for them. Beth and Eric trained together, traveled together, encouraged each other and together perfected their skating under Holum's expert coaching.

Told when she was in high school that she was too small for speed skating, Beth was nevertheless National Junior Girls' Outdoor Champion in 1975 when she was 14, and went to Europe to compete as a member of the US team. A year later at the Innsbruck Olympics the tiny skater broke an Olympic record set in 1972 and came in eleventh in the 3,000 meter race.

During her years at Madison West High School, Beth's commitment to skating required a daily trip to the Olympic Ice Rink at West Allis. In order to fit the 75 mile trip and three hours on the ice into her day, she scheduled her classes in the morning. School counselor Betty Perego remembers Beth's remarkable ability to get things done, to catch up when she had been out of town, and to remain involved with the school: "For most kids, being away for half of each day would mean losing touch with the school and with the other kids. Beth functioned as well with the other kids as if she was here all day long." She found time for soccer and played on the school tennis and track teams. During her senior year, she was elected prom queen. Beth graduated from high school with honors in 1977.

Intelligence and a capacity for hard work have characterized Beth's athletic development. She learned early the relationship between patient, diligent effort and success.

Women speed skating champions are usually sturdy, strapping women, often 40 to 50 pounds heavier than petite 5' 2" Beth Heiden, who has disciplined herself to get the maximum out of each stroke and whose strategy and technique compensate for sheer size and power.

1979 was extraordinarily busy and successful for Beth. In mid-January she won the women's 1,000 meters and 3,000 meters at West Allis, Wisconsin. At the end of January she was in Trondheim, Norway, for a three-nation event with skaters from Norway, the US and the USSR. Beth won all four women's races. In February she swept all four races in the World Speed Skating Championships at The Hague and captured her first all-around senior women's title. Beth Heiden was the first American to win the title since 1936. A few days later she won the 1,000 meters in the World Spring Championships and in March took the all-around title in the Golden Skates International, both at Inzell, and then at Grenoble, she won the Junior Worlds.

1980, the year of the Lake Placid Winter Olympics, began with the media focusing increasingly on Beth and Eric Heiden as the bright hopes of the USA. The two appeared on the cover of *Time* magazine. They had been famous for several years abroad—particularly in northern Europe where speed skating has long been a popular sport—and were suddenly in the limelight in the United States.

Beth arrived with an injured ankle which she valiantly tried to minimize, though it had seriously affected her training. It is a measure of her courage and resolve that she entered all four women's races. In the glare of publicity, pressured by comparisons with her brother and by the apparent demands of the press, the determined young lady skated as hard as she could. Before the Games began she had said she would be happy to win one medal; she won the Bronze in the 3,000 meters. What should have been a cause for rejoicing was a bittersweet experience for Beth.

After the last race she said: "I like to skate for myself, but this year I feel like I've been skating for the press."

By spring 1980, the bicycling that had always been part of Beth's training, became an end in itself. She rode 40 to 90 miles daily and by May she began entering and winning local, state, national and international races.

In September 1980, Beth announced her retirement from competitive skating. At the University of Wisconsin-Madison, the 1981 spring semester was her first on campus. Although she continued to spend several hours a day in training, Beth's first priority became her studies. Just before her final exams, Beth helped organize a Special Olympics event in Madison—"a seminar for the kids, with weight training, skating and soccer." Such concern and care for others sets Beth apart from the crowd.

She is modest, unaffected, interested in other people, generous and charming. Whatever she chooses to do in the future, one thing is certain: Beth Heiden is a winner.

(See Selected Honors, Accomplishments, Publications, page 309)

*Traveling has
given her perspective
on her own
country,
and has deepened
her appreciation
of it.*

appendix a: bibliography

Compiled by Linda Parker, Women's Studies Librarian-at-Large for the University of Wisconsin System, with the assistance of Donna Vukelich and Carolyn Platt.

This bibliography about Wisconsin women is the first in a series which will appear in *Feminist Collections: Women's Studies Library Resources in Wisconsin*. The series will include references to books, periodicals, manuscripts, reports, government documents, and nonprint media which cover the history of Wisconsin women. This first checklist was published to commemorate Wisconsin Women's History Week, March 8-14, 1981.

Brown, Victoria. THE UNCOMMON LIVES OF COMMON WOMEN: THE MISSING HALF OF WISCONSIN HISTORY. Madison: Wisconsin Feminists Project Fund, 1975.

Butler, Anna B., Emma C. Bascom and Katharine F. Kerr, eds. CENTENNIAL RECORDS OF THE WOMEN OF WISCONSIN. Madison: Atwood & Culver, 1876.

Catt, Carrie Chapman, 1859-1947. Papers, 1911-12. Published guide. State Historical Society of Wisconsin. Madison.

Danky, James P., and Eleanor McKay. WOMEN'S HISTORY: RESOURCES AT THE STATE HISTORICAL SOCIETY OF WISCONSIN. Madison: State Historical Society, 1975.

Delgado, Jeanne Hunnicutt. "Nellie Kedzie Jones' Advice to Farm Women: Letters from Wisconsin, 1912-1916." WISCONSIN MAGAZINE OF HISTORY, v. 57, no. 1 (1973), pp. 2-27.

Dexheimer, Florence Chambers. DAUGHTERS OF THE AMERICAN REVOLUTION: SKETCHES OF WISCONSIN PIONEER WOMEN. Fort Atkinson: W.D. Hoard & Sons Co., 1925.

Droste, Jean Rasmussen. WOMEN AT WISCONSIN. Madison: University of Wisconsin, 1968. (Thesis)

"First Assemblywomen Elected to State Legislature in 1924." WISCONSIN THEN AND NOW, v. 25, no. 9 (April 1979), pp. 2-3, 6.

Graves, Lawrence L. THE WISCONSIN WOMAN SUFFRAGE MOVEMENT, 1848-1920. Madison: University of Wisconsin, 1954. (Thesis)

Hass, Paul H. "Sin in Wisconsin: The Teasdale Vice Committee of 1913." WISCONSIN MAGAZINE OF HISTORY, v. 49, no. 2 (1966), pp. 138-151.

Hinding, Andrea. WOMEN'S HISTORY SOURCES: A GUIDE TO ARCHIVES AND MANUSCRIPT COLLECTIONS IN THE UNITED STATES. 2 vols. New York: R.R. Bowker, 1979. (Wisconsin entries, vol. 1, pp. 1061-1088.)

Hoeveler, Diane Long. MILWAUKEE WOMEN YESTERDAY, MILWAUKEE WOMEN TODAY. Milwaukee: University of Wisconsin Board of Regents, 1979.

Howie, Adda F., 1852-1936. Papers, 1904-26. State Historical Society of Wisconsin, Madison.

Hurn, Ethel Alice. WISCONSIN WOMEN IN THE WAR BETWEEN THE STATES. n.p.: Wisconsin History Commission, 1911.

Kidwell, Clara Sue. "The Power of Women in Three American Indian Societies." JOURNAL OF ETHNIC STUDIES, v. 6, no. 3 (1978), pp. 113-121.

Kohler, Ruth Miriam DeYoung. THE STORY OF WISCONSIN WOMEN. Kohler: Committee on Wisconsin Women for the 1948 Wisconsin Centennial, 1948.

Krueger, Lillian. MOTHERHOOD ON THE WISCONSIN FRONTIER. Madison: State Historical Society, 1951.

McBeath, Lida W. "Eloise Gerry: A Woman of Forest Science." JOURNAL OF FOREST HISTORY, v. 22, no. 3 (1978), pp. 128-135.

"Olympia Brown." Universalist Historical Society, Boston. ANNUAL JOURNAL (special issue), v. 4 (1963), pp. 1-76.

Pau On Lau, Estelle. "Ellen Sabin and the Founding of Milwaukee-Downer College." OLD NORTHWEST, v. 3, no. 1 (1977), pp. 39-50.

Rothaus, Leslie Gail. THE WOMEN'S STUDIES PROGRAM: A CASE STUDY OF THE POLITICAL SURVIVAL OF A NON-TRADITIONAL PROGRAM WITHIN THE UNIVERSITY OF WISCONSIN-MADISON. Madison: University of Wisconsin, 1980. (Thesis)

SPECIAL COLLECTION ON WISCONSIN WOMEN ARTISTS, THE. Golda Meir Library. Milwaukee: University of Wisconsin, 1979. (Features oral history tapes of women in the visual literary and performing arts. Accompanied by biographical sketches, slides, photographs, lists of works, catalogs and reviews.)

Stewart, Mary E., 1841-1931. Papers, 1828-1928. State Historical Society of Wisconsin, Madison.

Struna, Nancy, and Mary L. Remley. "Physical Education for Women at the University of Wisconsin, 1863-1913: A Half Century of Progress." CANADIAN JOURNAL OF THE HISTORY OF SPORT AND PHYSICAL EDUCATION, v. 4, no. 1 (1973), pp. 8-26.

Swoboda, Marian J., and Audrey J. Roberts, eds. UNIVERSITY WOMEN: A SERIES OF ESSAYS. Vol. 1: THEY CAME TO LEARN, THEY CAME TO TEACH, THEY CAME TO STAY. Vol. 2: WISCONSIN WOMEN' GRADUATE SCHOOL, AND THE PROFESSIONS. Vol. 3: WOMEN EMERGE IN THE SEVENTIES. Madison: Office of Women, University of Wisconsin System, 1980.

Thoms, Mildred Florence. WAR WORK OF WISCONSIN WOMEN 1860-1919. Madison: University of Wisconsin, 1921. (Thesis)

Waligorski, Ann Shirley. SOCIAL ACTION AND WOMEN: THE EXPERIENCE OF LIZZIE BLACK KANDER. Madison: University of Wisconsin, 1970. (Thesis)

White, Helen C., 1896-1967. Papers, 1917-65. Unpublished guide. UW-Madison, Archives.

Wisconsin. Governor's Commission on the Status of Women. Records. 1965-70. Unpubished guide. UW-Madison, Archives.

Wisconsin. Governor's Commission on the Status of Women. WISCONSIN WOMEN AND THE LAW. 3d ed. Madison: The Commission, 1979.

Wisconsin. State Historical Society. Women's Auxiliary, FAMOUS WISCONSIN WOMEN. 6 vol. Madison: State Historical Society, 1971.

Wisconsin. University. Dean of Women. Records. 1920-1968. Unpublished guide. UW-Madison. Archives.

Wisconsin Jewish Oral History Interview Project. Tapes and transcripts. Published guide. State Historical Society of Wisconsin, Madison.

Wisconsin Women's Suffrage Association. Records. 1892-1925. Published guide. State Historical Society of Wisconsin, Madison.

Women's International League for Peace and Freedom, Madison. Records. 1924-1965. State Historical Society of Wisconsin, Madison.

Further information and additional copies of this bibliographic checklist may be obtained from: Linda Parker, Women's Studies Librarian-at-Large, 112A Memorial Library, 728 State Street, Madison, WI 53706.

appendix b: selected honors,

accomplishments, publications

Assistance in the preparation of this appendix was graciously given by Mary Lueck Crouse.

MARGARET MARY McCORMACK ABARAVICH

Advocate for the deaf for: Milwaukee Schools two-track education; telephone devices for deaf customers; Wisconsin Bureau of the Hearing Impaired; television captioning.

Degrees: B.A., University of Wisconsin-Milwaukee.

JUSTICE SHIRLEY ABRAHAMSON

Justice, Wisconsin Supreme Court; American Bar Association.

Member: Commission on Undergraduate Education in Law and the Humanities; Council on Legal Education and Admission to the Bar.

Director: American Association for Advancement of the Humanities; Madison Trust for Historic Preservation; Wisconsin Civil Liberties Union; Madison League of Women Voters; Criminal Law Section, State Bar of Wisconsin.

Degrees: B.A., New York University; J.D., Indiana University Law School; S.J.D., University of Wisconsin Law School.

LOIS ALMON

Faculty member, Miles College, Birmingham, AL; nutrition researcher, Mississippi State Experimental Station.

Researcher, Wisconsin State Laboratory of Hygiene.

Degrees: Ph.D., M.S., B.S., University of Wisconsin-Madison.

Creator, Almon Recreation Area, Rhinelander.

MONICA E. BAINTER

Chairman, Dept. of Physics, University of Wisconsin-Stevens Point.

Awards: Distinguished Service Citation, American Association of Physics Teachers.

Degrees: B.A., College of St. Teresa; M.A., University of Minnesota; Ph.D., University of Wisconsin.

LORNA BALIAN

Honors: Four Junior Literary Guild Awards; Colorado Children's Picture Book Award; Georgia Children's Picture Book; Wisconsin's Little Archer.

Publications: HUMBUG WITCH; THE SWEET TOUCH; THE ANIMAL; I LOVE YOU, MARY JANE; SOMETIMES IT'S TURKEY, SOMETIMES IT'S FEATHERS; HUMBUG RABBIT; BAH! HUMBUG; A SWEETHEART FOR VALENTINE; WHERE IN THE WORLD IS HENRY?; LEPRECHAUNS NEVER LIE.

HELEN I. BARNHILL

President, Barnhill-Hayes, Inc.

Moderator, General Synod of the United Church of Christ.

(Continued)

Trustee, Lakeland College.

Board Member: Goals for Milwaukee, 2000; Northwest General Hospital; Better Business Bureau of Greater Milwaukee.

Member: United Way Planning and Allocations Council; Private Industry Council; Greater Milwaukee Committee.

Degrees: B.A., Marquette University.

Honors: Honorary Ph.D., Lakeland College.

Awards: Distinguished Service, Personnel-Industrial Relations Association; B'nai B'rith Interfaith Award for Community Service; Outstanding Business Achievement, Wisconsin Women's Political Caucus.

EVANGELINE HOYSRADT BERGSTROM

Collector of antique glass paperweights ranked among finest in the world.

Member, Mayflower Society of Massachusetts, the Colonial Dames of Wisconsin, Daughters of the American Revolution, Antiquarian Society of Wisconsin, State Historical Society of Wisconsin.

Publications: OLD GLASS PAPERWEIGHTS, 1940; "Pinchbeck but Precious," THE AMERICAN COLLECTOR.

ROBERTA REHBERG BOORSE

Founder, President, Managing Director, Milwaukee Ballet Company.

Founding Board Member: Great American Children's Theatre, Greater Milwaukee Council of Arts for Children.

Board Member: Ballet Foundation of Milwaukee, Inc., United Performing Arts Fund, Ko-Thi Dance Company.

Awards: Distinguished Service to the Performing Arts, University of Wisconsin-Milwaukee, School of Fine Arts; Theta Sigma Phi Community Service; First Lady of Milwaukee Ballet, MBC Ballet Board of Directors; Honorary Director, Ballet Foundation of Milwaukee, Inc.

GENE BOYER

Founder, National Organization for Women (NOW).

Treasurer, NOW.

National past president, NOW Legal Defense and Education Fund.

President, National Women's Conference Committee.

Secretary, Wisconsin Women's Education Fund.

Founder, Wisconsin Women's Network.

Member: Wisconsin Governor's Commission on Status of Women; Planning Commission, City of Beaver Dam.

Vice-Chair, Housing Authority, City of Beaver Dam.

Vice president, Wisconsin Retail Furniture Association.

Director, Midwest Home Furnishings Association.

Awards: Woman Activist of the Year, Wisconsin Zero Population Growth; Woman of the Year in Business, WISCONSIN STATE JOURNAL; Outstanding Community Leader, Beaver Dam Kiwanis Club; Woman Business Leader, Women's Equity Action League; Woman of the Year, Wisconsin NOW; Wisconsin Women's Political Caucus Toastee.

PEG BRADLEY

Trustee, Milwaukee Art Center.

Executive Board Member: Milwaukee Symphony; Wisconsin Arts Foundation Council.

Honors: Honorary Degree, D.F.A., Lawrence University.

Awards: Gimbel's Fashion; Pro-Urbe Medal for Civic Service, Mount Mary College; Headliner Award, Milwaukee Press Club.

ISABEL BROWN

Chairman, Arrowhead High School Board of Education.

Director: Wisconsin Polled Hereford Association; Wisconsin Livestock Breeders Association; Beef Superintendent, Waukesha County Fair.

President, Hartland Woman's Club.

Chairman, Cooperative Educational Service Agency.

Clerk, Village of Merton.

Awards: Premier exhibitor and breeder, numerous Midwestern state fairs.

FERNE CAULKER-BRONSON

Founder, Ko-Thi Dance Company.

Degree: B.A., University of Wisconsin-Milwaukee.

Awards: Outstanding Young Women of America, 1980 edition; Ko-Thi Dance Days, Milwaukee; one of "80 for the 80's," MILWAUKEE JOURNAL; Delta Sigma Theta, Distinguished Persons of Afro-American ancestry; Outstanding Achievement in the Creative and Performing Arts, YWCA Leader Luncheon.

MAUREE APPLEGATE CLACK

Professor: University of Wisconsin-La Crosse.

Awards: Meritorious Service to the English profession, Wisconsin Council of Teachers of English; Distinguished achievement in the language arts and the teaching profession, Arizona State University.

Degrees: B.A., Northwestern University, M.A. Northwestern University.

Publications: "Let's Write," Wisconsin School of the Air; HELPING CHILDREN IN WRITING; EVERYBODY'S BUSINESS—OUR CHILDREN; EASY IN ENGLISH; WINGED WRITING.

KATHRYN FREDERICK CLARENBACH

Chair, Wisconsin Governor's Commission on the Status of Women.

Member, Continuing Committee of the Houston National Women's Conference.

Consultant: National Manpower Institute, Center for Women and Work; National Advisory Council on Women's Educational Programs.

Chair, Board of Trustees, Alverno College.

Founder and First Chair of Board, National Organization for Women.

Awards: Wisconsin NOW—Woman of the Year; B'nai B'rith Human Rights; Wisconsin AFL-CIO Woman's Conference; Wisconsin Civil Libertarian of the Year, WCLU; Woman of Distinction, Madison, YWCA; Human Relations, Hall of Respect, Madison Public Schools.

Publications: "Continuing Education—A Personal View," chapter in UW System Monograph, UNIVERSITY WOMEN: WOME'

EMERGE IN THE SEVENTIES; UNFINISHED BUSINESS OF WOMEN'S RIGHTS, The Journal of Intergroup Relations, Vol. VII, No. 2, Sept. 1979; EDUCATIONAL NEEDS OF RURAL WOMEN, 1977 publication of National Advisory Council on Women's Educational Programs; WISCONSIN WOMEN AND THE LAW, co-author and editor, 1975, published by Wisconsin Status of Women Commission. (Second and third editions, 1977 and 1979.)

CATHERINE CLEARY

Adjunct professor of Business Administration, Graduate School of Business, UW-Milwaukee.

First woman president, board chairman, First Wisconsin Trust Co.

First woman director: Northwestern Mutual Life Ins. Co., American Telephone and Telegraph, Kraft, Kohler, General Motors.

Trustee: Lawrence University, Notre Dame, Mayo Foundation, Johnson Foundation, Faye McBeath Foundation, Milwaukee United Way.

Member: President's Committee on Education Beyond School; Commission on the Education of Women, American Council of Education.

Assistant Treasurer of the United States.

President, National Association of Bank Women; Milwaukee Children's Hospital.

Degrees: B.A., University of Chicago; L.L.B., University of Wisconsin Law School.

Honors: Eleven honorary degrees from major colleges and universities, including Babson College, Smith College, University of Notre Dame, Marquette University.

DR. FRANCES A. CLINE

Family Practice until February, 1980.

Part-time District Health Officer, Rhinelander.

Member: Wisconsin Public Health Association; consulting staff, St. Mary's Hospital, Rhinelander.

Life member: American Public Health Association; American Academy of Family Physicians.

Degrees: M.D., University of Illinois College of Medicine; M.P.H., John Hopkins University.

Honors: Francis A. Cline, M.D. Library, Rhinelander Hospital.

Awards: 1980 Woman of the Year, Rhinelander Business and Professional Woman's Club.

RUTH C. CLUSEN

Assistant Secretary for Environment, U.S. Department of Energy.

President, League of Women Voters, national, state and local.

Moderator, Presidential Campaign TV Debate, 1976.

U.S. Delegate, World Conference on Observance of Women's Year in Mexico City.

Degrees: B.A., University of Wisconsin-Eau Claire.

Honors: Honorary L.L.D., Colgate University, Wayne State University; Honorary L.H.D., St. Mary's College of Notre Dame.

Awards: Alumni Community Service, UW-Eau Claire, 1970; Doer of Decade, Wis. Chapter, Professional Women in Journalism, 1970; Woman of the Year, LADIES HOME JOURNAL, 1977; Natural

Resources Council Environmental, 1978; National Wildlife Federation, 1978; Listing in NOTABLE AMERICANS, 1976-77; WHO'S WHO IN AMERICA.

SIGNE SKOTT COOPER

Professor and Chairman, Continuing Education in Nursing, Health Sciences Unit, University of Wisconsin-Extension.

Associate Dean for Continuing Education, School of Nursing, University of Wisconsin-Madison.

Head Nurse, Obstetric Unit, University Hospitals, Madison.

President, Wisconsin Nurses Association.

Consultant: Clinical Center, National Institutes of Health; World Health Organization; PLATO Nursing Project (computer-assisted instruction), McGraw-Hill Book Company.

Degrees: B.S., University of Wisconsin School of Nursing; M.Ed., University of Minnesota.

Honors: Fellow, American Academy of Nursing.

Awards: Linda Richards, National League for Nursing for pioneering efforts in continuing education in nursing; Honorary Recognition, ANA; Pioneer, Adult Education Association of the USA.

Publications: CONTEMPORARY NURSING PRACTICE: A GUIDE TO THE RETURNING NURSE, New York: McGraw-Hill Book Company, 1970; and with May S. Hornback: CONTINUING NURSING EDUCATION, New York: McGraw-Hill Book Company, 1973; co-editor, PERSPECTIVE ON CONTINUING EDUCATION IN NURSING, Pacific Pallisades, CA: NURSECO, 1980; Editor, SELF-DIRECTED LEARNING IN NURSING, Wakefield, MA: Nursing Resources, 1980.

EMILY CONE HARRIS MURPHY COWLES

Finance Chairman, Green Bay-DePere YWCA.

Chairman, YWCA New Building Fund.

Board Member: Tank Cottage, Family Service.

FAY CROW

Executive Director, YWCA, Wausau, Wisconsin.

Founder, Marathon County Commission on Aging.

Degrees: B.A., Hiram College; M. Ed., Union Theological Seminary.

MARLENE CUMMINGS

Governor's Advisor, Women and Family Initiatives.

Coordinator for Human Relations, Madison Metropolitan School District.

Director of Public Relations, National Council for Adoptable Children.

Degree: R.N., Mount Sinai Hospital School of Nursing.

Awards: Woman of the Year, (1970), Jaycettes; Woman of Distinction in Education, Madison; Writer's Cup; one of "80 for the 80's," MILWAUKEE JOURNAL.

MARGUERITE DAVIS

Founder: Nutrition Laboratory, University of Wisconsin; School of Pharmacy, Rutgers University.

Co-author, THE NEWER KNOWLEDGE OF NUTRITION, 1913.

(Continued)

Degree: B.S., University of California at Berkeley.
Honors: Davis Hall of Natural History and Ecology in Racine County Historical Museum.
Awards: Women's Civic Council Award.

ADA DEER

Elected chairperson, Menominee Restoration Committee.
Lecturer, University of Wisconsin.
Director, Upward Bound, University of Wisconsin-Stevens Point.
Legislative Liaison, Native-American Rights Fund.
Member: President's Commission of White House Fellows; National Board, Americans for Indian Opportunity, OHOYO; Council on Foundations; Independent Sector; Rural America.
Degrees: B.A., University of Wisconsin-Madison; M.S.W., Columbia University School of Social Work.
Honors: Fellow, Institute of Politics, Harvard; Honorary Doctorate of Public Service, Northland College; Honorary Doctorate of Humane Letters, University of Wisconsin-Madison.

AUDREY JANE DERNBACH

Founder, Lazy Eye, Ltd. (amblyopia screening).
Degree: R.N., Columbia Hospital School of Nursing, Milwaukee.
Awards: Theodora Youmans Citizenship Award; Wisconsin Federation of Women's Clubs; National Center for Voluntary Action; American Legion Auxiliary; Sacred Heart Hospital Award for Lazy Eye Week; Eau Claire Exchange Club Book of Golden Deeds; Columbia School of Nursing Alumni; Eau Claire Chamber of Commerce Community Service.
Publication: CHARLIE'S LAZY EYE booklet.

HARRIET HARMON DEXTER

Acting President, Northland College.
Dean of Women, Northland College.
Visiting Professor, American University in Lebanon.
Teacher, Government Normal School for Boys, China.
Degrees: B.A., Cotner College; Master of Religious Education, Transylvania University.
Honors: Honorary L.L.D., Northland College.
Awards: Ashland's Outstanding Citizen of the Year, 1976, Veterans of Foreign Wars.
Publications: WHAT'S RIGHT WITH RACE RELATIONS, 1954; FINANCING FAITH, 1951; with William J. Hyde, DIG OR DIE, BROTHER HYDE, 1954; with Leila Anderson, PILGRIM CIRCUIT RIDER, 1960.

CLARE BLUETT DREYFUS

President, Wisconsin PTA, Milwaukee PTA, Milwaukee Board of School Directors.
Board member: Milwaukee School Board; Milwaukee Area Technical College; Milwaukee County Museum; Milwaukee Area Library System.
Secretary, Wisconsin Mental Health Association.
President, Milwaukee County Radio and TV Council.
Member, White House Committee on Children and Youth; White House Conference on Education.

Awards: "Mrs. PTA of Wisconsin," Wisconsin Mother of Year; Clare Dreyfus Scholarship.

EMMA DUERRWAECHTER

President, Germantown Bank.
Member: National Association of Bank Women, Wisconsin's Banker's Association.
Awards: Wisconsin's First Lady of Banking, Wisconsin Banker's Association; Listed in WHO'S WHO OF AMERICAN WOMEN, WHO'S WHO IN THE MIDWEST.

SUSAN SHANNON ENGELEITER

Wisconsin State Senator.
State Representative, Wisconsin State Assembly.
Governor's Legislative Liaison.
Attorney.
Degree: B.S., University of Wisconsin-Madison; J.D., University of Wisconsin Law School.

EDNA FERBER

Twelve Novels, including SHOW-BOAT, SO BIG, CIMARRON, GIANT, SARATOGA TRUNK, ICE PALACE.
Eleven volumes of short stories.
Six major plays with George S. Kaufman, DINNER AT EIGHT, ROYAL FAMILY, STAGE DOOR.
Two autobiographies.
Honors: Pulitzer Prize for SO BIG; Honorary Doctor of Letters Degree, Columbia University.

SISTER THOMASITA FESSLER, OSF

Chairperson, Art Department, Cardinal Stritch College.
Tour Guide: Europe, Far East, South America, United States, Mexico, Canada.
Member, Catholic Art Association, International Society for Education through Art, National Art Education Association, University Speaker's Bureau, Milwaukee Art Commission.
Degrees: B.Ed., University of Wisconsin-Milwaukee; B.F.A., M.F.A., Chicago Art Institute.
Major Exhibits: "The World is My Canvas"; "America is My Home"; "African Reflections"; "Reflections and Formations"; "Viewpoint."

ZONA GALE (BREESE)

Reporter: MILWAUKEE JOURNAL; NEW YORK WORLD.
Regent, University of Wisconsin.
Wisconsin representative, International Congress of Women.
Member, UW Board of Regents.
Degrees: B.A., M.A., University of Wisconsin.
Honors: Honorary L.L.D., Ripon College, University of Wisconsin.
Awards: Pulitzer Prize for play, MISS LULU BETT.
Novels: ROMANCE ISLAND; MOTHERS TO MEN; BIRTH.
Short Story Collections: FRIENDSHIP VILLAGE; FRIENDSHIP VILLAGE LOVE STORIES; WHEN I WAS A LITTLE GIRL; NEIGHBORHOOD STORIES; BRIDAL POND.

ROSALIE AGNES GANZ

County Superintendent of Schools, Buffalo County.
Founder, Sigma State Chapter, Delta Kappa Gamma.
Organizer, Alma American Legion Post No. 224.
Principal, Viroqua Junior High School.
Supervisor of Rural Schools, Juneau County.
Degree: B.A., University of Wisconsin-La Crosse.

JILL GEISLER

News Director, WITI-TV Channel 6, Milwaukee.
Campus chapter president, Sigma Delta Chi Professional Society of Journalists, UW-Madison.
Degree: B.A., University of Wisconsin School of Journalism.
Awards: Arc of Excellence, National Association for Retarded Citizens; Reporting: Northwest Broadcast News Association; Civic: Muscular Dystrophy, Big Brothers and Big Sisters, Toastmasters, Milwaukee Suburban Junior Women's Club, Milwaukee Fire Department and Association for Retarded Citizens.

GLORY OF THE MORNING

Chieftess, Thunder Clan of Winnebago Tribe.

BRETA LUTHER GRIEM

Home Economist, WTMJ-TV, "What's New in the Kitchen."
Chief Dietitian, Cook County Hospital, Chicago.
Degree: B.S., University of Wisconsin-Madison.
Publications: Co-author, THE BEST FROM MIDWEST KITCHENS.

SARAH HARDER

Assistant to Chancellor, University of Wisconsin-Eau Claire.
Founding Board Member, Wisconsin Women's Network.
Co-chair, National Women's Conference Committee.
Chair: AAUW National Committee on Women; Wisconsin State Division Committee on Women.
Degrees: B.A., B.S., University of Wisconsin-La Crosse; M.A., Bowling Green State University.
Presentations: "Barriers to Equality," "Programming for Disadvantaged Students"; "Equity in Academe"; "Women Making the System Work."
Awards: One of "80 for the 80's," MILWAUKEE JOURNAL.

MARGARET HAWKINS

Founder and conductor, Wisconsin Conservatory Symphony Chorus.
Regular Guest Conductor, Milwaukee Symphony Orchestra.
Art History Professor, Milwaukee School of the Arts.
Guest Conductor: Indiana All-State Chorus; New Mexico Honors Chorus; Racine Symphony Orchestra; Milwaukee Chamber Music Society; Blossom Festival.
Degrees: B.S., University of Wisconsin, Milwaukee; M.M. Indiana University.
Publications: Several articles, including monograph, "An Annotated Inventory of Distinctive Choral Literature for the High School Level."
Awards: Wisconsin Woman in the Arts, 1976.

MOTHER M. AGNES HAZOTTE. CSA

Co-Founder and Superior: Congregation of Sisters of St. Agnes.

FLORENCE PARRY HEIDE

Juvenile Novels: SECRET DREAMER, SECRET DREAMS; BANANA TWIST; GROWING ANYWAY UP; WHEN THE SAD ONE COMES TO STAY.
Picture Books: SOUND OF SUNSHINE, SOUND OF RAIN; THE SHRINKING OF TREEHORN; GIANTS ARE VERY BRAVE PEOPLE; ALPHABET ZOOP; MAXIMILIAN BECOMES FAMOUS; THE LITTLE ONE; WHO NEEDS ME? The Spotlight Club Mysteries; The Brillstone Adventures.
Short Stories: THE KEY; I NEVER LIKED HER.
Degrees: B.A., University of California at Los Angeles.
Honors: Honorary L.L.D., Carthage College.
Awards: Golden Archer Award; Jugendbuchpreis (best children's book in Germany); First Prize, juvenile fiction, Council for Wisconsin Writers.

BETH HEIDEN

Bronze Medalist, Lake Placid Winter Olympics, 1980.
World Speed Skating Champion, 1979.
World Road Bike Champion, 1980.
National Road Bike Champion, Senior Women's Division, 1980.
National Record holder, Time Trialing Event.
Awards: Madison Sportswoman of the Year; Madison Hall of Fame.

EDITH HEIDNER

Teacher, West Bend High School.
Volunteer curator, Historical Library and Museum, West Bend.
Degree: B.A., University of Wisconsin-Madison.
Awards: Service, Teacher's Recognition Day at State Fair; State Historical Society Local History Award of Merit.

MARGUERITE HENRY

Publications: KIND OF THE WIND; MISTY OF CHINCOTEAGUE; JUSTIN MORGAN HAD A HORSE; BLACK GOLD; SAN DOMINGO: THE MEDICINE HAT STALLION; WHITE STALLION OF LIPIZZA; BORN TO TROT.
Awards: Newberry; Lewis Carroll Shelf; Friends of Literature; William Allen White; Western Heritage; Sequoyah Children's Book.

HILDEGARDE

Star, NBC Network Radio Program, "The Raleigh Room."
Recorder of million-selling songs, "Darling, Je Vous Aime Beaucoup," "I'll Be Seeing You," "The Last Time I Saw Paris," "All of a Sudden My Heart Sings," and "Lili Marlene."
Co-star, touring company of Stephen Sondheim's Tony award winning musical "Follies."
Awards: George M. Cohen, Catholic Actors Guild.
Honors: Honorary Doctorate of Music, St. John's University.

JESSIE JACK HOOPER

National and state feminist.

(Continued)

Lobbyist, Wisconsin Woman Suffrage Association.

First President, Wisconsin League of Women Voters.

Chairman, Department of International Relations, General Federation of Women's Clubs.

Recording Secretary, Conference on the Cause and Cure of War.

ELLEN BENSON HUMLEKER

Associate Professor Emeritus, University of Wisconsin-Oshkosh, School of Nursing.

President, Fond du Lac City Council.

President, Fond du Lac Board of Education.

Vice-President, UW-Oshkosh, Association of University of Wisconsin Faculties.

Co-Chairperson, UW-Oshkosh Coordinating Council of Women in Higher Education.

President, Northern Wisconsin Dietetic Association.

Degrees: M.S., B.S., University of Wisconsin-Madison.

Awards: "Outstanding Contributions to the Community," Fond du Lac Area Chamber of Commerce; "Services Given Freely and Unselfishly," City of Fond du Lac; WHO'S WHO IN GOVERNMENT, 1976.

ADA JAMES

President, Political Equality League of Wisconsin.

Founder and Chairman, Children's Board of Richland County.

Vice-Chairman, Republican State Central Committee.

Chairman, Health Committee, Richland Center.

President, Wisconsin Women's Progressive Association.

ANITA HANKWITZ KASTNER

Professor Emeritus, University of Wisconsin-Milwaukee, School of Fine Arts, Department of Music.

Prior Teaching Experience: State Normal School, Natchitoches, LA; Central College, Fayette, MO; University of Wisconsin-Madison; Frances Shimer Junior College, Mt. Carroll, IL; Milwaukee Public Schools (Received state awards for student solo, ensemble, choral and orchestral competitions in tournaments.)

Degrees: B.Mus., M.Mus., Northwestern University; M.A., Columbia University; post master's degree study at both universities.

Honors conferred by Conservatoire Americaine, Fountainbleau, France: Diplome d'Execution, Piano; Diplome d'Aptitude a l'Enseignement du Piano; Diplome d'Aptitude a l'Enseignement du Solfege—Mention Bien.

Awards: Certificate of Recognition for Outstanding Civic Services, Sunday Morning Breakfast Club, Inc., Certificate of Appreciation Fourth District, Wisconsin Federation of Women's Clubs; Sword of Honor and Rose of Honor, Sigma Alpha Iota, International Professional Music Fraternity for Women.

Biographical Listings: WHO'S WHO IN MUSIC; DIRECTORY OF AMERICAN SCHOLARS; WHO'S WHO IN WISCONSIN; THE NATIONAL REGISTER OF PROMINENT AMERICANS AND INTERNATIONAL NOTABLES.

CLARE KIEPKE

Administrator, Volunteer Services Outagamie County Health Center.

Founding President: Casa Clare Halfway Houses I and II; Sunrise House for Chronically Mentally Ill Women, Appleton, WI.

Founder, Explorer Post for Health Care Fields; Acceptance, Inc. (Support group for Parents of Gays, Gays and Friends of Gays.)

Consultant, statewide on founding Halfway Houses; local, state and national levels on Fairweather Lodges.

Supervisor, Youthful Offenders from Circuit Court.

Co-Founder: LaRaza. Friends, Inc. (Drugs); Appleton Youth Drop-In Center; Christian Clothes Closet; Community Clothes Closet.

Awards: Howden Brotherhood from National Conference of Christians & Jews; Xavier Service to Humanity; Girl Scout Appreciation; Woman of the Year, APPLETON POST-CRESCENT; Woman's Club for help to the unfortunate.

RUTH DE YOUNG KOHLER

Vice-President and Curator, State Historical Society of Wisconsin.

Founding President, Women's Auxiliary of State Historical Society of Wisconsin.

President, Kohler Woman's Club.

Representative, Great Lakes Zone, National Trust for Historic Preservation.

Vice-President, Wisconsin State Division, AAUW.

Commissioner, Kohler Girl Scout Council.

Women's Editor, CHICAGO TRIBUNE.

Trustee: Lawrence College; Layton School of Art; Westminster Choir College; North Central Association of Colleges and Secondary Schools.

Degrees: B.A., Smith College.

Honors: Honorary L.L.D., Ripon College.

Awards: Theodora Youmans Citizenship Award.

MADAME LIANE KUONY

Instructor-Owner, Postillion School of Culinary Art and Postillion Great House Restaurant, Milwaukee.

BELLE CASE LA FOLLETTE

First woman to graduate from law school in Wisconsin.

Co-Founder, LAFOLLETTE WEEKLY MAGAZINE.

Organizer, Women's International League for Peace and Freedom.

Co-Founder, National Council for Prevention of War; Women's Committee for World Disarmament.

Degrees: LL.B., B.A., University of Wisconsin-Madison.

LILLIAN LEENHOUTS

Fellow: American Institute of Architects; Society of Women Engineers.

Founder: Architects' River Committee, Milwaukee Community Design Center.

Member, Wisconsin Architectural Licensing Board.

Degree: B.S. in Architecture, University of Michigan.

JILL ANN LIEBER

Reporter, SPORTS ILLUSTRATED

Sports Columnist, THE MILWAUKEE SENTINEL.
Degree: B.A., Stanford University.

MARY LINSMEIER

Founder and Co-Director, Mary Linsmeier Schools, Inc.
Instructor, Mount Mary College.
Degrees: Ph.B., Marquette University; M.S., University of Wisconsin-Milwaukee.
Publications: READING KIT; SENSORIAL MANUAL; PRE-STORIES; DISCUSSION TOPICS FOR PRE-SCHOOLERS; WHAT IS HAPPINESS?

LILLIAN MACKESY

Columnist and reporter, APPLETON POST-CRESCENT.
Co-Founder: Appleton Gallery of Arts; Appleton League of Women Voters.
Board member, Outagamie County Historical Society, Inc.
Degree: B.A., University of Wisconsin-Madison.
Awards: Golden Eaglet Pin, Girl Scouts; Historian of the Year, Outagamie County Historical Society; Local History Merit Award, Wisconsin State Historical Society.

MABEL RUBY MC CLANAHAN

Vice-President, Crane Engineering Sales, Inc.
President: Wisconsin Federation of Business and Women; National Federation of Business and Professional Women; Appleton Area School District Board of Education; Appleton Taxpayers' Association.
Board Member: Appleton Area Chamber of Commerce; Taypayers United to Control Spending; Appleton Area Goodwill, Inc.; Valley Northern Bank.
Awards: Woman of the Year, APPLETON POST-CRESCENT; WHO'S WHO IN THE WORLD COMMERCE AND INDUSTRY; WHO'S WHO IN THE MIDWEST.

MABEL MANNIX McELLIGOTT

Director, Continuing Education and Community Service, Mount Mary College.l
Assistant to Chancellor; Assistant to vice-president, Public Relations; Dean of Women — Marquette University.
President: Wisconsin Association of Women Deans and Counselors; Wisconsin Council of Catholic Women.
Vice-chairman, Governor's Commission on Status of Women.
Member: Wisconsin Legislative Council Committee; Wisconsin Development Authority.
Board member: Blue Cross/Blue Shield United of Wisconsin; AAUW Wisconsin State Division.
National President: Gamma Pi Epsilon, Jesuit Honor Society for women.
Degrees: B.Music, M.A., Marquette University.
Awards: Gimbel Forum Award; Milwaukee Council for Adult Learning Award; Germain Monteil Activist Award; AMUW Medallion, Bielefeld Award, Alumni Merit Award, Marquette University; Theta Sigma Phi Woman of the Year Award; Zonta Status of Women Award.

Honors: AAUW Wisconsin State Division Mabel Mannix McElligott Endowed Fellowship for Doctoral Studies.

GOLDA MEIR

Signer of Israel's Declaration of Independence (May 14, 1948).
Only woman member of first provisional legislature.
Israel's first minister to the Soviet Union.
Cabinet Posts: Minister of Labor and Social Insurance, Minister of Foreign Affairs; Chairman of Israel's United Nations delegation.
Fourth Prime Minister of Israel, first woman to hold post.
Teaching Certificate, Milwaukee Normal School.

CAROL HOUGH MERRICK

Founder and President, Kenosha Women's Network.
Co-Founder, Women's Horizons (battered women's shelter).
Board Member: Interagency Disability Board; CESA 18; Women Reading Women; State Displaced Homemaker's Board.
Wisconsin Delegate, Mini-White House Conference on Older Women.
Degrees: M.A., B.A., Northeastern Illinois University.

LILLIE ROSA MINOKA-HILL

Physician, Oneida, Wisconsin.
Degree: M.D., Woman's Medical College of Pennsylvania.
Awards: American Indian of the Year, Indian Fire Council of Chicago; Honorary membership, State Medical Society of Wisconsin.

GLADYS MOLLART

Volunteer curator of Watertown's Octagon House; Co-Founder, Watertown Historical Society.
Member, Watertown Memorial Hospital Board.
Degree: B.A., Vassar.
Awards: Outstanding Citizenship, Jefferson County chapter of Reserve Officers Association; "Gladys Mollart Tour Center," Watertown Historical Society Administration Building.

LUCY SMITH MORRIS

Founder: Wisconsin Federation of Women's Clubs; Athena Club.
Board member, Wisconsin Free Library Association.
Awards: Lucy Morris Memorial Scholarship, Wisconsin Federation of Women's Clubs.

MARY LOU MUNTS

State Representative, Wisconsin State Assembly.
Degrees: B.A., Swarthmore College, M.A., University of Chicago; J.D., University of Wisconsin-Madison.
Honors: Phi Beta Kappa, University of Chicago.
Awards: Citizen of the Year, Wisconsin Association for Mental Health; Wisconsin Environmental Decade Leadership; Commendation, International Association of Family Conciliation Courts; Madison Association for Retarded Children Annual Recognition; Center for Public Representation Public Service; Wisconsin Women's Political Caucus Annual; Madison YWCA Woman of Distinction; Wisconsin Association of Community Human Service Programs Certificate of Recognition.

BARBARA NICHOLS

Director, Hospitalwide Inservice Education, St. Mary's Medical Center, Madison.

President: American Nurses' Association; American Society for Health Manpower Education; Wisconsin Nurses' Association.

Vice-Chairman: Joint Practice Committee, Wisconsin Medical Society and Wisconsin Nurses Association; Region 5 Conference of the American Hospital Association on Educational Resources.

Degrees: B.S., Case Western Reserve University; M.S. University of Wisconsin-Madison.

Honors: Honorary D.Sc., University of Wisconsin-Milwaukee.

Writings: "ANA: A Multipurpose Representative Professional Association," JOURNAL OF NURSING ADMINISTRATION, May 1979; "Training in Transition," INSERVICE EDUCATION AND TRAINING MAGAZINE, Feb. 1975.

Awards: Navy Citation of Honor for Patients Undergoing Open Heart Surgery.

GEORGIA O'KEEFFE

Artist represented in the permanent collections of the Metropolitan Museum of Art, Whitney Museum of American Art, Brooklyn Museum, Museum of Modern Art, Albright-Knox Art Gallery, New York; Walker Art Center, MN; National Gallery of Art, Washington, D.C., Cleveland Museum of Art; Art Institute of Chicago; Amon Carter Museum of Western Art, Fort Worth; Milwaukee Art Center and 40 other museums throughout the U.S.

Honors: Honorary degrees from Minnesota College of Art and Design, Mt. Holyoke, University of Wisconsin, Harvard, Columbia, College of William and Mary, Mills College, University of New Mexico, Randolph-Macon Women's College.

Awards: Chosen one of the twelve outstanding women in the past fifty years, New York World's Fair, 1939; Presidential Medal of Honor; Outstanding Achievement in Visual Arts, by President Carter; Creative Arts, Brandeis University; Gold Medal, National Institute of Arts and Letters.

ROSALINE PECK

First white woman in Madison and Baraboo.

Namesakes: Rosaline Street in Baraboo.

Honors: Commemorative plaque, GEF-3, State Office Building, Madison.

ELIZABETH GIFFORD PECKHAM

Founding President, Association of Collegiate Alumnae (now AAUW), Milwaukee Branch.

Taxonomist noted for research on jumping spider, genus PECKHAMIA.

Degree: B.A., Vassar.

Publications: With her husband, published 31 works, including THE INSTINCTS AND HABITS OF SOLITARY WASPS.

MAREN CHRISTINE PEDERSEN

School Librarian: River Falls; Wisconsin Rapids; Eau Claire.

Chairman: Save South Hall Committee of Pierce County Historical Association; River Falls Public Library Board.

Founder, Senior Citizens Club; Telecare project and Awareness of Hazards to the Elderly, River Falls.

Member, UW-River Falls Foundation Board; Wisconsin Library Association; River Falls Area Retired Teachers Association; Wisconsin Retired Teachers Association.

Degrees: Teaching Certificate, River Falls Normal School; Library Science, University of Minnesota.

Awards: Service to the Elderly, Lions Club; AAUW Outstanding Woman Award.

KATE HAMILTON PIER

Founder, Psi Chapter, Kappe Beta Pi legal sorority, University of Wisconsin; Pier Law Firm, Milwaukee.

Vice-President, National Women Lawyers Association.

Degree: L.L.B., University of Wisconsin.

EDNA FRIDA PIETSCH

Composer, Music Teacher.

Honor: Edna Pietsch Scholarship Fund, MacFayden Club.

Awards: Career Achievement Award, Professional Fraternity Association; Honorary member, Seven Arts Society, Wauwatosa Music Club.

Performed Works: FANTASY FOR ORCHESTRA (two performances with the Chicago Symphony Orchestra in Milwaukee's Pabst Theatre with Dr. Frederick Stock conducting, 1942, and with Desire DeFauw, 1946; and with the Milwaukee Symphony, Uihlein Hall, Performing Arts Center, with John Covelli, 1975); FIVE ORIENTAL IMPRESSIONS (performed at National Gallery of Art, Washington, D.C., Richard Balles conducting, 1946; and in Milwaukee's Uihlein Hall, PAC, with Kenneth Schermerhorn conducting, 1978); Piano Concerto performed in Waukesha, 1956, with Milton Weber conducting.

GRETA LAGRO POTTER

Professor, Head of Department of Library Science, Clarion State College, PA.

Chairman: Better Broadcasts for Northwest Wisconsin; Policy Committee of the American Council for Better Broadcasts.

Degrees: B.A., University of Minnesota, B.S., M.S., Columbia University.

Published works: "An Appreciation of Sir Emery Walker," LIBRARY QUARTERLY; FOREVER REAL: CHEQUAMEGON VIEW HILLTOP AND OTHER POEMS.

Awards: Citations for work in Look-Listen Polls, Superior as Better Broadcasts chairman; Citation, League of Minnesota Poets.

SISTER JOEL READ

President, Alverno College

Chair, Advisory Committee for Project on Status and Education of Women, Association of American Colleges.

Board Member: Educational Communication Board, State of Wisconsin; Governmental Relations Committee, Wisconsin Association of Independent Colleges and Universities; National Council on the Humanities; United Community Services,

Milwaukee.

Degrees: B.S. Ed., Alverno College; M.A., Fordham University.

Honors: Honorary L.H.D., Lakeland College, Wittenberg University.

Awards: Teaching Excellence, Alverno College; Pope John XXIII; Viterbo College, Anne Roe; Harvard Graduate School of Education.

SISTER REMY REVOR

Art Professor, Mount Mary College.

Degrees: B.A., Mount Mary College; M.F.A., B.F.A., Art Institute of Chicago.

Exhibitor: Smithsonian Traveling Exhibition of Crafts; Museum of Art at Carnegie Institute, Pittsburgh.

Awards: Gold Medal for Craftsmanship, American Institute of Architects; Wisconsin Governor's Award for Achievement in the Arts; Wisconsin Designer-Craftsmen Exhibits; Alumnae Madonna Medal for Professional Excellence, Mount Mary College.

ELMA SPAULDING SCHUELE

Community Advocate

Founder: Oconomowoc Branch of the American Association of University Women; Oconomowoc Chapter of the League of Women Voters; PTA in Oconomowoc; Waukesha County Humane Society; LaBelle Garden Club.

Degree: B.A., Pullman University (Washington State University).

BERNICE M. SCOTT

Founder, Marinette-Menominee Branch AAUW.

President, Sheboygan Branch AAUW.

Wisconsin State Division AAUW Board Member, almost continuous service, 1941-1971, including elected positions of Vice-President and Recording Secretary.

President: Sheboygan County Halfway House; Sheboygan County Retired Teachers' Association; Wisconsin Council of Social Studies; Wisconsin Association of College and Secondary School Counsellors.

Board Member: Sheboygan County Mental Health Association, Sheboygan County Receiving Home, Lake Shore Technical Institute Foundation, Sheboygan Arts Foundation.

Degrees: B.A., M.A. (2), University of Wisconsin-Madison.

Honors: Bernice M. Scott Endowed Fellowship, Wisconsin State Division, AAUW.

Awards: Good Citizen, Sheboygan Rotary Club; Distinguished Service, Sheboygan County Mental Health Association.

AUDREY SICKINGER

Farmer and Farm Manager, Manitowoc County.

President: Wisconsin Women for Agriculture; Grimms Helping Hands Homemakers.

Treasurer, Port Cities Business & Professional Women.

Chairman, Dairy Commodity, American Agri-Women.

Member, Advisory Committee on "Right to Farm," Wisconsin Department of Agriculture, Trade and Consumer Protection.

Wisconsin Representative, President's Rural American Women Conference.

Awards: Master Agriculturists, THE WISCONSIN AGRICULTURIST; Farm Wife of the Year.

MARY SPELLMAN

Mayor, Beaver Dam, Wisconsin.

Co-Founder, Beaver Dam Women's Club.

President, Service Club of St. Joseph's Hospital (Beaver Dam Community Hospital).

Degree: Teaching Certificate, Oshkosh Normal School.

Honors: "Spellman Award," for Junior High Student excelling in mathematics, Beaver Dam Junior Chamber of Commerce.

MARIE SPERKA

Founder, Woodland Acres Nursery.

Developer, Dicentra Luxuriant PP3324, everblooming bleeding heart.

Publications: GROWING WILD FLOWERS—A GARDENER'S GUIDE, Harper and Row.

HANNAH WERWATH SWART

Curator, Hoard Historical Museum, Fort Atkinson, WI.

Formerly Registrar, Milwaukee School of Engineering.

Past President, Women's Auxiliary, State Historical Society.

Member, Woman's Club of Wisconsin.

Publications: FOOTSTEPS OF OUR FOUNDING FATHERS; MARGARETHA MEYER SCHURZ; KOSHKONONG COUNTRY: A HISTORY OF JEFFERSON COUNTY; KOSHKONONG COUNTRY REVISITED.

Awards: Numerous local, state and national including: Girl Scouts USA, Legislative, State Historical Society, and service; included in WHO'S WHO since 1970.

ANGELINE THOMPSON

President, Village of Haugen.

Founder, Haugen Senior Citizen's Center; co-founder, Haugen Community Club.

Awards: Plaques of appreciation from Haugen Kiwanis Club; Citizens of the Village of Haugen; Haugen Area Senior Citizens Club; Distinguished American, Rice Lake Branch AAUW; listed in WORLD'S WHO'S WHO; WHO'S WHO OF AMERICAN WOMEN; INTERNATIONAL REGISTER OF PROFILES.

BARBARA THOMPSON

Superintendent of Public Instruction, State of Wisconsin.

Chairperson, Agency for Instructional Television, Bloomington, Indiana.

Board Member: College Board, New York; Wisconsin Council on Drug Abuse; National Council for Accreditation of Teacher Education; Jackson Clinic, Madison.

Degrees: B.S., University of Wisconsin-Platteville; Ph.D., M.S., University of Wisconsin-Madison.

Honors: Honorary L.H.D., Carroll College.

Awards: Distinguished National Alumnus Recognition, National 4-H Clubs of America; Distinguished Alumnus, University of

(Continued)

Wisconsin-Platteville; Honorary American Farmer, National Future Farmers of America; State Conservation, Madison Lions Club.

HELEN F. THOMPSON
State Representative, Wisconsin State Assembly.
President: Red Cross and Public Library Board, Park Falls.
Manager-owner, Park Hotel.
Chair, Women's Study Club.
Degree: Teaching Certificate, Milwaukee Normal School.

CLARISSA TUCKER TRACY
Teacher, Brockway (Ripon) College.
Charter member and first program chairman, vice-president, Educational Club of Ripon.
Honors: Honorary M.A., Ripon College; "Mother of Ripon College."
Publication: PLANTS GROWING WITHOUT CULTIVATION IN RIPON AND NEAR VICINITY.

DOROTHY VON BRIESEN
Volunteer Attorney: Legal Aid Society; Counseling Center of Milwaukee, Inc.
Wisconsin Chairman, American Field Service.
Board Member: National Council for International Visitors; United Way of Greater Milwaukee; Young Women's Christian Association of Milwaukee; Curative Rehabilitation Center.
Degrees: B.A., Northwestern University; LL.B., University of Wisconsin Law School.
Honors: "Mrs. AFS Wisconsin"; Special Service, Milwaukee Civic Alliance; Woman of Achievement, Quota Club of Milwaukee; Woman of the Year, Theta Sigma Phi.

DELLA MADSEN WENDT
President: Wisconsin State Division American Association of University Women; Young Women's Christian Association, Racine; Racine Branch AAUW.
Board Member: Racine Board of Education; League of Women Voters, Racine Women's Club; Racine Education Association, PTA; Mental Health Association, Racine County.
Chair, Great Decisions discussion groups, Foreign Policy Association; Red Cross Membership Drive; Building Fund Drive (for national AAUW headquarters bldg).
Degree: B.A., University of Wisconsin-Madison.
Honors: Della Madsen Wendt Endowed Fellowship Wisconsin State Division, AAUW; Racine Branch AAUW Named Grant.
Awards: Woman of the Year, Racine Women's Civic Council.

RUTH WEST
Developer, "West of the Lake," Manitowoc.
Chairman of the Board, Rahr-West Museum and Civic Center.
Awards: Distinguished Service, Lion's Club; Lydia Shafer Silver Bowl, Wisconsin Garden Club Federation; Distinguished Service, Manitowoc-Two Rivers YMCA; "Speak Up", YMCA.
Namesake: Ruth West Library of Beauty, Manitowoc Public Library.

HELEN CONSTANCE WHITE
Chairman, Department of English, University of Wisconsin.
President: American Association of University Women; American Association of University Professors.
Vice-President, International Federation of University Women.
First woman to hold full professorship in College of Letters and Science at UW-Madison.
Board Member: National Conference of Christians and Jews; American Council on Education; Phi Beta Kappa Senate.
Degrees: B.A., Radcliffe College; Ph.D., University of Wisconsin-Madison.
Novels: A WATCH IN THE NIGHT; NOT BUILT WITH HANDS; DUST ON THE KING'S HIGHWAY. Other publications: TUDOR BOOKS OF PRIVATE DEVOTION; ENGLISH DEVOTIONAL LITERATURE, 1600-1640.
Honors: Guggenheim Fellowship Grants (2); AAUW Achievement; 23 Honorary Degrees.

ELLA WHEELER WILCOX
Author, 40 volumes, mainly poetry; numerous articles for COSMOPOLITAN and other national magazines.
Honors: Included among famous women honored at World's Fair, 1893; Presented at Court of St. James; Honorary member of Sioux Indian tribe.
Awards: "Poet of the Day," Women's Congress, Chicago; Included in NOTABLE AMERICAN WOMEN.
Publications: POEMS OF PASSION; MAURINE; DROPS OF WATER; PERDITA AND OTHER STORIES; AN ERRING WOMAN'S LOVE; THE HEART OF THE NEW THOUGHT; THE ART OF BEING ALIVE; SONNETS OF SORROW AND TRIUMPH.

FRANCES WILLARD
President: Evanston College for Ladies; National Women's Christian Temperance Union; National Council of Women; World WCTU Convention, Faneuil Hall, Boston.
Honors: Honorary LL.D., Ohio Wesleyan University.

SHEILA YOUNG (OCHOWICZ)
Gold Medal Speed Skater, Innsbruck Winter Olympics.
First Place Winner, World Cycling Championships, Sprint Event, Italy.
Member, Executive Board, United States Olympic Committee.
Board member, United States International Skating Association.
1981 Amateur Athlete of the year by US Olympic Committee.

appendix c: source listing

ABARAVICH, MARGARET, written by Vincent Abaravich
1. Personal knowledge as husband of honoree.

ABRAHAMSON, SHIRLEY, written by Marion V. Bates
1. Personal interview.

ALMON, LOIS, written by Allan Bell
1. Personal letters and files of Lois Almon.
2. Newspaper articles—RHINELANDER DAILY NEWS, OUR TOWN, TOMAHAWK LEADER.
3. Resource persons of Rhinelander Branch, AAUW: Jane Binkley, Dr. Frances Cline, Marion Fletcher, Joan Heide, Betty McCleary, Rose Nelson.
4. Resource persons from the community: Pat Folgert, Mardell Penca, Cedric Vig, Dr. James Zimmerman.

BAINTER, MONICA, written by Marilyn Thompson
1. Personal interview.

BALIAN, LORNA, written by Sue Roemer
1. Interview with Lorna Balian.
2. Anderson, Jack, "Lorna Balian: Book Ideas from Gumball Machines," WEST BEND NEWS, October 10, 1975.
3. ABINGDON PRESS NEWSLETTER.

BARNHILL, HELEN, written by Mary Crouse
1. Vita and personal interviews from Helen Barnhill, Milwaukee.
2. MILWAUKEE SENTINEL, April 25, 1979, article by Ira Jwan Hadnot, "Boss meets own demands."
3. MILWAUKEE SENTINEL, April 26, 1979, Kent R. Krauss, "Women, Blacks making it."
4. MILWAUKEE JOURNAL, August 26, 1979, David Beal, "Where Opportunity Knocked."
5. APPLETON POST-CRESCENT, July 3, 1981, "Milwaukeean is Moderator."

BERGSTROM, EVANGELINE, written by Andrea Bletzinger
1. GLASS PAPERWEIGHTS OF THE BERGSTROM ART CENTER, by Evelyn Campbell Cloak (Crown Publishers, 1969).
2. EVANGELINE H. BERGSTROM COMMEMORATIVE PAPERWEIGHT, news release of March 14, 1974; Bergstrom Art Center files.
3. PIONEER PROFILES, a program presented by Mary Corry, Gretchen Maring and Florence Wilterding at the Y Community Center, Neenah, Wis., February, 1976.
4. PIONEER PROFILES: COLLECTOR'S INTEREST GREW TO BECOME GIFT OF BEAUTY from Northwestern newspaper, Friday, Oct. 8, 1976, by Andrea S. Bletzinger.

BOORSE, ROBERTA, written by Alice Sedgwick & Patricia Wilmeth
1. MILWAUKEE JOURNAL, October 7, 1979.
2. MILWAUKEE JOURNAL, May 7, 1980.
3. Interview, Friday, April 10, 1981.

BOYER, GENE, written by Iris Grundahl
1. Excerpt from a speech by Kathryn Clarenbach at a Wisconsin NOW Convention at Stevens Point in June, 1979, honoring Gene Boyer as Women of the Year.
2. Information in this biography was gained in interviews with the subject, unless otherwise noted.
3. Article in BEAVER DAM DAILY CITIZEN of Dec. 9, 1975.
4. Article about Gene Boyer from THE FEMINIST CONNECTION of October 1980.

BRADLEY, PEG, written by Margaret Park
1. Interviews with: Barbara Brown at Milwaukee Art Museum; Mrs. Valencourt at Zita's on Astor; Irene Braeger of the Allen-Bradley Company; Annabel Douglas McArthur of Milwaukee, historian; Alice Nelson, docent at the Bradley sculpture garden.
2. MILWAUKEE JOURNAL articles: Jan. 28, 1962; March 19, 1967, Lois Hagen; May 3, 1970; Sept. 14, 1975, James Auer, "A Visit with Peg Bradley"; Feb. 5, 1978, James Auer, "She had no pretensions . . . "
3. MILWAUKEE SENTINEL article, January 28, 1962.
4. WOMEN'S WEAR DAILY, March 20, 1956.
5. CHRISTIAN SCIENCE MONITOR, Aug. 24, 1956.

BROWN, ISABEL, written by Bette Brown and Mary Ellen Stone
1. Personal knowledge as daughter of honoree, Bette Brown

CAULKER-BRONSON, FERNE, written by Olive Caulker
1. NEW YORK TIMES, "Dance-Drama from India Opens Asia Society Hall," April 24, 1981.
2. Reviews, MILWAUKEE SENTINEL, MILWAUKEE JOURNAL.
3. Letter recommendation, Jack Waldheim, Associate Professor, UW-M School of Fine Arts.

CLACK, MAUREE APPLEGATE, written by Patt Boge
1. Archives room, LaCrosse Public Library.
2. LACROSSE TRIBUNE, July 14, 1969, and obituary, July 11, 1969.
3. Files of Neenah Joint School District, Neenah, Wisconsin.
4. Historical Files of University of Wisconsin-LaCrosse.

CLARENBACH, KATHRYN, written by Constance Threinen
1. Personal Interview

CLEARY, CATHERINE, written by Patricia Smith Wilmeth
1. Interview with Catherine Cleary, February 18, 1981.
2. Biographical Data: Northwestern Mutual Life Insurance Company, May, 1979.

CLINE, DR. FRANCES, written by Marion E. Miller and Lisbeth Kretlow
1. Personal interview with Dr. Frances Cline.
2. Resource persons: AAUW members, Rhinelander Branch—Jane Binkley and Rose Nelson.
3. Resource persons from community—Pat Folgert, Tom Michele, Mardell Penca.
4. Article by Tom Michele, OUR TOWN, November 25, 1979.

CLUSEN, RUTH, written by Lucille Katas
1. Personal interview.

COOPER, SIGNE SKOTT, written by Anne Niles
1. Cooper, S.S., "Nursing in the university system," UNIVERSITY WOMEN, A SERIES OF ESSAYS (Vol. II, (edited by M.S. Swoboda, A.J. Roberts). Madison: University of Wisconsin System, 1980, pp. 41-53.
2. Nichols, B.L. CONTINUING EDUCATION IN NURSING: A PROFESSIONAL IMPERATIVE. Paper presented at the 16th Invitational Conference for Nursing In-service and Staff Development Educators, University of Wisconsin-Extension, Madison, February 23, 1981.
3. CONTEMPORARY AUTHORS. Detroit: Gale Research, Vols. 53-56, 1975, p. 120.
4. DICTIONARY OF INTERNATIONAL BIOGRAPHY. London: Dictionary of International Biography Company, 1969-70, 6th Edition, Part I, p. 189.
5. WHO'S WHO IN AMERICAN EDUCATION. Hattiesburg, MS. Who's Who in American Education, Inc., Vol. 23, 1967-68, p. 165.
6. WHO'S WHO IN AMERICAN WOMEN. Chicago: Marquis Who's Who, Inc., 11th Edition, 1978-80, p. 169.

COWLES, EMILY, written by Diana C. Margotto
1. History of Green Bay-DePere YWCA 1919-1961.
2. History of Green Bay-DePere YWCA 1961-1968.
3. Interviews with daughters: Margaret Cowles (Mrs. Robert, Jr.), Green Bay, WI; Emily Ann Cowles (Mrs. Ray Hutson), LaCrosse, WI.
4. GREEN BAY PRESS GAZETTE: "Obituary"—Emily Cone Harris Murphy Cowles, 1969; "Braebourne revisited" October 1976; "Braebourne Big Hit" 1976.
5. Personal contacts: Mildred Smith (Mrs. Ralph), and Vesta Myller (Mrs. E.H.).

CROW, FAY, submitted by Marian Seagren Hall
1. Nikolai, Geri. WAUSAU DAILY HERALD. December 12, 1975.
2. Obituary. WAUSAU DAILY HERALD, July 20, 1979.

CUMMINGS, MARLENE, written by Jeanne Lamsam
1. Personal interview.

DAVIS, MARGUERITE, written by Elizabeth Walker
1. Colbert, Lucy, "Diplomat, Author, Vitamin Co-discoverer, Has Occupied 'House on the Hill'," JOURNAL-TIMES. October 7, p. 19.
2. Cooper, Barbar, Mitchell, Rynbergen, NUTRITION-IN-HEALTH AND DISEASE Lippincott, 12th Edition, Philadelphia and Montreal, 1957, p. 78.
3. "Developer of Vitamins, Marguerite Davis, Dies," JOURNAL-TIMES, September 19, 1957, p. 1.
4. Flynn, Helen, VENTORES, VOYAGES, VITAMINS,—National Dairy Council, Chicago, 1944, p. 8.
5. Jones, Edith Seymour and Jean Matheson, "Dr. Davis' Plant Specimens Still Used in Studies at University of Wisconsin," JOURNAL-TIMES, March 5, 1972.
6. Kaiser, Douglas, "Eating Habits Were Fortified by Miss Davis," JOURNAL TIMES, July 2, 1978.
7. McCollum, E.V., MY EARLY EXPERIENCES IN THE STUDY OF FOODS AND NUTRITION, Annual Review of Biochemistry, Vol. 22, 1953, p. 8.
8. "Trust Fund of Racine Doctor Will Aid Botanical Research," JOURNAL-TIMES, July 1, 1955.
9. "Vitamins," ENCYCLOPEDIA BRITANNICA, Vol. 23, 1945, pp. 219-20.
10. Interviews: Joyce Dahlberg, Kenosha, WI; Carolyn Gertenbach, Racine, WI; Estelle Keech, Racine, WI; James Molbeck, Molbeck's Health and Spice Sho-, Pacine, WI; Mildred Bo-'

Racine, WI; Murval Weidlein, Racine, WI.

DEER, ADA, written by Lois Kliefoth
1. Shames, Deborah (ed.) FREEDOM WITH RESERVATION, National Committee to Save the Menominee People and Forests, Madison, WI 1972.
2. Periodicals: Madison: CAPITAL TIMES. February 4, 1975, February 11, 1975, May 3, 1976, June 9, 1978, September 4, 1979; MILWAUKEE JOURNAL: December 28, 1976, October 30, 1976, December 3, 1976; NATIONAL OBSERVER. February 15, 1976; NATIONAL OBSERVER. February 15, 1975; MS. MAGAZINE. April, 1973; WASHINGTON POST, 1981.
3. Interviews: Ada Deer, Jody Schmitz, Anne Minahan.
4. Curriculum Vita for Ada Deer.

DERNBACH, AUDREY, written by Barbara Zellmer
1. "Community Communique." MD's WIFE, January, 1974.
2. "Amblyopia Detection." AMERICAN JOURNAL OF NURSING, 74:6:1084, June, 1974.
3. "Vision Testing by Parents of 3½ Year Old Children." PUBLIC HEALTH REPORTS, July, 1970.
4. Interview with Audrey Dernbach, R.N., March, 1981.
5. CAPITAL TIMES, Madison, WI, December, 1970.
6. EAU CLAIRE PRESS, October 25, 1970; August 6, 1971; October 9, 1972; July 22, 1973 and July 27, 1974.
7. MILWAUKEE JOURNAL, August 22, 1971; November, 1972 and April 27, 1974.

DEXTER, HARRIET HARMON, written by Eileen Carlsen and Ida Bobb
1. Anderson, Andra, ed. CABLE CULLINGS. Centennial Issue, 1980.
2. Dexter, Nathaniel B. HISTORY OF NORTHLAND COLLEGE. Ashland, Wisconsin.
3. Dodd, Florence. HISTORY OF ASHLAND BRANCH OF AMERICAN ASSOCIATION OF UNIVERSITY WOMEN (including incorporated scrapbooks).
4. Minutes of Vaughn Library Board.
5. NORTHLAND COLLEGE ALUMNI NEWS. "The Highway". Vol. 80, No. 1 (Winter, 1980).
6. "Northern Light" of Northland College (Fall, 1963).
7. News items from Ashland Daily News: January 22, 1958; July 7, 1958; September 17, 1959; June 2, 1961; June 16, 1962; November 27, 1963; January 23, 1971; January 26, 1971; February 13, 1980.
8. News release: Northland College. January 19, 1971.

DREYFUS, CLARE, written by E. Frankie Dreyfus
1. Personal knowledge as daughter-in-law of honoree.
2. Personal recollections of Governor Lee S. Dreyfus, son.

DUERRWAECHTER, EMMA, written by Janice Strauss
1. Interviews: Mrs. Arnold Kannenberg, Menomonee Falls, WI; Mr. and Mrs. Melvin Kelling, Germantown, Wisconsin; Mrs. Emmy Kinkead, Germantown, Wisconsin; Howard Reingruber, Germantown, Wisconsin.

ENGELEITER, SUSAN, written by Catherine DePledge
1. Interviews with Susan Engeleiter and with Ruth Humphries, her secretary.

FERBER, EDNA, written by Beverly Prieto
1. APPLETON EVENING CRESCENT, 1903-04.
2. Edna Ferber, A PECULIAR TREASURE, 1939.
3. Edna Ferber, A KIND OF MAGIC, 1964.
4. "Ferber," by Julie Goldsmith Gilbert, 1978.
5. Ryan High School Clarion, 1899-1903.
6. The Ferber books to 1926.
7. Clippings from Outagamie County Historical Society files.

FESSLER, SISTER THOMASITA, written by Sr. Margaret Peter
1. Personal interview.

GALE, ZONA, written by Judith Eulberg
1. Ridgely Torrence Collection, Princeton University Library.
2. Zona Gale papers, State Historical Society of Wisconsin, Madison.
3. Deegan, Dorothy Zost. THE STEREOTYPE OF THE SINGLE WOMAN IN AMERICAN NOVELS. New York: King's Crown Press, Columbia University, 1951.
4. Derleth, August. STILL SMALL VOICE: THE BIOGRAPHY OF ZONA GALE. D. Appleton-Century, 1940.
5. Farrar, John. "Zona Gale Ventures Into the Asylum", BOOKMAN. January, 1927.
6. Simonson, Harold Peter. ZONA GALE. New York: Twayne Publishers, 1962.
7. Interview with Dorothy Walker, Portage Attorney, March 23, 1981.

GEISLER, JILL, written by Barbara F. Clapp
1. Block, Allan. "Personal Letter to Henry Davis", Vice President and General Manager of Channel 6. May 29, 1979.
2. Clapp, Barbara. Interview with Jill Geisler. March 3, 1981.
3. Drew, Mike. "Critic Is Up in the Air." MILWAUKEE JOURNAL, Accent Section, September 7, 1979.
4. Hickey, Sue. "Jill Geisler Remains Jill Geisler." SOUTH SIDE spirit, Aug. 20, 1980, Vol. II, No. 33, pp. 1-2.

GLORY OF THE MORNING by Joann L. Oh
1. Adrian, Sylvester. Telephone interview regarding the Decorah family museum he formerly operated in Montello. April 3, 1981.
2. Carver, Jonathan. THE JOURNALS OF JONATHAN CARVER AND RELATED DOCUMENTS 1766-70. Ed John Parker. St. Paul: Minnesota Historical Society Press, 1976.
3. Carver, Jonathan. TRAVELS THROUGH THE INTERIOR PARTS OF NORTH AMERICA IN THE YEARS 1766, 1767, 1768. 3rd ed., 1781; facsimile rpt. Minneapolis: Ross and Haines, 1956.
4. Corry, Mary, Gretchen Maring, and Florence Wilterding. "Pioneer Profiles." Oshkosh NORTHWESTERN, June 1976.
5. Durrie, Daniel Steele. "Jonathan Carver and 'Carver's Grant.'" WISCONSIN HISTORICAL COLLECTIONS. Ed. Reuben Gold Thwaites. Madison: Wisconsin Historical Society, 1908. VI, 224-25.
6. Grignon, Augustin. "72 Years' Recollections of Wisconsin." WISCONSIN HISTORICAL COLLECTIONS. Ed. Lyman Copeland Draper. Madison: Wisconsin Historical Society, 1904. III, 286-88.
7. HISTORY OF THE FOX RIVER VALLEY, LAKE WINNEBAGO, AND THE GREEN BAY REGION. Ed. William Titus. Vol. 1. Chicago: S.J. Clarke Publishing Co., 1930.
8. HISTORY OF WINNEBAGO COUNTY. Ed Publius V. Lawson. Vol. 1. Chicago: Cooper and Co., 1908.

9. Horan, James D. THE McKENNEY-HALL PORTRAIT GALLERY OF AMERICAN INDIANS. New York: Crown Publishing, 1972.
10. THE INDIANS' BOOK. Ed. Natalie Curtis. New York: Harper and Brothers, 1935.
11. Kellogg, Louise Phelps. "Glory of the Morning: A Winnebago Chieftess." WISCONSIN MAGAZINE OF HISTORY, Aug. 1927.
12. Kohler, Ruth DeYoung. THE STORY OF WISCONSIN WOMEN. Committee on Women for the 1948 Centennial.
13. La Ronde, John T.D. "Personal Narrative." WISCONSIN HISTORICAL COLLECTIONS. Ed. Lyman Copeland Draper. Madison: Wisconsin Historical Society, 1908. VII, 245-265.
14. Lawson, Publius, V. HABITAT OF THE WINNEBAGO. Madison: State Historical Society of Wisconsin, 1907.
15. Leonard, William Ellery. "Glory of the Morning." In WISCONSIN PLAYS. Ed. Thomas Dickinson. New York: B.W. Huebsch, Inc., 1922.
16. Lurie, Nancy Oestreich. "Winnebago." HANDBOOK OF NORTH AMERICAN PLAYS. Ed. Thomas Dickinson. New York: B.W. Huebsch, Inc., 1922.
17. Patterson, Elsie. "The Decorah Family." BADGER HISTORY, Nov. 1967, pp. 4-15.
18. Radin, Paul. THE STORY OF THE AMERICAN INDIAN. New York: Liveright, 1954.
19. Radin, Paul. THE WINNEBAGO TRIBE. Lincoln, Nebraska: University of Nebraska Press, 1923.
20. Sieber, Nadine. Telephone interview regarding her forebear Glory of the Morning. March 23, 1981.

GRIEM, BRETA LUTHER, written by Maxine Ellis
1. Armstrong, Alicia. THE MILWAUKEE JOURNAL, September 18, 1955, p. 6.
2. Arndt, Jessie Ash. CHRISTIAN SCIENCE MONITOR, November 22, 1961, p. 10.
3. Daniell, Constance, MILWAUKEE JOURNAL, March 8, 1970.
4. "Working with Breta Griem," a personal interview, April, 1981.
5. DeMasters, Carol. MILWAUKEE SENTINEL, April 5, 1979.
6. Dooley, Donald H. MILWAUKEE JOURNAL, March 1, 1959.
7. Hinkamp, Mary. MILWAUKEE JOURNAL, September 28, 1947.
8. Hood, Joan. "Breta Griem Tells Restaurant Story," THE WISCONSIN RESTAURATEUR, January, 1959, 6.
9. Pilarski, Laura. MILWAUKEE JOURNAL, October 6, 1957.
10. MILWAUKEE JOURNAL, July 23, 1961; July 12, 1962; January 20, 1966; and April 7, 1980.

HARDER, SARAH, written by Kathy Mitchell
1. Personal interview with Sarah Harder, June 1, 1981.

HAWKINS, MARGARET, written by Marie Frank
1. Article on Margaret Hawkins, Barbara Moake, her secretary.
2. Biographical material and resume, Mary L. Crouse.
3. Kenngoff, Louise, "You can't . . . 'they said," MILWAUKEE JOURNAL, January 28, 1979.
4. Telephone interview with Margaret Hawkins.

HAZOTTE, MOTHER M. AGNES, written by Sr. Margaret Lorimer, CSA
1. Unpublished letters from the Archives of the Sisters of Saint Agnes, Fond du Lac, Wisconsin.
2. Life Sketches of the Deceased Sisters of the Congregation of St. Agnes from the Archives of the Sisters of Saint Agnes, Fond du Lac, Wisconsin. (Unpublished)

3. Palen, Sister Imogene. FIELDSTONES '76: THE STORY OF THE FOUNDERS OF THE SISTERS OF SAINT AGNES. Oshkosh, Oshkosh Printers, 1976.
4. Naber, Sister M. Vera. WITH ALL DEVOTEDNESS: CHRONICLES OF THE SISTERS OF SAINT AGNES. New New York, P.J. Kenedy & Sons, 1959.

HEIDE, FLORENCE PARRY, written by Linda S. Noer
1. Personal interview.

HEIDEN, BETH, written by Mary Helen Becker
1. Personal interview.

HEIDNER, EDITH, written by Marion Haebig
1. Personal interview.

HENRY, MARGUERITE, written by Anne Megna Dunst
1. Interviews with Gertrude Breithaupt Jupp (Marguerite Henry's sister).
2. WHO'S WHO IN AMERICA.
3. The World's WHO'S WHO OF WOMEN.
4. "Life is a Fast Track for Author" by Charles Hillinger Staff Writer for Los Angeles Times and Washington Post.
5. Brochure: "Meet Marguerite Henry". Rand McNally & Company.
6. HORNBOOK MAGAZINE, January-February, 1950.
7. ELEMENTARY ENGLISH, published by the National Council of Teachers of English, November 1954, January 1968, October 1974.

HILDEGARDE written by Alice Zillmer
1. OVER 50—SO WHAT! by Hildegarde with Adele Whitely Fletcher.
2. Hildegarde Biography. Compiled by Tommy Wonder and Don Dellair, Personal Managers of Hildegarde.

HOOPER, JESSIE JACK, written by Dorothy and Lee Newcomer.
Unpublished Sources:
1. Catt, Carrie Chapman. Carrie Chapman Catt Papers, Library of Congress.
2. Graves, Lawrence Lester. "The Wisconsin Women Suffrage Movement, 1846-1920," Ph.D. dissertation, University of Wisconsin, 1954.
3. Hooper, Jessie Jack. Jessie Jack Hooper Papers, State Historical Society of Wisconsin.
4. Miller, Josephine. Interviews by Dorothy Newcomer, Feb. 9, April 13, 1978.
5. Smith, Sophia. Sophia Smith Collection, Women's History Archives, Smith College.
6. Van Valkenburgh, Lois. Taped reminiscences, March, 1981, in possession of Dorothy and Lee Newcomer.
7. Walker, Lola Carolyn. "The Speeches and Speaking of Carrie Chapman Catt," Ph.D. dissertation, Northwestern University, 1950.
8. Whittemore, Helen. Interview by Dorothy Newcomer, Feb. 8, 1981.
Published Sources:
1. Allen, Hazel L. "Jessie Hooper." FAMOUS WISCONSIN WOMEN. Madison: State Historical Society of Wisconsin, 1975, 4.
2. DICTIONARY OF AMERICAN BIOGRAPHY. SUPPLEMENT ONE. Ed. by Harris E. Starr. New York: Charles Scribner's Sons, 1944.

3. Epstein, Leon D. POLITICS IN WISCONSIN. Madison: University of Wisconsin Press, 1958.
4. Ferrell, Robert H. PEACE IN THEIR TIME: THE ORIGINS OF THE KELLOGG-BRIAND PACT. New Haven: Yale University Press, 1952.
5. Graves, Lawrence Lester. "Two Noteworthy Wisconsin Women: Mrs. Ben Hooper and Ada James." WISCONSIN MAGAZINE OF HISTORY, 41 (Spring, 1958), 174-84.
6. MILWAUKEE JOURNAL.
7. NEW YORK TIMES.
8. NOTABLE AMERICAN WOMEN, 1607-1950. 3 vols. Ed. by Edward T. James. Cambridge: Harvard University Press, 1971.
9. O'Neill, William L. EVERYBODY WAS BRAVE: THE RISE AND FALL OF FEMINISM IN AMERICA. Chicago: Quadrangle Books, 1969.
10. OSHKOSH DAILY NORTHWESTERN.
11. Smith, James Howell. "Mrs. Ben Hooper of Oshkosh: Peace Worker and Politician." WISCONSIN MAGAZINE OF HISTORY, 46 (Winter, 1962-63), 124-135.
12. WHO'S WHO IN AMERICA. Ed. by Albert Nelson Marquis. Chicago: The A.N. Marquis Co., 1930-35.

HUMLEKER, ELLEN BENSON, written by Mary D. Fischer
1. FOND DU LAC COMMONWEALTH REPORTER: March 7, 1960, "Board Studies '61 Contracts;" March 11, 1979, "Council Presidents Review Progress"; January 22, 1976, "Ellen Humleker has Served Well".
2. June 20, 1966, "Good Educational Program Not Same as Building Plan".
3. January 11, 1960, "State Industrial Commission Will Close Roosevelt unless Major Repairs are Completed".
4. March 4, 1972, "Woman Runs for Council Re-election on Past Record".
5. Myron J. Medin, Jr., Letter dated May 1, 1980 to Dorothy Lane (Ms in possession of Ellen B. Humleker).
6. Jerome N. Strupp, letter dated May 1, 1980 to College of Nursing, University of Wisconsin-Oshkosh.

JAMES, ADA, written by Jane Nee Marr
1. Clark, James I., WISCONSIN WOMEN FIGHT FOR SUFFRAGE. Madison: State Historical Society, 1965.
2. James, Ada. Papers, State Historical Society of Wisconsin, Madison.
3. Kay, Carolyn, "Ada James", FAMOUS WISCONSIN WOMEN, Volume 3. Women's Auxiliary, State Historical Society of Wisconsin. Madison, 1973.
5. Scott, Margaret Helen, RICHLAND CENTER, WISCONSIN—A HISTORY, Richland County Publishers, 1972.
6. WISCONSIN STATE JOURNAL, Madison, September 30, 1952.

KASTNER, ANITA HANKWITZ, written by Frank J. Prince
1. Black, Anita, "Her Life Is Set to Music", MILWAUKEE SENTINEL, October 23, 1980 section of "The Organization Women 1980, pp 6-7.
2. Kastner, Anita—Biographical materials supplied by the subject.

KIEPKE, CLAIRE, written by Marilynn Richter
1. Personal interview.

KOHLER, RUTH DE YOUNG, written by Dolores Flader
1. Chase, Mus. Lucius P. "Ruth De Young Kohler". FAMOUS WISCONSIN WOMEN, Volume One. Women's Auxiliary, State Historical Society of Wisconsin, 1971.

2. Special Wade House Edition. KOHLER OF KOHLER NEWS. Kohler, WI: Kohler Company, 1957.
3. "People", Kohler Company, Kohler, Wisconsin, March 11, 1953.
4. "Let's Talk It Over", DECATUR (IL) HERALD, March 18, 1937.
5. Parnell, Dorothy, MILWAUKEE SENTINEL, March 9, 1953.
6. Interview with Ruth De Young Kohler II.
7. John Flader, personal letter to Dolores Flader.

KUONY, MADAME LIANE, written by Marilyn Stuckey
1. Personal interview.

LA FOLLETTE, BELLE CASE, written by Maria Bode
1. "Belle Case La Follette: a Progressive", WISCONSIN THEN AND NOW, Feb. 1972.
2. Clark, James I., WISCONSIN WOMEN FIGHT FOR SUFFRAGE, Madison: State Hist. Soc. of Wisconsin, 1956.
3. Doan Edward N., THE LA FOLLETTES AND THE WISCONSIN IDEA. New York: Reinhardt. 1947.
4. La Follette, Belle Case, LA FOLLETTE'S WEEKLY MAGAZINE, LA FOLLETTE'S MONTHLY MAGAZINE (numerous articles in the Home and Education Department) 1909-1931.
5. La Follette, Belle Case, and La Follette Middleton, Fola, ROBERT M. LA FOLLETTE, JUNE 14, 1855-JUNE 18, 1925. New York: Hafner. 1953, 1971 (reprint).
6. La Follette, Robert M., Sr., LA FOLLETTE'S AUTOBIOGRAPHY: a personal narrative of political experience, Madison: U. of Wisc. Press. 1960.
7. NOTABLE AMERICAN WOMEN: a biographical dictionary, 1607-1950, Cambridge, MA: Belknap Pres of Harvard U. Press, 1971.
8. Obituary, NEW YORK TIMES, Aug. 19, 1931, p. 21.
9. THE PROGRESSIVE, "Memorial Edition," Nov. 7, 1931.
10. Thelen, David P., THE EARLY LIFE OF ROBERT M. LA FOLLETTE, 1855-1884, Chicago: Loyola U. Press, 1966.
11. Wisconsin State Historical Society Women's Auxiliary, FAMOUS WISCONSIN WOMEN, vol. 5, pp. 1-9, Madison: State Historical Society, 1971.

LEENHOUTS, LILLIAN, written by Ruth Swaziek
1. Personal interview.

LIEBER, JILL ANN, written by Janet L. McBride
1. Cooper, Kenneth, THE NEW AEROBICS, Philadelphia, J.B. Lippincott, 1970.
2. Copland, Aaron, WHAT TO LISTEN FOR IN MUSIC, New York, McGraw-Hill, 1929.
3. Lieber, Jill, "You Can't Go Back, Beth Heiden Learns," MILWAUKEE SENTINEL, Feb. 21, 1980.
4. "Beth Heiden Over-Coached," MILWAUKEE SENTINEL, Feb. 18, 1980.
5. "Heiden Family Ruining Things for Eric," MILWAUKEE SENTINEL, Feb. 29, 1980.
6. Lieber, Jill, "Shouldering The Pain: Hisle, Slaton Join List of Players Sidelined by Rotator Cuff Injuries" MILWAUKEE SENTINEL, Aug. 4, 1980.
7. "Doctor Prefers To Shun Surgery," MILWAUKEE SENTINEL, August 6, 1980.
8. Lieber, Jill, "Dusting Off the Gold: Leah looking for End to Roller Coaster Life," MILWAUKEE SENTINEL, 1980.
9. "Baby Girl Warms Heart of 'Ice Maiden' ", MILWAUKEE SENTINEL, 1980.

10. Machlis, Joseph, THE ENJOYMENT OF MUSIC, New York, W.W. Norton & Company, Inc., 1957.
11. Mirkin, Gabe, "Why Every Athlete Needs Muscle-Stretching Exercises," WASHINGTON POST, April 1, 1976.
12. Suinn, Richard M., "Psychology for Olympic Champs," PSYCHOLOGY TODAY, June 1976.

LINSMEIER, MARY, written by Kathleen Winkler
1. Personal interview.

MACKESY, LILLIAN, written by Anne Biebel
1. Documents, papers, photographs bequeathed to the Outagamie Historical Society.

McCLANAHAN, MABEL RUBY, written by Jean Gaecke
1. Personal interview.

McELLIGOTT, MABEL MANNIX, written by Violet E. Dewey
1. WHO'S WHO IN AMERICA.
2. MILWAUKEE JOURNAL: January 3, 1975, "Mrs McElligott Changes Jobs;" May 8, 1977, "Advice to Others Was Good For Her;" 1977, "Mrs. McElligott Gets New Title at Mt. Mary."
3. MILWAUKEE SENTINEL, October 23, 1980, "Women Alumnae Vital to MU Growth."
4. Personal interviews.

MEIR, GOLDA, written by Mary Podell
1. Mann, Peggy, GOLDA: THE LIFE OF ISRAEL'S PRIME MINISTER, New York, Cowand, McCann & Georghegan, 1971.
2. Marlow, Moan, THE GREAT WOMEN, New York, A & W Publishers, Inc., 1979.
3. Meir, Golda, A LAND OF OUR OWN: AN ORAL AUTOBIOGRAPHY, ed. by Marie Syrkin, New York, G.P. Putnam's Sons, 1973.
4. "Meir, Golda," CURRENT BIOGRAPHY YEARBOOK, New York, The H.W. Wilson Company, 1970, pp. 284-287.
5. Meir, Golda, MY LIFE, New York, G.P. Putnam's Sons, 1975.
6. Syrkin, Marie, "Golda Meir: A Woman With a Cause", New York, G.P. Putnam's Sons, 1963.

MERRICK, CAROL, written by Elaine Edwards
1. Personal interview.
2. Newspaper articles from the KENOSHA NEWS and the MILWAUKEE SENTINEL.

MINOKA-HILL, LILLIE ROSA, written by Rima D. Apple
1. Rima D. Apple, "Lillie Rosa Minoka-Hill", NOTABLE AMERICAN WOMEN, supplement edited by Barbara Sicherman, Cambridge: The Belknop Press of Harvard University Press, 1980.
2. Rima D. Apple, "In Recognition of . . . Lillie Rosa Minoka-Hill (1876-1952), WOMEN & HEALTH, 1980.
3. Victoria Brown, "Dr. Rosa Minoka-Hill, "UNCOMMON LIVES OF COMMON WOMEN: THE MISSING HALF OF WISCONSIN HISTORY" Madison, Wisconsin Feminists Project Fund, Inc.
4. "An Indian Physician Remembers," THE CRUSADER: THE WISCONSIN ANTI-TUBERCULOSIS ASSOCIATION, May, 1951.
5. Sally Rogow, "Indian Doctor: Rosa Minoka-Hill, M.D."
6. Archives Division, State Historical Society of Wisconsin.
7. Appraisal of our work by Minoka-Hill in possession of granddaughter, Carol O'Loughlin Smart.

8. Other information provided by children: Norbert S. Hill and Jane Hill O'Loughlin.

MOLLART, GLADYS, by Evelyn Rose
1. News items in WATERTOWN DAILY TIMES, MILWAUKEE JOURNAL.
2. Records of Watertown Historical Society: minutes of Saturday Club.
3. Personal interviews: Gladys Mollart, Theodora Taras (Red Cross, AAUW), Rev. Robert Tully, pastor of First Congregational United Church of Christ.

MORRIS, LUCY SMITH, written by Vicki Gooding and Joan Wucherer
1. TRI-COUNTY NEWS: May 27, 1935, May 28, 1935, June 6, 1935.
2. BERLIN EVENING JOURNAL, May 29, 1935.
3. Personal letter, Lucy Smith Morris to Mrs. Coke, Oct. 17, 1931.
4. EDUCATIONAL HISTORY OF WISCONSIN, edited by Charles McKenney, A.M., The Delmont Co., Chicago Publishers, 1912.

MUNTS, MARY LOU, written by Marion Bates
1. Personal interview.
2. ISTHMUS, Madison, July 18, 1980.
3. MILWAUKEE SENTINEL, January 21, 1980.

NICHOLS, BARBARA L., written by Louise C. Smith
1. WISCONSIN STATE JOURNAL, May 20, 1979.
2. Personal interview, February 16, 1981.
3. Interview with Dennis Day, PhD, director of Inservice Education St. Mary's Hospital Medical Center, Madison.
4. Interview with Ellen Patterson, Associate Director, St. Mary's Hospital Medical Center.
5. Nichols, Barbara, AMERICAN JOURNAL OF NURSING, January, 1980.
6. Nichols, Barbara, URBAN HEALTH, July-August, 1980, p. 36.
7. AMERICAN JOURNAL OF NURSING' May, 1980, p. 881; "ANA President Barbara Nichols discusses Issues Due for Action at June Convention in Houston."

O'KEEFFE, GEORGIA, written by Catherine Krueger
1. O'Keeffe, Georgia. GEORGIA O'KEEFFE. New York: Viking Press, 1976.
2. Kotz, Mary, "A Day With Georgia O'Keeffe", ART NEWS, December, 1977.
3. Looney, Ralph, "Georgia O'Keeffe", ATLANTIC, April, 1965.
4. Sieberling, Dorothy, "Horizons of a Pioneer", LIFE, March 1, 1968.
5. Tomkins, Calvin, "the rose in the eye looked pretty fine." NEW YORKER, March 4, 1974.

PECK, ROSALINE, written by Betty Geisler
1. Butterfield, C.W., HISTORY OF DANE COUNTY, Chicago: 1880; HISTORY OF SAUK COUNTY, Chicago: 1880.
2. Canfield, W.H., OUTLINE SKETCHES OF SAUK COUNTY, 1899.
3. Durrie, Daniel Steele, A HISTORY OF MADISON, THE CAPITAL OF WISCONSIN, INCLUDING THE FOUR LAKE COUNTRY, Madison: 1874.
4. WISCONSIN STATE JOURNAL, "Madison Past and Present, 1851-1902", Semi-centennial edition, 1902.
5. Geisler, Betty Schlimgen, "Rosaline Dished Up Gemutlichkeit,

Yankee Style". THIS IS MADISON, July, 1976; "Capitol Fever", THIS IS MADISON, August, 1976.
6. Thwaites, Reuben Gold, THE STORY OF MADISON, Madison: 1900.
7. WISCONSIN HISTORICAL COLLECTIONS, Volume 6, 343-363.
8. Personal interview with Mrs. Victoria Peck Fillhouer, great granddaughter of Rosaline Peck, Madison, Wisconsin, April 2, 1981.

PECKHAM, ELIZABETH, written by Annabel Douglas McArthur
1. Bruce, William G., HISTORY OF MILWAUKEE, CITY AND COUNTY, Volume One.
2. Gregory, John C., HISTORY OF MILWAUKEE, WISCONSIN, Volume II, IV.
3. Jass, Joan, "The Peckham Spider Collection", LORE, Volume 29, No. 1, 1979, Milwaukee Public Museum.
4. Ogden, Marion, HOMES OF OLD SPRING STREET, 1946.
5. Stark, William, PINE LAKE, Sheboygan: Zimmerman Press, 1971.
6. Youmans, Theodora, "How Wisconsin Women Won The Vote," WISCONSIN MAGAZINE OF HISTORY, Madison: State Historical Society of Wisconsin, September, 1921.

PEDERSEN, MAREN CHRISTINE, written by Jane S. Huelskamp
1. Personal interview with Christine Pedersen.
2. Dagmar P. Frye, family anecdotes.

PIER, KATE HAMILTON, written by Joan Des Isles
1. DICTIONARY OF WISCONSIN BIOGRAPHY, Madison: State Historical Society of Wisconsin, 1960.
2. Doyle, Ruth B., "Women and the Law School, From a Trickle to a Flood," UNIVERSITY WOMEN, Madison: University of Wisconsin Office of Women, 1980.
3. HISTORY OF FOND DU LAC COUNTY, WISCONSIN, Chicago: Western Historical Company, 1880.
4. Kohler, Ruth DeYoung, THE STORY OF WISCONSIN WOMEN, Kohler: The Committee on Wisconsin Women, 1948.
5. Smith, Laura Grover. "A Law Firm of Women," LADIES HOME JOURNAL, September, 1892.
6. FOND DU LAC COMMONWEALTH REPORTER, June 10, 1956.
7. FOND DU LAC DAILY COMMONWEALTH, April 15, 1895.
8. FOND DU LAC DAILY REPORTER, April 1, 1922; June 22, 23, 1925.
9. FOND DU LAC JOURNAL, June 16, 1887; September 5, 1889.
10. FOND DU LAC WEEKLY COMMONWEALTH, September 16, 1887; June 26, 1891.

PIETSCH, EDNA FRIDA, written by Gloria D. Prince
1. KENNGOTT, Louise, "At Age 83, She Takes Her Bow", MILWAUKEE JOURNAL, 1968.
2. Grass, Mrs. Whitaker, Appleton Wisconsin Sunday POST CRESCENT, November 23, 1969.
3. Austin, Dorothy, "Honor for Miss Pietsch," MILWAUKEE SENTINEL, World of Women, June 5, 1971.
4. Johnson, Lawrence B., "Edna Pietsch: An Ageless Musician," MILWAUKEE SENTINEL, March 31, 1978.
5. Pietsch, Edna Frida, personal interview.

POTTER, GRETA, written by Paul H. Gaboriault
1. Telephone interview with Dr. Mary Leslie Spence, July 29, 1980.
2. Manuscript and other source materials, Superior Public Library.
3. Greta Potter file, Carlson Library, Clarion State College, Pennsylvania.
4. THE ECHO, Senior Number, University of Minnesota, May-June, 1911.
5. Bernard, Effie, "At 79, Superior Woman Has A Concerned Interest in Many Scholarly Pursuits," DULUTH NEWS-TRIBUNE, July 16, 1972.
6. Bunce, Alan, "Quality Television: What You Can Do," CHRISTIAN SCIENCE MONITOR, February 26, 1971.
7. Spence, Dr. Mary Leslie, "Veteran Workers in ACBB: Greta Lagro Potter." ACBB POST, November, 1969.

READ, SISTER JOEL, written by May Murphy Thibaudeau
1. Personal interviews: Sister Joel Read, Lois Rice, Dolores Schuda.
2. News Releases, Alverno Public Relations Department, Wittenberg University.
3. Article: NEWS-SUN, Springfield, Ohio, May 23, 1978.
4. Article: MILWAUKEE SENTINEL, November 7, 1975.

REVOR, SISTER REMY, written by P.T. Casey
1. THE AUTOBIOGRAPHY OF A COLLEGE, Milwaukee: Bruce Publishing Company, 1939.
2. SSND, MOTHER CAROLINE AND THE SCHOOL SISTERS OF NOTRE DAME IN NORTH AMERICA, Saint Louis: Woodward & Tiernan Co. 1928.

SCHUELE, ELMA SPAULDING, written by Shirley Whipple Hinds
1. Haegg, Margaret S., Letters and Tape Recording.
2. Hoeft, Mae G., Telephone interview.
3. Johnson, Jean Lindsay, ILLUSTRIOUS OCONOMOWOC, Milwaukee, 1977.
4. Kinkel, Irma K., Telephone interview.
5. Kile, W.W., Letter.
6. OCONOMOWOC ENTERPRISE, Reprint of 10-7-65 article.
7. Slemmons, Sarahbelle, Letter.

SCOTT, BERNICE, written by Betsy Hodson
1. WISCONSIN, A LEADER IN EDUCATION, Bicentennial project of Wisconsin Retired Teachers Association, 1976.
2. Jarvis, Shirley. "Miss Scott: Common Sense Counselor," SHEBOYGAN PRESS, June 5, 1967.
3. Personal interview with Bernice M. Scott, February 11, 1981.
4. Personal letters from John G. Buchen, Robert Leverenz, Howard Vieth, Mary Jo Ballschmider, Kathryn Hill, Eileen Scott, Nancy Schreiber.

SICKINGER, AUDREY, written by Anne Ernst
1. Kinderman, Wendy, "Farm Wife of Year Plans to Promote State Agriculture," Colby (WI): THE COUNTRY TODAY, May 7, 1980.
2. Menard, Maggie, "Top Farm Wife Prefers 'Farmer' Title," MILWAUKEE SENTINEL, May 3, 1980.
3. Miller, Patricia, "Farm Wife: She Lobbies for Farm Laws," Superior (WI): November 19, 1979.
4. Vogel, Jo Ann, Nomination for Master Agriculturist, March 26, 1980.
5. Zipperer, J.J., "Farm Wife of Year Is Rural Activist," Green Bay (WI): COMPASS, July 26, 1980.
6. Articles in: FARMER'S FRIEND AND RURAL REPORTER, Denmark (WI), May 22, 1980; VALDERS (WI) JOURNAL,

April 17, 1980; WISCONSIN WOMEN FOR AGRICULTURE NEWSLETTER, June-July, 1980.

SPELLMAN, MARY, written by Margaret Lamoreux Macfarlane
1. Butler, Genevieve, GRASS ROOTS, pamphlet on the 25th anniversary of Mary Spellman's death, 1970.
2. Butler, Roy G., CAROLINE SHERMAN BEULE, 1967.
3. Historical Committee, Centennial History, Beaver Dam, Wisconsin, dedicated to the Dodge County Historical Society, 1941.

SPERKA, MARIE, written by Cheryl Maxwell
1. Personal interview.

SWART, HANNAH, written by Jean Tyler
1. Personal interview with Hannah Swart
2. Botton, Harry, editor, PIONEER IN PROGRESS, 75TH ANNIVERSARY HISTORY, MILWAUKEE SCHOOL OF ENGINEERING, Milwaukee, 1977.
3. Walton, Ruby, "Hannah + Hoard = History," WISCONSIN TRAILS, Madison, Winter 1978.

THOMPSON, ANGELINE, written by Jane Manske
1. Personal interview

THOMPSON, BARBARA, written by Myrna M. Toney
1. Personal interview

THOMPSON, HELEN F., by Grace Draxler
1. PARK FALLS HERALD news items—1924, 1925, 1926, 1937.
2. St. Anthony's Church Bulletin, February 18, 1935.
3. Scrapbook of Miss Thompson, with clippings from PARK FALLS HERALD, STEVENS POINT JOURNAL, Madison CAPITAL TIMES, WISCONSIN STATE JOURNAL, MILWAUKEE JOURNAL, WISCONSIN BLUE BOOK, 1925.

TRACY, CLARISSA TUCKER, written by Beverly Thomann
1. Brown, Victoria, THE UNCOMMON LIVES OF COMMON WOMEN: THE MISSING HALF OF WISCONSIN HISTORY, Wisconsin Feminists Project Fund, 1976.
2. Merrill, Ada Clark, CLARISSA TUCKER TRACY, R.A. Donnelly & Sons: Chicago, IL, 1908.
3. Pedrick, Miller, A HISTORY OF RIPON, WISCONSIN, Worzalla Publishing Company: Stevens Point, 1964.
4. RIPON COMMONWEALTH, June 21, 1905.
5. Ripon Educational Club. MINUTES, 1878-1905.
6. Tracy Memorabilia, Ripon Historical Museum.

VON BRIESEN, DOROTHY, written by Ann Andersen
1. Personal interview.

WENDT, DELLA MADSEN, written by Esther Kaufmann
1. Personal interview.

WEST, RUTH, written by Dolly Stokes
1. Manitowoc HERALD-TIMES REPORTER.
2. Ruth West interview.
3. Mrs. Lee Layman, National Protocol Chairman, National Federation of Garden Clubs.
4. Late Dr. Puestow, in presenting Distinguished Service Award of Manitowoc Lions Club.
5. Green Bay PRESS GAZETTE.

WHITE, HELEN C. written by Hazel McGrath
1. Agard, Joan, Biography of Helen Constance White, unpublished manuscript, State Historical Society of Wisconsin Archives.
2. Butler, Anna P., "Dr. Helen Constance White, A Great and Gracious Teacher," Delta Kappa Gamma publication, 1947.
3. Roberts, Audrey, "Helen C. White Remembered," UNIVERSITY WOMEN—THEY CAME TO LEARN, THEY CAME TO TEACH, THEY CAME TO STAY, Volume I, Chapter 6, Madison: University of Wisconsin Office of Women, 1980.
4. Letters of Helen C. White, University of Wisconsin Archives.
5. Newspaper articles: Madison CAPITAL TIMES, June 20, 1961; MILWAUKEE JOURNAL, April 7, 1946; WISCONSIN STATE JOURNAL, June 20, 1961.

WILCOX, ELLA WHEELER, written by Kathy Van Sistine and James P. Koltes
1. Ballou, Jenny. PERIOD PIECE. Boston: Houghton Mifflin Company, 1940.
2. Wheeler, M.P. EVOLUTION OF ELLA WHEELER WILCOX AND OTHER WHEELERS. Madison, 1921.
3. Wheeler, Sarah Burdge. Private collection. Unpublished letter to Marcus P. Wheeler.
4. Wilcox, Ella Wheeler. THE WORLDS AND I. New York: George Doran Company, 1918. The Beautiful Land of Nod. Morrill, 1892.

WILLARD, FRANCES, written by Ann Allen
1. Trowbridge, Lydia Jones. Frances Willard of Evanston. Chicago: Willet, Clark & Company, 1938.
2. Willard, Frances E. GLIMPSES OF FIFTY YEARS; THE AUTOBIOGRAPHY OF AN AMERICAN WOMAN. Chicago: Women's Temperance Publication Association, 1889.
3. This sketch appeared in WE WERE HERE: CONTRIBUTIONS OF ROCK COUNTY WOMEN. Janesville Branch, American Association of University Women, 1975.

YOUNG OCHOWICZ, SHEILA, written by Anne Silvis O'Brien
1. Interview with Sheila Young, March 20, 1981.
2. Article by Jill Lieber, MILWAUKEE SENTINEL, January 9, 1981.
3. GOOD HOUSEKEEPING WOMAN'S ALMANAC. New York: Newspaper Enterprise Association, 1977.

index:

A

ABARAVICH, MARGARET MARY, 202
Abaravich, Vincent:
    MARGARET MARY ABARAVICH, 202
ABRAHAMSON, SHIRLEY, 263
Allen, Ann:
    FRANCES WILLARD, 32
ALMON, LOIS, 148
Andersen, Ann:
    DOROTHY VON BRIESEN, 176
Apple, Rima D.:
    LILLIE ROSA MINOKA-HILL, 75

B

BAINTER, MONICA, 168
BALIAN, LORNA, 250
BARNHILL, HELEN, 268
Bates, Marion:
    SHIRLEY ABRAHAMSON, 263
    MARY LOU MUNTS, 232
Becker, Mary Helen:
    BETH HEIDEN, 298
Bell, Allan:
    LOIS ALMON, 148
BERGSTROM, EVANGELINE, 66
Biebel, Anne:
    LILLIAN MACKESY, 162
Bletzinger, Andrea:
    EVANGELINE BERGSTROM, 66
Bobb, Ida & Eileen Carlson:
    HARRIET HARMON DEXTER, 128
Bode, Maria:
    BELLE CASE LA FOLLETTE, 53
Boge, Patt:
    MAUREE APPLEGATE CLACK, 130
BOORSE, ROBERTA, 254
BOYER, GENE, 244
BRADLEY, PEG, 104
Brown, Bette & Mary Ellen Stone:
    ISABEL BROWN, 220
BROWN, ISABEL, 220

C

Carlson, Eileen & Ida Bobb:
    HARRIET HARMON DEXTER, 128
Caulker, Olive:
    FERNE CAULKER-BRONSON, 286
CAULKER-BRONSON, FERNE, 286
Casey, Phyllis Tikalsky:
    SISTER REMY REVOR, 212

CLACK, MAUREE APPLEGATE, 130
Clapp, Barbara:
    JILL GEISLER, 284
CLARENBACH, KATHRYN, 208
CLEARY, CATHERINE, 186
CLINE, FRANCES, 142
CLUSEN, RUTH, 223
COOPER, SIGNE SKOTT, 216
COWLES, EMILY, 101
Crouse, Mary Lueck:
    HELEN BARNHILL, 268
CROW, FAY, 82
CUMMINGS, MARLENE, 280

D

DAVIS, MARGUERITE, 92
Davis, Sally Ann:
    BRIEF HISTORY OF AAUW, 14
DEER, ADA, 265
De Pledge, Catherine:
    SUSAN ENGELEITER, 292
DERNBACH, AUDREY JANE, 240
Des Isles, Joan Stebbins:
    KATE HAMILTON PIER, 35
Dewey, Violet E.:
    MABEL MANNIX MC ELLIGOTT, 164
DEXTER, HARRIET HARMON, 128
Draxler, Grace:
    HELEN THOMPSON, 58
DREYFUS, CLARE, 109
Dreyfus, E. Frankie:
    CLARE DREYFUS, 109
DUERRWAECHTER, EMMA, 84
Dunst, Anna Megna:
    MARGUERITE HENRY, 170

E

Edwards, Elaine:
    CAROL HOUGH MERRICK, 258
Ellis, Maxine:
    BRETA LUTHER GRIEM, 126
ENGELEITER, SUSAN SHANNON, 292
Ernst, Anne:
    AUDREY SICKINGER, 260
Eulberg, Judith:
    ZONA GALE, 70

F

FERBER, EDNA, 89

FESSLER OSF, SR. THOMASITA, 178
Fischer, Mary D.:
    ELLEN BENSON HUMLEKER, 194
Flader, Dolores C.:
    RUTH DE YOUNG KOHLER, 156
Frank, Marie:
    MARGARET HAWKINS, 272

G

Gaboriault, Dr. Paul H.:
    GRETA POTTER, 112
Gaecke, Jean:
    MABEL RUBY MC CLANAHAN, 196
GALE (BREESE), ZONA, 70
GANZ, ROSALIE, 94
Geisler, Betty Schlimgen:
    ROSALINE PECK, 26
GEISLER, JILL, 284
GLORY OF THE MORNING, 22
Gooding, Vicki & Joan Wucherer:
    LUCY SMITH MORRIS, 40
GRIEM, BRETA LUTHER, 126
Grundahl, Iris:
    GENE BOYER, 244

H

Haebig, Marion:
    EDITH HEIDNER, 106
Hall, Marian Seagren:
    FAY CROW, 82
HARDER, SARAH, 274
HAWKINS, MARGARET, 272
HAZOTTE, MOTHER M. AGNES, 43
HEIDE, FLORENCE PARRY, 205
HEIDEN, BETH, 298
HEIDNER, EDITH, 106
HENRY, MARGUERITE, 170
HILDEGARDE, 160
Hinds, Shirley Whipple:
    ELMA SPAULDING SCHUELE, 86
HISTORY OF AAUW, BRIEF, 14
Hodson, Betsy:
    BERNICE SCOTT, 145
HOOPER, JESSIE JACK, 63
Huelskamp, Jane:
    MAREN CHRISTINE PEDERSEN, 140
HUMLEKER, ELLEN BENSON, 194

J

JAMES, ADA, 79

K

KASTNER, ANITA HANKWITZ, 154
Katas, Lucille H.:
    RUTH CLUSEN, 223
Kaufmann, Esther:
    DELLA MADSEN WENDT, 151
KIEPKE, CLARE, 192

Kliefoth, Lois:
    ADA DEER, 265
KOHLER, RUTH DE YOUNG, 156
Koltes, James & Kathy Van Sistine:
    ELLA WHEELER WILCOX, 46
Kretlow, Liz & Marion E. Miller:
    FRANCES CLINE, 142
Krueger, Catherine:
    GEORGIA O'KEEFFE, 96
KUONY, MADAME LIANE, 189

L

LA FOLLETTE, BELLE CASE, 53
Lamson, Jeanne:
    MARLENE CUMMINGS, 280
LEENHOUTS, LILLIAN, 173
LIEBER, JILL ANN, 295
LINSMEIER, MARY, 247
Lorimer CSA, Sr. Margaret:
    MOTHER M. AGNES HAZOTTE, 43

M

Macfarlane, Margaret Lamoreaux:
    MARY SPELLMAN, 60
MACKESY, LILLIAN, 162
Manske, Jane:
    ANGELINE THOMPSON, 226
Margotto, Diana:
    EMILY COWLES, 101
Marr, Jane Nee:
    ADA JAMES, 79
Maxwell, Cheryl:
    MARIE SPERKA, 166
McArthur, Annabel Douglas:
    ELIZABETH PECKHAM, 50
McBride, Jann:
    JILL ANN LIEBER, 295
MC CLANAHAN, MABEL, 196
MC ELLIGOTT, MABEL MANNIX, 164
McGrath, Hazel:
    HELEN C. WHITE, 122
MEIR, GOLDA, 136
MERRICK, CAROL HOUGH, 258
Miller, Marion E. & Liz Kretlow:
    FRANCES CLINE, 142
MINOKA-HILL, LILLIE ROSA, 75
Mitchell, Kathy:
    SARAH HARDER, 274
MOLLART, GLADYS, 120
MORRIS, LUCY SMITH, 40
MUNTS, MARY LOU, 232

N

Newcomer, Dorothy & Lee:
    JESSIE JACK HOOPER, 63
NICHOLS, BARBARA, 278
Nikolai, Geri:
    FAY CROW, 82
Niles, Anne G.:
    SIGNE SKOTT COOPER, 216

Noer, Linda S.:
    FLORENCE PARRY HEIDE, 205

O

O'Brien, Anne Silvis:
    SHEILA YOUNG OCHOWICZ, 289
Oh, Joann L.:
    GLORY OF THE MORNING, 22
O'KEEFFE, GEORGIA, 96

P

Park, Margaret Jane:
    PEG BRADLEY, 104
PECK, ROSALINE, 26
PECKHAM, ELIZABETH, 50
PEDERSEN, MAREN CHRISTINE, 140
Peter OSF, Sr. Margaret:
    SR. THOMASITA FESSLER OSF, 178
PIER, KATE HAMILTON, 35
PIETSCH, EDNA FRIDA, 116
Podell, Mary:
    GOLDA MEIR, 136
POTTER, GRETA CELIA LAGRO, 112
Prieto, Beverly:
    EDNA FERBER, 89
Prince, Frank J.:
    ANITA HANKWITZ KASTNER, 154
Prince, Gloria:
    EDNA FRIDA PIETSCH, 116

R

READ, SISTER JOEL, 236
REVOR, SISTER REMY, 212
Richtor, Marilynn:
    CLARE KIEPKE, 192
Roemer, Sue:
    LORNA BALIAN, 250
Rose Evelyn:
    GLADYS MOLLART, 120

S

Schneider, Blanche:
    ROSALIE GANZ, 94
SCHUELE, ELMA SPAULDING, 86
SCOTT, BERNICE, 145
Sedwick, Alice & Patricia Smith Wilmeth:
    ROBERTA BOORSE, 254
SICKINGER, AUDREY, 260
Smith, Louise C.:
    BARBARA NICHOLS, 278
SPELLMAN, MARY, 60
SPERKA, MARIE, 166
Stokes, Dolly:
    RUTH WEST, 133
Stone, Mary Ellen & Bette Brown:
    ISABEL BROWN, 220
Straus, Janice & Lois Turba:
    EMMA DUE

Stuckey, Marilyn:
    MADAME LIANE KUONY, 189
SWART, HANNAH, 182
Swaziek, Ruth:
    LILLIAN LEENHOUTS, 173

T

Thibaudeau, May Murphy:
    SISTER JOEL READ, 236
Thomann, Beverly:
    CLARISSA TRACY, 29
THOMPSON, ANGELINE, 226
THOMPSON, BARBARA, 229
THOMPSON, HELEN, 58
Thompson, Marilyn:
    MONICA BAINTER, 168
Threinen, Constance:
    KATHRYN CLARENBACH, 208
Toney, Myrna M.:
    BARBARA THOMPSON, 229
TRACY, CLARISSA, 29
Turba, Lois & Janice Straus:
    EMMA DUERRWAECHTER, 84
Tyler, Jean:
    HANNAH SWART, 182

V

Van Sistine, Kathy & James Koltes:
    ELLA WHEELER WILCOX, 46
VON BRIESEN, DOROTHY, 176

W

Walker, Elizabeth:
    MARGUERITE DAVIS, 92
WENDT, DELLA MADSEN, 151
WEST, RUTH, 133
WHITE, HELEN C., 122
WILCOX, ELLA WHEELER, 46
WILLARD, FRANCES, 32
Wilmeth, Patricia Smith:
    CATHERINE CLEARY, 186;
    & Alice Sedgwick:
    ROBERTA BOORSE, 254
Winkler, Kathleen:
    MARY LINSMEIER, 247
Wucherer, Joan & Vicki Gooding:
    LUCY SMITH MORRIS, 40

Y

YOUNG C

the committee

Thanks to the efforts of this committee — whose members by now have become forever friends who value each other's talents with a whole new perspective — and thanks to the contributions of time, enthusiasm and support of the Wisconsin State Division AAUW Branch State Project Chairs (page 328), this publication has at last materialized!

JEANNINE GOGGIN

PAT MANSKE

LOIS KLIEFOTH

MARY CROUSE

JANICE MC CARTHY

JANET ROBERTSON ⫠

MARGE